Cover image © Shutterstock, Inc.

Kendall Hunt
publishing company

www.kendallhunt.com
Send all inquiries to:
4050 Westmark Drive
Dubuque, IA 52004-1840

Copyright © 2012, 2017, 2018 by Kendall Hunt Publishing Company

ISBN 978-1-5249-4989-1

All rights reserved. No part of this publication may be reproduced,
stored in a retrieval system, or transmitted, in any form or by any means,
electronic, mechanical, photocopying, recording, or otherwise,
without the prior written permission of the copyright owner.

Printed in the United States of America

To Marie

CONTENTS

	Preface	xi
Chapter 1	**Some Economic Concepts: Macroeconomics and the Global Economy**	**1**
	Some National Accounting Definitions	1
	Trade and Protectionism	2
	The Balance of Payments	5
	Exchange Rates	7
	Fiscal and Monetary Policy	12
	REFERENCES	16
Chapter 2	**The First Era of Globalization**	**17**
	The First Era of Globalization and the Second Industrial Revolution	17
	Globalization Through Imperialism	18
	International Trade	21
	Factor Mobility	22
	Exchange Rate Stability and the Classical Gold Standard	23
	Monetary Policy in the Era of the Gold Standard	25
	REFERENCES	27
Chapter 3	**Legacy of the First World War**	**29**
	First World War and the Economic Role of Government	30
	Immediate Costs of the War	31
	The Postwar Boom and Slump	33
	Hyperinflation	34
	Restoration of the Gold Standard	40
	The Chain of Debt	42
	Changing Patterns of Production and Demand	43
	International Trade	44
	Demographic Changes	45
	Protectionism	46
	Diminishing Trade	47
	REFERENCES	48

v

Chapter 4	**The Great Depression**	**49**
	Introduction	49
	The Depression in the United States	50
	Monetarism and Wage Rigidity	54
	Wage Rigidity	60
	Other Explanations of the Depression in the United States	61
	Recovery and the Recession of 1937–1938	63
	International Aspects of the Depression	64
	The International Economy, 1933–1940	68
	The Great Depression and the Great Recession	72
	REFERENCES	73
Chapter 5	**Bretton Woods and the International Institutions**	**75**
	The Legacy of the Second World War	76
	The Marshall Plan and the European Payments Union	77
	The Bretton Woods System	80
	The Triffin Dilemma	84
	The General Agreement on Tariffs and Trade	86
	The World Trade Organization	88
	The Rise and Fall of the Bretton Woods System, 1947–1973	88
	Post–Bretton Woods	91
	Labor and Environmental Issues and the International Institutions	91
	REFERENCES	94
Chapter 6	**International Institutions and International Financial Crises**	**95**
	Macroeconomic Imbalances	95
	Contagion	96
	Globalization and Capital Mobility	97
	Crisis Avoidance	100
	Role of the IMF and the World Bank	102
	Major International Economic Crises Since 1980	105
	REFERENCES	115

Contents   vii

Chapter 7   **Regional Trade Agreements**   **116**

Trade Creation and Trade Diversion   117

The North American Free Trade Agreement (NAFTA)   118

The European Union   127

The European Sovereign Debt Crisis   139

Brexit   145

Mercosur   149

REFERENCES   150

Chapter 8   **The Soviet Union and the Socialist Economies of Europe**   **151**

Historical Development of the Soviet Economic System   151

Collectivization of Agriculture in the USSR   154

Economic Planning in the Soviet Union and the Other
  Socialist Economies   156

Attempts at Reform   158

The Socialist Economies of Central and Eastern Europe   159

Comecon   161

Failure of the Socialist Economies   163

REFERENCES   164

Chapter 9   **Emerging Economies: The BRICS Countries**   **165**

Russia   165

China   172

China and Russia: "Shock Therapy" versus "Gradualism"   180

India   181

Brazil   184

South Africa   187

REFERENCES   189

Chapter 10   **East Asia: The Development State**   **190**

Economic Growth and Exports   190

Japan   193

The Emerging Economies of East Asia   199

REFERENCES   207

viii   Contents

Chapter 11   The Middle East and Africa   **209**

OPEC and the Oil-Exporting States   209

Non-Oil-Exporting States   212

The Arab Spring   215

Sub-Saharan Africa   215

REFERENCES   220

Index   221

ABOUT THE AUTHOR

Michael Jolly received his PhD from the University of Toronto after receiving degrees from Auckland University and the London School of Economics. He currently teaches in the Department of Economics at Ryerson University in Toronto and has previously taught at the University of Saskatchewan in Saskatoon and Auckland University in New Zealand. His primary research interests are in international economics, economic history, and the Asian economies.

PREFACE

Until very recently it was possible to believe that we were living in a new world in which the economic problems of the past had little or no relevance. A general economic collapse such as the Great Depression of the 1930s was held to be no longer possible because the international economy was fundamentally different from that which had existed before the Second World War or indeed that of twenty years ago. In any case, policy makers and their economic advisers now had the tools to prevent such an event. There were, of course, disturbances in the global economy, such as the Debt Crisis of the 1980s and the Asian Crisis of 1997, but it was felt in the West that these mainly affected non-Western countries which had failed to adopt sound market policies. The subprime mortgage crisis of 2008, along with the subsequent "Great Recession" and sovereign debt crisis, shattered this complacency. The world came dangerously close to repeating the experience of the 1930s and, while it is certainly true that the international economy of the twenty-first century *is* different in many respects from that of the years immediately preceding the Great Depression, it turned out that there are also worrisome similarities between the two periods.

The fact that a second Great Depression was avoided was in large part due to the fact that, perhaps belatedly, lessons were learned from the earlier catastrophe. Accordingly, some familiarity with the recent history of the international economy is necessary for an understanding of current economic issues. By understanding how economic institutions developed, how the world economy has evolved and is still evolving, through some familiarity with the similarities and differences between our current problems and the problems of the recent past, we gain a sense of perspective and some guidance as to the nature of the challenges facing the global economic system. The purpose of this book, however, is not primarily historical and accounts of current economic issues are given at least as much emphasis as the events of the recent past. The fact that events are still unfolding places limits on the usual certainty of hindsight, and there is often considerable controversy surrounding the topics covered in this book. In describing both current and historical issues I have aimed to discuss fairly the differences of opinion which exist where there is no consensus.

Any understanding of the global economy requires some knowledge of economic theory. I have tried to avoid being overly technical, but for those who are not familiar with economic theory the first chapter of the book provides an introduction to some of the basic building blocks and terminology of international macroeconomics. Brief asides with respect to economic theory are also provided in other chapters where useful.

The book is organized as follows. As has already been pointed out, chapter 1 provides an introduction to some economic concepts and theories. Chapters 2 through 4 provide an historical account of the international economy between the two world wars with an emphasis on the causes and economic consequences of the Great Depression of the 1930s. Chapter 5 describes the Bretton Woods System of fixed exchange rates, which was in operation throughout

xi

xii   Preface

the 1950s and 1960s, and the development of the international institutions that play such a prominent part in the international economy today. Finally, chapters 6 through 11 describe and discuss current and recent developments in the global economy, including international crises (chapter 6), regional trade agreements (chapter 7), the socialist economies (chapter 8), the BRICS emerging economies (chapter 9), the "development states" of East Asia (chapter 10), and the economies of the Middle East and Africa (chapter 11).

Chapter 1

Some Economic Concepts: Macroeconomics and the Global Economy

While this book is not intended to be a macroeconomics textbook, some knowledge of basic macroeconomic concepts is useful for an understanding of later chapters in the book.[1] This chapter introduces some terms and theories that may be helpful to readers, especially those who have no previous exposure to economics. The first section of the chapter describes some national accounting definitions. The second section focuses on international trade, introducing the theory of comparative advantage and briefly describing some of the economic effects of restrictions on trade. The third section describes the balance of payments. The fourth section provides an account of the determination of exchange rates. Finally, the fifth section describes fiscal and monetary policy, the tools used by governments for macroeconomic management, and relates them to the balance of payments and exchange rates.

Some National Accounting Definitions

A country's economic activity during the space of a year is summarized in the national income and expenditure accounts, in which total expenditures are shown for the different sectors of the economy and checked against total incomes. Since all expenditures generate income somewhere in the economy, total expenditure must equal total income if both are correctly calculated. It is not necessary to the purposes of this book to describe the national accounts in any detail, but some terms from the expenditure side of the national accounts will be used from time to time. The first of these is gross domestic product (GDP), which is the most commonly used measure of the total production of goods and services in a country during a fixed period of time, usually a year. When the GDP is expressed in current monetary terms, it is more precisely referred to as "nominal GDP" and is to be distinguished from "real GDP," which is GDP adjusted to take account of changes in prices over time. Real GDP is useful in comparing the performance of an economy over several years since it is valuable to know whether an increase in GDP over time is due to an increase in the quantity of goods produced or merely to a rise in prices. The expenditures included in GDP are divided up into four categories: consumption, investment, government expenditure, and net exports. The first of these, consumption, refers to expenditure on goods and services for immediate use and is the largest component of GDP. Investment refers to expenditure on capital goods (which are used to

---

[1] Macroeconomics is the branch of economics concerned with broad economic aggregates such as national income or unemployment, as opposed to microeconomics, which is concerned with individual decision-making units in the economy such as firms.

1

produce other goods) and consumer goods (which are produced but not consumed in the current year). Government expenditure on goods and services is largely self-explanatory, though it should be noted that it does not include "transfers" such as pensions or welfare payments since these will already be implicitly included in GDP through the consumption expenditures of their recipients. The final component of GDP is net exports (exports minus imports). Some of the goods and services produced are sold, or exported, to foreign firms and individuals. Since these exports generate incomes in the home country they are included in the national expenditure calculations. By the same logic, some goods and services purchased in the home country are imported from abroad. Since these imports do not directly generate incomes in the home country (apart from local sales services) they are *deducted* from national expenditure.

"You ever get the feeling that this economy benefits some people more than others?"

A concept similar to GDP but now less widely used, is gross national product (GNP), the market value of all goods and services produced by the residents of a country in one year. GNP differs from GDP in that it includes foreign investment, and transfers (such as payments of foreign pensions). It therefore includes consumption, investment, and government expenditure, but instead of net exports it incorporates the current account balance (described below in the section on the balance of payments and exchange rates).

Trade and Protectionism

Comparative Advantage

The theory of comparative advantage was first described by David Ricardo in 1817 and, after almost two hundred years, it still provides one of the most powerful arguments for free trade. Ricardo used an example involving trade in wine and cloth between England and Portugal. As a courteous Englishman he assumed that Portugal could produce both goods at a lower absolute cost than England and demonstrated that even under such circumstances trade could still be beneficial to both countries. This would be so provided that the *relative* costs of the two goods were different in the two countries. Using Ricardo's example, suppose that England is a very high cost producer of wine and only a moderately high cost producer of cloth, while Portugal is a moderately low cost producer of cloth and a very low cost producer of wine. Then it would be beneficial to both countries if Portugal specialized in wine production, importing cloth from England, while England specialized in cloth, importing wine from Portugal. A simple numerical example illustrates the argument. Suppose Portugal can produce one unit of wine with 80 hours of labor and one unit of cloth with 90 hours of labor, while the corresponding labor inputs for England are 120 hours per unit of wine and 100 hours per unit of cloth, as indicated in Table 1.1. In this case Portugal has an *absolute* advantage in the production of both goods, and England has an *absolute* disadvantage in both goods.

Some Economic Concepts: Macroeconomics and the Global Economy   3

TABLE 1.1. Unit Labour Costs in the Production of Wine and Cloth (in Hours)

	1 Unit of Wine	*1 Unit of Cloth*
Portugal	80	90
England	120	100

Source: Statistics Canada. Available at: http://www.statcan.gc.ca/tables-tableaux/sumsom/101/cst01/eco-n01a-eng.htm. Accessed on April 23, 2012. Reproduced and distributed on an "as is" basis with the permission of Statistics Canada

England, however, has a *comparative* advantage in cloth production, while Portugal has a *comparative* advantage in wine but a *comparative* disadvantage in cloth. This becomes clear if we express the costs of the two goods in terms of each other, using a concept referred to by economists as "opportunity costs." In Portugal one unit of wine costs 0.889 ($\frac{8}{9}$) units of wine since 80 hours of labor could produce one unit of wine or $\frac{8}{9}$ units of cloth ($^{80}\!/_{90}$). Using the same logic, one unit of cloth would cost 1.125 ($1\frac{1}{8}$) units of wine. In England the corresponding costs are one unit of wine for 1.2 units of cloth ($^{120}\!/_{100}$) and one unit of cloth for 0.833 ($^{100}\!/_{120}$) unit of wine, as indicated in Table 1.2.

TABLE 1.2. Opportunity Costs of Wine and Cloth

	1 Unit of Wine *(in terms of cloth)*	*1 Unit of Cloth* *(in terms of wine)*
Portugal	0.889	1.125
England	1.200	0.833

On the assumption that shipping costs are negligible, Portugal would benefit from buying cloth from England provided that England was willing to sell cloth at a price of less than 1.125 units of wine per unit of cloth. Similarly, England would buy wine from Portugal in exchange for cloth provided that Portugal demanded a price of less than 1.2 units of cloth per unit of wine. If, for example, the two countries traded at a rate of one unit of wine for one unit of cloth, Portugal would be able to import cloth from England at a lower cost (in terms of wine) than it would obtain if it produced cloth domestically and England would acquire wine from Portugal at a lower cost than would be the case if it produced its own wine. Thus *both* countries would benefit from engaging in trade rather than producing and consuming in isolation, even when one of them is the lower cost producer (in terms of labor hours) in both goods.

Trade Restrictions

The theory of comparative advantage provides a powerful argument for free trade but in fact few, if any, countries practice completely unrestricted trade. Instead, they practice "protectionism," a term that refers to the practice of restricting access to a country's domestic market

4   Chapter 1

by imposing barriers to trade on foreign exporters. Barriers to trade are common for a variety of reasons. One obvious reason is that while society as a whole may benefit from free trade, this is not necessarily true for all sections of society. In the simple example of comparative advantage illustrated by Tables 1.1 and 1.2, if the adoption of free trade by England and Portugal occurred after a period in which the two countries produced both wine and cloth in isolation, the producers in the English wine industry and the Portuguese cloth industry would both lose their markets to imports. In principle they could be compensated for their losses out of the gains made by English cloth exporters and Portuguese wine exporters, but in practice this sort of compensation is rarely paid. That being so, those who lose from free trade will lobby their governments for protection from imports. Therefore, a major reason for protectionism is political lobbying by pressure groups who stand to lose from the adoption of free trade.

In some circumstances barriers to trade can be justified on economic grounds as well as on grounds of political expediency. An economic argument for temporarily limiting international trade is based on the concept of *dynamic* comparative advantage. Ricardo's theory is a static one. In his example Portugal has a comparative advantage in wine and England has a comparative advantage in cloth. No explanation is given as to how they acquired these comparative advantages and no account is taken of whether comparative advantage can change over time. It may, however, be possible for a country to gain a comparative advantage that it did not initially have. By repeatedly producing a specific good or service, firms and workers in a country may become more efficient in that activity. If faced with import competition, however, they may never get the opportunity to gain this proficiency. *Dynamic* comparative advantage is therefore sometimes used as a justification for *temporary* restrictions on trade. The most common variant of this argument is known as the "infant industry argument," which states that it may be desirable to temporarily protect a new industry in order that it can become a mature industry capable of competing internationally. A problem with applying this argument, of course, is that unfortunately the infant sometimes never grows up, in which case the country becomes saddled with an industry that will never be competitive internationally but is now supported by a politically influential lobby that stands to lose from free trade.

Tariffs and Quotas

Barriers to trade are of three types: tariffs, quotas, and other nontariff barriers. Tariffs are taxes or duties imposed on imported goods. They may be levied as a fixed sum per unit of the imported good, such as a tax of X dollars per ton or per liter, but more common are *ad valorem* tariffs, which are expressed as a percentage of the value of the goods. In either case the objective is to raise the cost of imported goods and hence raise the price received by domestic producers. In doing so, a tariff reduces the supply of the good available to domestic consumers. Unless it is a *prohibitive* tariff, which imposes such a high duty that imports are kept out altogether, it will also add to the government's tax revenues.

A quota is a *quantitative* restriction on imports of a specific commodity. By reducing supply of the good to the domestic market it raises the price received by domestic producers. In this respect it has a similar effect to a tariff but quotas differ from tariffs in two important ways. First, the government receives tax revenue from a tariff but not from a quota unless it auctions or otherwise sells the right to import the permitted quota. Second, a quota represents a more severe restriction on trade than a tariff since in the latter case it is, in principle, possible for foreign exporters to gain access to the home country's market if they cut their pre-tariff prices sufficiently. It is, however, impossible by legal means to overcome quota restrictions no matter how efficient or low cost foreign producers may be.

In addition to imposing tariffs or quotas, governments can restrict access to their countries' domestic markets through a variety of "nontariff barriers." Such measures have become more widely used as international agreements have closed off the more obvious barriers to trade, tariffs, and quotas. Examples of nontariff barriers are "health and safety" regulations, which are strictly applied with respect to imports but disregarded when it comes to domestic producers, and very slow, bureaucratic inspection procedures imposed on imports. No one could deny the right of governments to require that imports meet health and safety requirements, but regulations in those areas can be a disguised form of protectionism.

The Balance of Payments

The balance of payments is a summary of a country's international transactions during a year. It is divided into three subheadings: the current account, the capital account, and the financial account. For each of these accounts there are credit items and debit items. The credit (positive) items generate inflows of payments from the rest of the world into the country, while debit items represent outflows of payments to the rest of the world.

The Current Account

The current account includes three major categories of transaction.

1. *Trade in goods and services.* Trade in goods, such as exports of cars or imports of oil, is referred to as "merchandise trade"; internationally traded services, such as tourism, are sometimes known as "invisibles." Exports of goods and services are credit items since they generate an inflow of funds from other countries, while imports are debit items since they require an outflow of funds to pay for them.

2. *Investment income.* When companies or local residents of a country (country A) own investments in other countries, they receive dividends, interest payments, or other types of investment income. These are credits. Similarly, residents of other countries will receive income from their investments in country A. These are debits. If the credits exceed the debits there will be a positive overall balance of investment income. This would be expected for a country that has high levels of foreign investment. Countries for which a large proportion of the economy is foreign owned are more likely to have a negative overall balance.

6   Chapter 1

3. *Current transfers.* There are many receipts and payments that are not associated with trade or investments. Examples are foreign aid and payments to individuals, such as foreign pensions. These flows of funds are called "transfers." Countries that have large numbers of foreign or guest workers may have a large negative balance in terms of transfers as foreign workers send payments to their families back home, while other countries, which "export" their population, would be more likely to have a positive balance as they receive payments from their citizens currently living and working overseas.

The difference between total receipts (credits) and total payments (debits) for the transactions included under the aforementioned three headings gives the current account balance. If the receipts exceed the payments there is a "current account surplus." If the payments exceed the receipts there is a "current account deficit."

The Capital Account

Under an older definition, the "capital account" summarizes all a country's financial transactions with the rest of the world, but a more narrow definition used by international institutions such as the International Monetary Fund (IMF) limits it to certain types of capital transfers such as migrants' funds and superannuation benefits. Other transactions usually included in the broader definition of the capital account are instead placed under a "financial account."

The Financial Account

Under the IMF definition, the financial account summarizes a country's financial capital transactions with foreign countries, apart from those listed under the capital account. There are two major types of private sector capital movements: foreign direct investment (FDI) and portfolio investment. Foreign direct investment refers to transactions that lead to a change in control over a business, such as a foreign takeover of an existing business or the building of a foreign factory or branch plant. This is sometimes regarded with suspicion by nationalists who fear foreign domination, but such investment has the advantage of being relatively stable since it generally involves a long-term commitment. Portfolio investment represents financial flows that do not result in a change in control, such as purchases of government or corporate bonds or shares in companies that do not give the purchaser control over a company. Portfolio investment may seem to present less of a threat to national sovereignty than foreign direct investment, but it has the disadvantage of being highly volatile since it implies no long-term commitment. Portfolio investment is very sensitive to such factors as interest rate differentials between countries and rumors about government policies or debt sustainability. In addition to private sector investment, the financial account includes changes in official reserves, which represent the net purchases or sales of the government's official reserves of foreign currency. These transactions are generally made to enable the government to achieve its exchange rate targets and will be described below in the description of exchange rates.

Like the current account, the capital and financial accounts have surpluses or deficits. In principle, a current account surplus (or deficit) will be exactly offset by deficits (or surpluses)

Some Economic Concepts: Macroeconomics and the Global Economy   **7**

TABLE 1.3. Balance of International Payments. Canada (2011) ($ Millions)

Current Account	Total Receipts (Inflows)	Total Payments (Outflows)	Balance
Goods and services	532,393	−555,594	−23,201
Investment income	66,640	−87,724	−21,084
Transfers	8,008	−12,026	−4,018
Total	607,041	−655,345	**−48,304**
Capital Account	5,483	−670	**4,813**
Financial Account	159,115	−108,412	**50,703**
Foreign direct investment			
- Canadian FDI abroad		−45,215	
- FDI into Canada	40,345		
Portfolio investment			
- Canadian investment abroad		−17,592	
- Foreign investment in Canada	96,636		
Other investments (including change in official reserves)	23,134	−46,605	
Statistical Discrepancy		**−7,213**	

Source: Statistics Canada, http://www.statcan.gc.ca/tables-tableaux/sumsom/101/cst01/econ01a-eng. htm. Accessed on April 23 <http://www.statcan.gc.ca/tables-tableaux/sumsom/101/cst01/econ01a-eng. htm.%20Accessed%20on%20April%2023>, 2012. Reproduced and distributed on an "as is" basis with the permission of Statistics Canada.

on the capital and financial accounts. If the sum of the debit items on a country's current account exceeds the sum of the credit items, the difference will have to be paid for by selling financial assets, which would produce a surplus on the financial account. In practice the sum never exactly equals zero because of errors and omissions in collecting information. This is why the balance of payments always includes a "statistical discrepancy."

Table 1.3 shows the Canadian balance of payments in 2011.

Exchange Rates

The Exchange Rate Model

The *exchange rate* describes the external value of a currency relative to another currency. When the currency appreciates, it buys more of the foreign currency per unit and when it depreciates it buys less. To analyze how exchange rates are determined we need to consider why people or firms choose to hold foreign currencies. A major reason is to engage in international trade since foreign currencies may be needed to pay for imports of goods and services. There are also other reasons for holding foreign currencies, and these will be described below, but the use of foreign currencies for trading purposes provides the basis for the standard demand and supply model of exchange rate determination.

This can be illustrated by an example of trade between the United States and France. Suppose an American car producer exports cars to France and is paid in dollars. The French importer will buy American dollars on the foreign exchange market. Hence exports of American goods and services create a demand for dollars. Since those goods will be cheaper and more desirable in France the lower is their price in terms of euros, it follows that the lower the price of the dollar in terms of euros, the larger will be American exports to Europe and the larger will be the quantity of dollars demanded. We can now graph the quantity of dollars demanded against the exchange rate of the dollar in terms of euros.

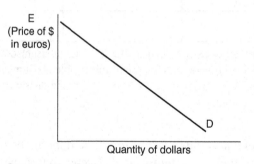

Demand for Dollars

The supply of foreign exchange can be analyzed in a similar fashion. Suppose now that an American company imports wine from France, paying in U.S. dollars. In doing so, it supplies the foreign exchange market with dollars. Clearly the supply of dollars will be greater the larger the value of European goods imported into the United States. Since those goods will be cheaper and more desirable in the United States the lower their price is in terms of dollars, it follows that the lower the price of the euro in terms of dollars, the larger will be American imports from Europe and the larger will be the quantity of dollars supplied. Since currency values are relative, a cheap euro is equivalent to an expensive dollar. We can now graph the quantity of dollars supplied against the exchange rate of the dollar in terms of euros.

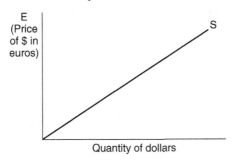
Supply of Dollars

The demand and supply curves together determine the equilibrium exchange rate (E*) and the equilibrium quantity of dollars, where "equilibrium" describes the value at which these variables will remain unless something happens to disturb either demand or supply.

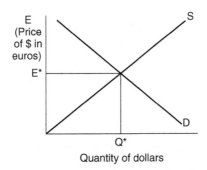
Foreign Exchange Market Model

The exchange rate model described above incorporates only trade in goods and services, but in fact currencies are held and exchanged for other reasons as well. Trade in goods and services are described in the current account of the balance of payments, but transactions that belong to the capital and financial accounts also affect the foreign exchange market. The effect on the exchange rate of changes in foreign investment can be illustrated by the example of American investment in France and French investment in the United States. First consider the case of an increase in French investment in the United States. The buying of American financial assets will create a demand for dollars in the same way that an increase in French imports of American goods would have done. This can be shown on the foreign exchange market diagram by a rightward shift in the demand curve because more dollars will now be demanded at every exchange rate. As a result, the dollar will appreciate in value. Now consider the case of increased American investment in France. In this case, the supply of dollars will increase and the dollar will depreciate.

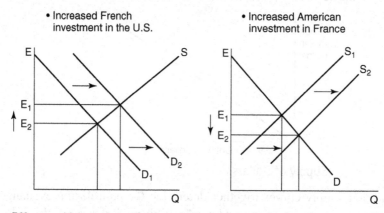

Effect on Value of the Dollar of Changes in Foreign Investment

Short-term fluctuations in exchange rates are largely driven by shifts in portfolio investment, which is very sensitive to differences in interest rates between countries and expectations about future exchange rates. In the above examples of foreign investment, the increased French investment in the United States could be generated by a rise in interest rates in the United States relative to those in France. Such an increase in interest rate differentials would bring about an appreciation in the U.S. dollar. Similarly, a rise in European interest rates would cause the euro to appreciate. Trading in currencies entails the possibility that exchange rates will change, so expectations about future exchange rates are also important. Speculators hope to take advantage of future changes in exchange rates by buying currencies that they expect to appreciate and selling currencies that they expect to depreciate. Clearly such expectations can become self-fulfilling as the demand for a currency increases or decreases due to the actions of speculators.

The long-run trend in exchange rates is generally assumed to be determined by "purchasing power parity," which predicts that long-run exchange rate changes should reflect differences in national rates of inflation. It is based on the idea that a given "basket" of goods should cost the same in all countries when its price is converted into a common currency. It then follows that if, for example, Mexico has a higher rate of inflation than Canada, the value of the Mexican peso will fall relative to the Canadian dollar so that the rise in prices of goods in terms of Mexican pesos would not affect the prices of Mexican goods exported to Canada once the cheaper pesos have been converted into the more expensive Canadian dollars. For example, if the exchange rate now is 12 pesos to the dollar and a Mexican good costs 120 pesos, this will convert into a Canadian price of $10. Now suppose that in one year's time Canada has experienced no inflation but Mexican has experienced 10 percent inflation. The product that used to cost 120 pesos now costs 132 pesos, but if it is to sell at a competitive price in Canada it will still have to cost $10 because prices have not changed in that country. This would imply that the exchange rate must now be 13.2 pesos to the dollar, so the peso has depreciated by 10 percent.

Fixed and Flexible Exchange Rates

In the description of the exchange rate model and the factors affecting exchange rates, it has been assumed that relative currency values are allowed to fluctuate in accordance with shifts in market demand and supply. This is true if the exchange rate is "flexible" or "floating." Historically, however, exchange rates have not generally been allowed to fluctuate in this manner, and it is still the case that many countries intervene in the foreign exchange market to prevent or at least minimize fluctuations in the external value of their currency. Such countries have "fixed" exchange rates. In this case the country's currency is "pegged" to something else. In the earlier part of the twentieth century currencies were generally pegged to gold, but in more recent times the peg has usually been a foreign currency, most often the U.S. dollar. Under a fixed exchange rate system, the monetary authority intervenes to stabilize the exchange rate by buying or selling foreign exchange. Consider an example in which a country has pegged its currency to the U.S. dollar or to gold at some fixed rate. Suppose that the fixed exchange rate is E*, but there is now a decrease in demand for a country's currency from D1 to D2, perhaps because of a fall in exports or because of shifts in foreign investment. The authorities have to prevent the exchange rate from decreasing.

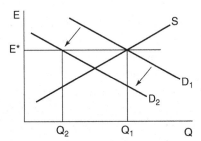

Fixed Exchange Rate

There are three ways to achieve this objective.

1. *Buy (Q1-Q2) domestic currency, purchasing it with foreign exchange reserves.* This is feasible if the decrease in demand is small and temporary, but if it is large and prolonged there is a danger that the country will run out of foreign exchange reserves, in which case the peg will have to be abandoned.

2. *Raise interest rates.* This should attract foreign investment, reversing the decrease in demand, and reduce supply as local investors keep their money at home to take advantage of the higher interest rates.

3. *Increase taxes and reduce government spending.* This is known as "fiscal tightening" and has the effect of reducing domestic incomes. People with lower incomes buy fewer goods, including imported goods, so fiscal tightening will reduce imports and hence decrease the supply of the country's currency on the foreign exchange market. This will prevent a currency depreciation.

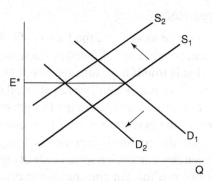

Decreased Supply of Currency

The Gold Standard of the early twentieth century and the Bretton Woods System of the mid-twentieth century are both examples of fixed exchange rate systems, which will be described in later chapters.

Managed Exchange Rates

Many countries have exchange rates that are neither fixed nor wholly flexible. More usual are "managed" exchange rate systems, under which the authorities try to prevent extreme fluctuations in exchange rates while allowing long-term trends to take their course. At one time it was possible to do this directly through buying and selling foreign exchange, but the reserves available to central bankers acting on behalf of their governments are now far too small to be able to overrule the financial markets. Daily flows of currency are in the order of U.S.$1.2 trillion *per day,* and not even the richest countries can counter a market of this size. Instead the authorities seek to encourage "herd effects" in the markets by influencing expectations. Signals to the market may include a change in interest rates and some buying or selling of foreign currency using foreign exchange reserves. Alternatively, a few well-chosen words by the minister of finance or the head of the central bank may encourage investors to buy or sell currencies. Naturally this is as much an art as a science and can very easily lead to overshooting. The hoped-for herd effect may turn into a stampede. There are frequent examples of countries, such as Mexico in 1995 and Thailand in 1997, for which a hoped-for modest currency depreciation turned into a currency collapse.

Fiscal and Monetary Policy

Three macroeconomic policy tools are available to governments to influence the economy. One of these is exchange rate policy or the exchange rate "regime." As discussed in the previous section, a country may choose to have a fixed or floating exchange rate. The other policy tools are "fiscal policy" and "monetary policy." As will be seen, these three policy tools are interconnected.

Fiscal Policy

Fiscal policy is the part of government policy concerned with taxation and government expenditure. If the government wishes to increase the total level of spending in the economy, it may increase spending directly through expanding government programs or increase spending by the private sector through tax cuts, which increase after-tax incomes and allow households to spend more on consumer goods and firms to invest more. A policy of increased government spending and tax cuts is described as a "fiscal expansion" or an "expansionary fiscal policy." The opposite policy of increasing taxes and reducing government expenditure, which will reduce overall spending in the economy, is described as "fiscal restraint" or a "contractionary fiscal policy." Clearly the fiscal policy adopted will affect the government's budget balance. If government spending exceeds tax revenues there will be a budget "deficit." The effect would be expansionary but would also increase government debt. A contractionary fiscal policy will reduce the budget deficit or, if tax revenues end up exceeding government spending, create or enlarge a "budget surplus." A budget surplus would be desirable if overall spending in the economy is too high, causing price inflation. A budget deficit is more appropriate when the economy is in recession and the government wishes to bring about higher levels of spending.

"Call it a hunch, Hal, but are you having debt problems?"

Monetary Policy

In addition to modifying their exchange rate policies or fiscal policies, governments can affect the economy through changes in "monetary policy." Monetary policy is the part of economic policy that controls the amount of money or liquidity in the economy. It is generally managed by the "central bank," a usually autonomous agency that acts as the government's bank and the banker for the commercial banks. By providing loans to commercial banks and accepting deposits from them, the central bank is able to set interest rates, which in turn affect borrowing and spending in the economy and, through their effects on foreign investment, influence the exchange rate. Almost all countries or monetary zones have a central bank, such as the U.S. Federal Reserve, the European Central Bank (ECB), the Bank of England, or the Bank of Canada. More detailed accounts of the economic effects of monetary policy and how central banks implement it will be found in chapters 2 and 4.

Fiscal Policy and Monetary Policy

Fiscal policy and monetary policy are closely linked through the "public financing identity":

$$\text{Fiscal Deficit Financing} = \text{Money Financing} + \text{Domestic Debt Financing} + \text{External Debt Financing}$$

which indicates that governments can finance budget deficits in three ways. First, the deficit could be financed through money creation. In this case the central bank essentially creates money by buying government bonds. The danger is that this increase in the money supply

14   Chapter 1

could lead to inflation. Second, the deficit could be financed through domestic borrowing. In this case the government borrows from the general public and, by competing with the private sector for funds, "crowds out" private investment. Finally, the deficit can be financed through borrowing abroad. This brings about an appreciation of the exchange rate and can also, in time, lead to an external debt crisis. Hence fiscal policy can affect both the money supply and the exchange rate. If, as is true for most low-income countries, domestic financial markets are poorly developed, budget deficits will be mainly covered by money financing and foreign borrowing. This will inevitably result in inflation and a rising external debt.

Fiscal Policy and the Balance of Payments

The government's fiscal stance can affect the balance of payments in other ways. The budget balance and the current account balance often, though not always, move in the same direction so that countries in which the government has a budget deficit also frequently have a current account deficit. The "twin deficit hypothesis," described in sidebar I, explains this phenomenon by means of national accounting definitions. In essence a budget deficit may be financed through foreign borrowing, which would cause a financial account surplus as foreign investors buy government bonds. This will create or increase the size of a current account deficit since, as seen earlier, financial account surpluses are associated with current account deficits. This relationship between the budget and current account deficits has important implications.

Because of the relationship between the current and financial accounts, every time a country runs a current account deficit, the proportion of its economy that is foreign owned increases. The cumulative effect of current account deficits over time determines the country's international investment position, which is the total value of all foreign assets owned by the residents of the home country minus the value of domestic assets owned by foreign residents. A current account deficit causes the size of a country's international investment position to decrease. When this happens, its international investment position is said to "deteriorate." Conversely, the international investment position improves when there is a current account surplus.

Is a current deficit therefore necessarily a bad thing? The answer to this question depends on the circumstances of the country. Countries that are rapidly industrializing or in a pioneer stage of development, such as the United States, Canada, and Australia in the nineteenth century, often have a current account deficit. This is generally considered to be a good thing since such countries offer enormous investment opportunities relative to the savings available from their relatively small populations. It would have made little sense for the United States or Canada to have postponed the building of railroads and cities because they could only be built with foreign investment. Such a strategy would have held back development for decades. For developed, high income countries, however, the situation is different. For these countries a large current account deficit is likely to be due to a low propensity to save and makes them dangerously dependent on continued inflows of foreign capital.

What can be done if a country has a dangerously large current account deficit? Unfortunately, no easy options are available. Government policies to reduce current account deficits fall into two categories. Expenditure switching policies are policies designed to shift domestic spending from imported goods and services to locally produced goods. In the past, trade restrictions, such as tariffs and quotas, were widely used but these are now frowned upon and

Some Economic Concepts: Macroeconomics and the Global Economy   15

SIDE BAR I

THE TWIN DEFICIT HYPOTHESIS

The twin deficit hypothesis is based on two identities. In the national accounts, gross national product (Y_N), the market value of all goods and services produced by the residents of a country in one year, is defined as the sum of private consumption spending (C), investment (I), government expenditure (G), and the current account balance (CA). There is also another national accounting identity by which all income is consumed, saved, or paid to the government in taxes. Therefore GNP (Y_N) is equal to the sum of consumption spending (C), private sector saving (S_P), and taxes (T). Therefore, combining the two identities:

$$Y_N = C + I + G + CA = C + S_P + T$$

Rearranging these terms and eliminating C, we get

$$S_P + (T - G) = I + CA$$

The left of the equation is equal to total saving, private plus government, since (T − G) is the budget surplus, which is the same as government saving. The right of the equation equals total investment since the current account balance is always of equal size but of opposite sign to the sum of the capital and financial accounts.

If there is a government budget deficit, G > T and (T − G) is negative. This budget deficit could be covered in three ways. First, it could be balanced by an increase in private saving (S_P). Second, it could be balanced by a decrease in investment (I). When this occurs it is referred to by economists as the 'crowding-out effect' and is a result of the public sector competing with the private sector for loans. Finally, the budget deficit might be associated with a current account deficit. In this case, the twin deficit case, the budget deficit is financed by foreign borrowing, which creates a financial account surplus and a current account deficit.

---

would be counterproductive if they cause other countries to retaliate by imposing their own trade restrictions. The beneficial effects of a reduction in imports would then be cancelled by a fall in exports. An alternative expenditure switching policy is to engineer an exchange rate depreciation. As seen in the description of fixed exchange rates, this can result in a currency crisis and even if successful will cause a rise in the cost of living by increasing import prices. An exchange rate depreciation will only work if there is a decrease in real incomes, in which case incomes increase by less than the price level.

Expenditure reducing policies are achieved through cuts in government spending and increases in taxes. This brings about a reduction in imports, which are sensitive to changes in domestic incomes. In terms of the twin deficit hypothesis, the government is reducing the current account deficit by reducing the budget deficit. It goes without saying that cuts in spending and increases in taxes are never pleasant.

Monetary Policy and Exchange Rates (The Trilemma)

Since the 1980s and especially since the 1990s, there has been a huge increase in international flows of financial capital following the removal of restrictions on capital mobility, which had been in place since the Great Depression of the 1930s. This has brought into prominence a phenomenon known as the "Open Economy Trilemma" or "Impossible Trinity," which highlights conflicting objectives that governments may have with respect to monetary policy, exchange rate policy, and policy with respect to capital mobility. In the early 1960s Robert Mundell and J. Marcus Fleming pointed out that in a world of free capital mobility, it is impossible for a country with a small economy and a fixed exchange rate to

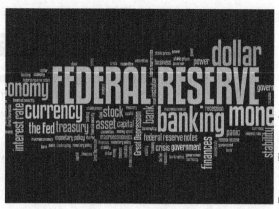

pursue an independent monetary policy. More generally, the trilemma suggests that governments cannot achieve the following three objectives at the same time: (1) a fixed exchange rate, (2) free capital movements, and (3) an independent monetary policy. If the government wishes to achieve the first two objectives—a fixed exchange rate and free capital mobility—it cannot pursue an independent monetary policy because its interest rates would have to be the same as those of other countries whose currencies were similarly pegged. If it tried to lower domestic interest rates through an expansionary monetary policy, capital would flee the country seeking higher foreign interest rates. Faced with a balance of payments deficit, the country would be unable to maintain the fixed exchange rate. It is possible to achieve the first and third objectives of having a fixed exchange and an independent monetary policy but only by imposing capital controls and thereby abandoning the second objective. Finally, it is possible to achieve the second and third objectives—free capital mobility and an independent monetary policy—but only if the exchange rate is allowed to float. In an increasingly globalized world it has become difficult to prevent capital movements even if governments wish to do so and, as a result, governments are faced generally with a choice between a fixed exchange rate and an independent monetary policy. Governments, especially in small or less-developed countries, often prefer fixed exchange rates if a large proportion of their foreign debt is denominated in a foreign currency, such as the U.S. dollar, since a currency depreciation would increase the real burden of the debt in terms of local currency. Some countries also peg their currency to that of a country with a low rate of inflation as part of a strategy to combat domestic inflation. If they adopt a fixed exchange rate, however, they lose the ability to reduce interest rates, which is a desirable policy in the event of a recession.

References

Articles

Fleming, J. Marcus. (1962). Domestic financial policies under fixed and floating exchange rates. *IMF Staff Papers, 9*.

Mundell, Robert A. (1963). Capital mobility and stabilization policy under fixed and flexible exchange rates. *Canadian Journal of Economic and Political Science, 29*(4).

Rodrik, Dani. (2000). How far will international economic integration go? *Journal of Economic Perspectives, 14*(1).

Chapter 2

The First Era of Globalization

The late nineteenth and early twentieth centuries, immediately prior to the outbreak of the First World War, may be described as the "first era of globalization." This era was followed by a more fragmented world economy during the period between the two world wars. A "second era of globalization" began in the 1970s and is still underway. There are some definite similarities between the two globalization eras but also some differences. In particular, the two eras have both exhibited considerable transnational mobility of factors and rapidly growing international trade but differ in respect to exchange rate stability. The world economy between 1918 and 1939 contrasted strongly with both eras of globalization in terms of factor mobility and trends in international trade.

The First Era of Globalization and the Second Industrial Revolution

The "first era of globalization" began about 1880 and ended with the outbreak of the First World War (1914), overlapping to a considerable extent the period sometimes referred to as the "second industrial revolution." Between about the 1860s and 1914 there was an acceleration in the pace of technological change. In some ways this was a continuation of the first industrial revolution, which began in Britain in the late eighteenth century and is usually considered to have been completed by about 1850, but it differed from the earlier industrial revolution in some significant ways. The pace of change was greater and technological leadership was no longer concentrated in Britain but was more widely dispersed among the Western industrial countries. In fact, the United Kingdom was overtaken in terms of total industrial production by the United States in the 1880s and by Germany in the first decade of the twentieth century.

The history of technological developments in the late nineteenth and early twentieth centuries is beyond the scope of this book, but it is worth noting that they included major discoveries and modifications in the following areas, which intensified globalization.

1. *Steel.* The Bessemer (1856) and Siemans-Martin (1865) processes produced steel at rapidly falling prices.

18   Chapter 2

2. *Chemicals.* The period saw developments in the production of chemical fertilizers, synthetic materials (such as plastic), and pharmaceuticals.

3. *Electricity.* The use of electricity expanded rapidly in the 1870s and subsequent decades saw the introduction of electric streetcars, transformers, improved generators, and electric lighting

4. *Transportation.* The switch from wooden to steel ships and the introduction of the steam engine resulted in a sharp decline in long-distance transportation costs. Slightly later, the development of the internal combustion engine led to the emergence of the automobile industry. Prior to the First World War the car remained largely the preserve of the wealthy. But in 1913, on the eve of the war, Henry Ford introduced the assembly line into his automobile plant and brought cars within the reach of a much wider section of the population.

5. *Agriculture and food processing.* By the outbreak of the First World War tractors and combine harvesters were coming into wider use, while the development of mechanical refrigeration brought about a huge expansion in the international meat trade.

Associated with these developments in technology was the growth of industrialization in some regions where it had previously been lagging, such as Italy, Russia, and Austria-Hungary. Italy's industrial revolution is widely regarded as having occurred between 1896 and 1914, although it was mainly confined to the north of the country, while Russia became a major industrial power in the 1890s.

Globalization Through Imperialism

A renewed wave of imperial expansion in the late nineteenth century also served to promote globalization. Until this time most of Asia and Africa had remained only marginally attached to the global economy, but Western imperial expansion forced these regions into full participation in international trade and commerce. Some parts of Asia, such as India, Malaya, and the Dutch East Indies (now Indonesia), had long been exposed to European commerce but others, notably China, Korea, and Japan, had sought to minimize political and economic contacts with the West. Sub-Saharan Africa had previously suffered the depredations of the slave trade, but its interior had been largely inaccessible to Europeans because of its climate, the prevalence of tropical diseases, and a lack of navigable rivers. These circumstances were to change in the late nineteenth century.

Africa

During the course of the nineteenth century, European influence was extended over southern, northern, and central Africa.

Cape Colony had been settled by the Dutch in the seventeenth century, but European influence in southern Africa really began to grow after the conquest of the colony by the British during the Napoleonic Wars. Opposed to the abolition of slavery by the British, the Boers (or

Afrikaners), the descendants of Dutch settlers, began their Great Trek to the north in 1835, founding new colonies in what was later to become South Africa. Subsequently, diamonds were discovered (in 1867) and then gold (in 1886), which led to an influx of immigrants and a great expansion of African trade with the rest of the world. One of the new immigrants was Cecil Rhodes, who became the principal exponent of British imperial expansion in Africa. It was Rhodes who, through his British South Africa Company, gained control for Britain of the vast territory later called Rhodesia, which later still was divided into the countries of Zimbabwe, Zambia, and Malawi.

The Arab countries of North Africa had ostensibly been part of the Ottoman Turkish Empire since the sixteenth century but had long been effectively independent. This independence ended in the late nineteenth and early twentieth centuries. The French, who had already conquered Algeria earlier in the nineteenth century, completed their conquests with the acquisition of Tunisia and Morocco between 1881 and 1912, while the British gained de facto control of Egypt in 1882 and of the Sudan in 1898. There remained only Libya, which was ceded to Italy by the Ottoman Empire in 1912.

Central Africa also came under European domination. The discovery of diamonds in South Africa and the occupation of North Africa by Britain and France had given rise to the "Scramble for Africa," in the course of which Belgium and Germany also acquired African territories. Most notoriously King Leopold of the Belgians established what he called the Congo Free State as his private domain in Africa. Leopold's rule became infamous for the brutal exploitation of the Congo's inhabitants and the plundering of its natural resources.

Asia

By the beginning of the nineteenth century India and Indonesia had long been ruled by European powers, but it was only during the course of that century that the other regions of Asia were forced into closer economic ties with Europe and the Americas through a process of "gunboat diplomacy."

China had long held aloof from trade with Europe because, although Europe desired Chinese tea and silks, the Europeans had little to offer to China in exchange. This situation changed when British traders found a ready market for opium. When a Chinese official confiscated a large shipment of opium, local British representatives launched the Opium War (1839–1842). At the end of the war the defeated imperial government of the Qing (or Manchu) Dynasty was forced to grant substantial trading and commercial concessions to Britain and cede the island of Hong Kong. The defeat of the Manchu government encouraged Western powers to demand concessions, and so began the era of unequal treaties, during which China was repeatedly forced to grant concessions to Western traders and their governments. This process accelerated with the outbreak of the Taiping Rebellion (1850–1864), which marked the beginning of China's disintegration into chaos. Periodic outbreaks of antiforeign violence, such as the Boxer Rebellion of 1900, simply led to further defeats and concessions. Only rivalries and mutual suspicion among the great powers prevented the division of China between the colonial powers. The situation did not significantly change when the Qing Dynasty was

20   Chapter 2

overthrown and replaced in 1912 in a revolution led by Dr. Sun Yat-sen. The new republic remained weak and divided.

Until the mid-nineteenth century Japan held itself even more separate from the outside world than did China, but this isolation was forcibly ended in 1853 when Commodore Matthew Perry of the U.S. Navy sailed into Tokyo Harbor and forced Japan to accept a treaty permitting entry by U.S. merchant ships. Other Western countries soon followed the American example. The Japanese reaction to the incursion of Western powers, however, differed from that of the Chinese. While some Japanese leaders called for the expulsion of the foreigners, others recognized that Japan would need to adopt Western industrial methods to retain its independence. It was this view that prevailed, and during the Meiji period (1868–1912) Japan became a major trading and industrial power. By the turn of the century it had joined with the other powers in colonial expansion, annexing Taiwan in 1895 and Korea in 1910.

In Southeast Asia the British extended control over Burma and the Malay states during the course of the nineteenth century, while the French gained control over substantial territory in the region. French missionaries, who had long been active in the southeast Asian peninsula, were increasingly persecuted by local rulers during the first half of the nineteenth century; this provided the French government with a reason for intervention. Between 1858 and 1893 France took control of Vietnam, Cambodia, and Laos, which it organized into French Indo-China. Only Thailand (or Siam, as it was then called) retained its independence. Like other Asian countries it was opened to Western influence by force but, unlike the rulers of those other countries, the kings of Thailand responded with conciliatory gestures and sought to modernize their kingdom.

The Economic Effects of Imperialism

While the imperialism of the nineteenth and early twentieth centuries did serve to extend the economic reach of industrialized countries into Africa and Asia, its importance to the economies of those countries has often been exaggerated. Despite the decline of communism in recent decades, the Marxist, or rather Leninist theory of imperialism, which was expounded in 1915 by Lenin in his pamphlet "Imperialism, the Highest Stage of Capitalism," remains influential. In Lenin's analysis, competition in capitalist countries leads to the formation of larger and larger enterprises, which accumulate more and more capital. At the same time the masses lack the means to buy all the products of these large-scale enterprises. Faced with accumulating capital and unsold products, the capitalists support imperialism in order to gain control over foreign regions where they can invest their capital and sell their products.

Lenin was hardly an advocate of imperialism, but some supporters of acquiring colonies put forward very similar views. Colonial expansion was often justified as providing new markets and outlets for investment. Certainly there was some selling of European goods in colonial markets. This was especially true of Britain, but even for Britain only about 30 percent of exports between 1900 and 1913 went to Asia and Africa; the balance went to independent countries in Europe and the Americas, and to the self-governing dominions of Australasia. Nor was it the case that Britain depended overwhelmingly on imports from colonial territories. Between 1900 and 1913, between 15 and 20 percent of British imports came from Asia and Africa. For other Western countries colonies were far less important in terms of trade. Before 1914, about 10 percent of French exports went to French colonies.[1]

In Marxist theory the colonies not only provided markets but also opportunities for investment of surplus capital, and there was indeed investment in colonial territories. Again, however, this should not be exaggerated. Britain had by far the largest empire and was the largest foreign investor. Even though British colonial investments were substantial, they amounted to less than half the total of British investments overseas, and other countries invested far less in their colonies. Less than 10 percent of French investments before 1914 went to French colonies, and Germany invested very little in its colonial empire. In fact, colonial expansion in this period was driven more by geopolitical concerns and nationalist pride than by economic needs. Nevertheless, although its economic importance to the colonial powers was limited, it obviously had a great deal of importance to the colonized peoples and, for good or ill, brought them more closely into the global economy.

International Trade

The heyday of free trade occurred in the mid-nineteenth century, and the period after 1879 saw a shift toward more protectionist policies in a number of countries. It is important not to exaggerate this shift, however, and throughout the late nineteenth and early twentieth centuries international trade continued to grow at a faster pace than world income.

Opening of the Suez Canal.

From the late 1870s, as improved transportation systems exposed local farmers and manufacturers to greater competition from abroad, a number of countries sought to protect their home markets from foreign competition. The shift to increased protectionism began with Germany, which increased tariffs on both agricultural and manufactured products in 1879. France, Austria-Hungary, Italy, and Russia all followed with tariff increases in the 1880s and 1890s, while the United States, which had always been protectionist, retained its high import duties. Only Britain and a number of smaller countries, which were highly dependent on the international economy, remained wedded to free trade; even in Britain there was a campaign for higher tariffs after 1903. Nevertheless, while tariffs rose they were not prohibitive. In contrast to the situation after World War I, governments of the time were heavily dependent on import duties as a source of revenue and prohibitive duties, by drastically cutting imports, would have slashed tax revenues. Indeed, land abundant and labor scarce countries such as Canada and Argentina clearly increased import duties more for revenue than

---

[1] William Ashworth. (1969). *An Economic History of England* (London: Methuen & Co.), Tables VI and VII, shows the distribution of British exports by continent.

for protectionist purposes. Certainly the increase in tariffs did not prevent a rapid growth in international trade during the two decades before 1913.

International trade during the decades preceding the First World War grew rapidly as a proportion of world output, in contrast to the interwar period, when trade fell relative to output. Exports as a proportion of world GDP rose from less than 5 percent in 1870 to almost 8 percent on the eve of the First World War, only to fall back to 5.5 percent by 1950. This is despite the fact that there were more countries in existence after the First World War than there had been before as a result of the peace treaties of 1919, which broke up the Austro-Hungarian and Ottoman empires and also created new countries out of territories that had previously been parts of Germany and Russia.

Factor Mobility

In the late nineteenth and early twentieth centuries both capital and labor were far more mobile internationally than they were to be again until late in the twentieth century. This is clear despite the fact that comparisons of labor mobility between the early and late twentieth century are complicated by data limitations. Because of factors such as return migration and multiple visits it is difficult to get an accurate estimate of international migration. For the late twentieth century there is the added complication of the introduction of tighter regulations covering migration, which has led to a growth in illegal migration. Making allowance for such uncertainty, however, it appears that international labor mobility fell sharply during the First World War, recovered during the 1920s, and fell sharply in the 1930s during the Great Depression. By the 1990s international migration was undoubtedly larger in absolute numbers than was the case in the pre-1913 era, but as a proportion of the world population, it was probably similar or even slightly lower than was the case before World War I.

Immigrants at New York.

Statistics for capital flows, although far from perfect, are more readily available than those for labor mobility. Foreign investment provided a significant proportion of the incomes of a number of countries in the period 1870–1910, most dramatically for the United Kingdom, which largely explains why the city of London was the dominant financial center in the pre-1914 world. As with labor mobility, there was a sharp drop in capital mobility in the 1930s and it is clear that it was only in the mid-1980s that international capital movements again reached their pre-World War I share of world GDP. Even then, it is worth noting that in the years between 1870 and 1910 the United Kingdom was regularly investing over 5 percent of its national income overseas and Canada was receiving inflows of foreign investment equal to more than 7 percent of national income. Nothing of this magnitude was experienced after

TABLE 2.1. Net International Capital Flows as a Proportion of GNP for Selected Countries (%)[2]

	1870	1890	1910	1938	1958
France	–	–	3	0	0
Germany	–	2	1	–	0
United Kingdom	5	6	7	0	1
United States	–2	–2	–1	1	0

Sources: Data for France, Germany, and the United Kingdom calculated from Tables J1 and J3 from B. R. Mitchell (1978). *European Historical Statistics 1750–1970* (New York: Columbia University Press); data for the United States calculated from Series U 1-25 and F 47-70 in U.S. Bureau of the Census (1975). *Historical Statistics of the United States.*

World War II. This can be seen from Table 2.1, which shows estimated net international capital flows as a proportion of GDP in the late nineteenth and early twentieth centuries for the countries with the largest foreign investments. Changes in the volume of capital flows, however, give only a partial impression of the changes in the pattern of international investment that occurred during the interwar period. In 1914, short-term investments were very small compared to long-term investments, but after World War I, short-term investments grew much larger and became more volatile.

Exchange Rate Stability and the Classical Gold Standard

The two decades immediately before the First World War, the first era of globalization experienced remarkable stability in exchange rates when compared with both the interwar period and the second era of globalization. The late nineteenth and early twentieth centuries were the age of the "classical gold standard," during which the national currencies of most major countries

were fixed relative to gold. Prior to that time a variety of standards were in use, such as a silver standard in China and a bimetallic standard (silver and gold) in the United States. Britain

---

[2] Because foreign investment is difficult to estimate directly for the nineteenth century, the current account balance has been used to obtain an approximation of international capital flows.

24   Chapter 2

adopted the gold standard as early as 1821, while most other major trading countries adopted the standard later in the century, though China never adopted it and Russia did so only in 1897. The gold standard, therefore, lasted for only a relatively brief period as the dominant world monetary system, but it was held to be the ideal system during the decade prior to the Great Depression and there have occasionally been calls for its restoration since 1945. It is therefore worth describing the theory underlying the gold standard and some of its institutional features in the years immediately before 1913.

The international monetary system adopted by many countries, including all the major industrial countries, in the 1890s and early 1900s was one of fixed exchange rates which were set indirectly by fixing the domestic monetary price of a unit of gold. The gold prices adopted by the various countries then determined their relative exchange rates. For example, between 1880 and 1914 the official gold price in the United States was $20.67 per ounce and the official price in the United Kingdom was £4.24 per ounce. Consequently, the "mint parity" between the dollar and sterling was $4.87 to £1.00. The actual exchange rate fluctuated within a narrow range determined by the cost of shipping gold between the two countries. These costs determined the so-called "gold points." Since the cost of shipping gold between London and New York (including insurance and brokerage charges) was about 2 cents an ounce, the gold import point from New York to London was reached when the pound became worth $4.89, at which point it would be worthwhile for British exporters to the United States to demand payment in gold rather than in dollars. Similarly, the gold export point was $4.85, so that the actual rate of exchange between the pound and the dollar could fluctuate slightly. The rates of exchange between other pairs of currencies were established in a similar fashion. These exchange rates were supposed to be permanent, not periodically adjustable, as with the Bretton Woods system, which was to be established after 1945, or continuously fluctuating, as with floating exchange rates. The question then arises as to how countries could maintain fixed rates in the face of fluctuations in trade and flows in international investment.

The basic theory underlying the gold standard was the "price-specie flow mechanism" described by David Hume (1711–1776) in the eighteenth century. This mechanism linked the domestic quantity of money to balance of trade surpluses or deficits and domestic prices to the quantity of money. Later versions of the mechanism brought investment flows into the picture and incorporated the balance of payments rather than merely the balance of trade. To see how this mechanism works, consider a simplified example in which Britain has a balance of trade surplus and international payments are made in gold. Because Britain is selling to other countries more than it is buying, there will be a net inflow of gold, which will increase the British domestic money supply. In the most extreme form of the gold standard, in which the money supply consists entirely of gold, the inflow will have a direct effect on the quantity of money. In a fiat money system, in which the money supply is backed by gold reserves, the banks will acquire more reserves and be able to increase the money supply by creating more loans. In this case gold represents "high-powered money." Under the quantity theory of money, prices and incomes are determined by the amount of money in the economy under the relationship

$$MV = PY$$

where M is the quantity of money, V is the velocity of circulation (the number of times a unit of currency circulates per period, assumed to be constant), P is the price level, and Y is real income. Clearly this implies that an increase in M will result in an increase in P and/or Y. Therefore, the trade surplus causes an inflow of gold, which increases the domestic money supply, which in turn increases the domestic price level and possibly the level of real income. Since the exchange rate is fixed, higher domestic prices translate into higher foreign prices for England's exports, making them less competitive, and British exports decrease. At the same time, higher incomes in Britain, in combination with rising prices of British goods, cause an increase in imports. In time the balance of trade surplus will automatically be eliminated. In summary, the following occurs:

Balance of trade surplus $\Rightarrow$ inflow of gold $\Rightarrow$ increase in domestic money supply $\Rightarrow$ increase in domestic prices and real incomes $\Rightarrow$ decrease in exports and increase in imports

In the event of Britain having a balance of trade deficit, this will automatically disappear as a result of gold outflows, as follows:

Balance of trade deficit $\Rightarrow$ outflow of gold $\Rightarrow$ decrease in domestic money supply $\Rightarrow$ decrease in domestic prices and real incomes $\Rightarrow$ increase in exports and decrease in imports

The automatic characteristic of the gold standard is the source of its appeal to economists, and politicians who dislike the use of discretionary policies by governments or central banks. The above description, however, leaves two questions unanswered. How were exchange rates initially established and how quickly would adjustments occur? The first of these questions is easily answered. The actual exchange rates were established by different countries at different times without any kind of international coordination, but this was assumed not to matter since the specie flow mechanism itself would bring about adjustments in domestic economies if countries initially had trade imbalances. Of crucial importance, as countries were to find out during the interwar period, was the speed with which these adjustments would occur since slow adjustment would be associated with unacceptably severe and prolonged periods of falling real incomes or rising prices. Prior to the First World War it was generally taken for granted that adjustments would occur quickly and smoothly and, indeed, that appeared to be the case in the two decades prior to the war. Even so, central banks, governments, and commercial banks found it useful to have stocks of gold to cope with short-term fluctuations in trade and investment flows. Prior to 1914 these stocks were usually in the form of gold coins since gold coins were still circulating as part of the domestic money supply, alongside bank notes. When the gold standard was temporarily restored in the 1920s it was more usual to hold gold bars (bullion).

Monetary Policy in the Era of the Gold Standard

An example of the way in which national monetary systems operated under the gold standard is shown by the monetary system of the United States, as it developed at the beginning of the twentieth century.

26   Chapter 2

Banks and Money

Under a fractional reserve system, banks keep only a fraction of their deposit liabilities as reserves. Under the gold standard these reserves were in the form of gold or currency (notes or coins). Relatively small changes in reserves can create much larger changes in the money supply, as was shown in the banking crisis of 1907. In October 1907 five banks in New York experienced difficulties as a larger than normal number of depositors began converting their deposits into currency. Soon a nationwide banking panic developed. Since most of their deposits were held in income-earning securities rather than currency or gold, the banks could not pay out cash to most of their customers. They could, of course, sell those securities on the open market to obtain cash, but this would drive down the price of the securities, and the banks might then have insufficient assets to cover their liabilities and be driven into bankruptcy. In 1907 the banks began suspending redemption of deposits into currency or gold but continued to clear checks and make loans. The panic subsided, but the banks increased the proportion of their deposits kept as cash reserves while depositors increased their holdings of currency and reduced the size of their bank deposits. This caused the money supply to shrink, and the resulting reduction in spending led to falling prices and a sharp but brief recession.

The Federal Reserve System

It was the need to deal with such banking crises that led Congress to create the Federal Reserve System in 1913. One of its major functions was to help the commercial banks acquire additional cash reserves when faced with nervous depositors. It did this by "discounting commercial paper" (buying up securities received by banks as a result of their loans). To prevent a monopoly, the Congress created twelve regional reserve banks rather than a single federal reserve bank. The activities of the reserve banks were to be coordinated by a Federal Reserve Board in Washington, D.C., but its responsibilities were not clearly spelled out. In the 1920s, the regional Federal Reserve banks tended to operate with a large degree of independence. The New York Federal Reserve bank was especially influential because of New York's role as the financial center of the United States.

When commercial banks needed additional cash reserves they could borrow them from the Federal Reserve banks, which would accept short-term commercial paper (claims by banks on their debtors) from the banks as security. This was referred to as "discounting." To make these loans to the commercial banks the Federal Reserve banks could print Federal Reserve notes, which were backed by gold and the commercial paper submitted by the borrowing banks. The commercial banks could then pay depositors wishing to withdraw funds with either gold or Federal Reserve notes.

The intention was to end bank panics by providing commercial banks with the ability to borrow from the Federal Reserve banks using their commercial paper as security. The Federal Reserve banks could control the amount of bank borrowing, and hence the money supply, by varying the interest rate they charged on their loans to commercial banks (the "discount rate"). They soon discovered that they could also influence the money supply by entering the open market and buying or selling commercial paper. Through these "open market operations" they affected the quantity of commercial bank reserves. The reserve banks would provide commercial banks with more reserves when they bought commercial paper and would draw reserves to themselves and away from commercial banks when they sold back the commercial paper.

Commercial banks that were members of the Federal Reserve system (not all commercial banks were) had to deposit their reserves at their regional Federal Reserve bank. Under the gold standard these Federal Reserve banks had to have enough gold to back up 35 percent of the reserve deposits of their members and 40 percent of the Federal Reserve notes outstanding. The remaining 60 percent of the outstanding Federal Reserve notes had to be backed by either gold or eligible securities (primarily short-term commercial paper with maturities of less than one year). Therefore, the system was constrained by the availability of gold.

The Gold Standard and Monetary Policy

The period from about 1880 to 1914, a relatively short period, is usually considered to be the heyday of the gold standard. Under the gold standard no country held gold reserves sufficient to cover its entire money stock, but gold had to cover a proportion of the money supply—a very common required ratio was about 40 percent. Most central banks, however, tried to keep some excess reserves above this required minimum to avoid the need for sudden and drastic changes in prices and output as a result of temporary economic disturbances. Faced with such disturbances, "central banks" such as the Bank of England and the U.S. Federal Reserve might adopt other measures in addition to or instead of making use of excess reserves. They might raise interest rates to attract gold or, if the disturbance involved inflows of gold, they might "sterilize" these inflows by increasing their holdings of excess gold reserves rather than allowing the domestic money supply to increase. Such violations of the "rules of the game" of the gold standard became more obvious in the 1920s but were not unknown before 1914. In the earlier period, however, they were less significant because economic disturbances tended to be temporary and less severe.

References

Books

Ashworth, William. (1969). *An economic history of England*. London: Methuen & Co.

Cameron, Rondo. (1989). *A concise economic history of the world*. New York: Oxford University Press.

Foreman-Peck, James. (1995). *A history of the world economy: International economic relations since 1850* (2nd edition). New York: Harvester Wheatsheaf.

Maddison, Angus. (2006). *The world economy: Historical statistics*. Paris: Organisation for Economic Co-operation and Development.

Mitchell, B. R. (1978). *European historical statistics 1750–1970*. New York: Columbia University Press.

Smiley, Gene. (2002). *Rethinking the great depression*. Chicago: Ivan R. Dee.

U.S. Bureau of the Census. (1975). *Historical statistics of the United States. Colonial times to 1970*. Part 2.

28 Chapter 2

Articles

Irwin, Douglas A. (2002). Interpreting the tariff-growth correlation of the late nineteenth century. *NBER Working Paper 8739.*

McKeown, Adam. (2007). Periodizing globalization. *History Workshop Journal,* 63.

Mokyr, Joel. (1998). The second industrial revolution, 1870–1914. In Valerio Castronono (Ed.), *Storia dell' economia Mondiale.* Rome: Laterza.

Chapter 3

Legacy of the First World War

The period between the two world wars was marked by a failure to adjust to the changes brought about by the First World War. Throughout the 1920s there were unsuccessful or only partially successful attempts to recreate what had come to be seen as the golden age before the First World War. Governments and their advisers were unable, however, to come to grips with the adjustment problems bequeathed by the war. A conflict on the scale of the First World War was bound to require massive rebuilding by the countries involved, but it also transformed the international economy in the following long-term ways.

Canadian troops on the Western front.

1. The gold standard was effectively suspended. During the war the supply of paper currency and bank credit expanded so that convertibility of currency into gold was impossible. At the same time governments prohibited gold exports to prevent losses of gold reserves. Official exchange rates generally remained the same as in 1913 but under the circumstances of war they bore little or no relationship to the relative economic strengths of the countries in question.

2. Patterns of production were distorted. In particular there had been a substantial increase in agricultural production by food importing countries. Once peace was restored it emerged that there was a glut of some agricultural products on the world markets. Adjustments were not, however, limited to the primary sector. There were also problems related to some manufacturing industries.

3. Demographic changes, already apparent during the late nineteenth century, were accelerated as a result of the war. Population growth slowed sharply in the industrialized countries, while some poorer countries were beginning to experience the population explosion, which was to characterize them for most of the twentieth century.

4. Ever since the late nineteenth century, the European countries in general, and Britain in particular, had been experiencing a decline in their share of world exports. This

30   Chapter 3

was a natural result of industrial development in other parts of the world. The war, however, greatly accelerated the pace of change.

5. Protectionism increased to the degree that even though there were more countries on the map after 1919 than before 1914, international trade declined as a proportion of world production.

Governments in the 1920s were therefore faced with difficult long-term problems in addition to having to manage the transition to peacetime conditions after having geared their countries' economies to total war. At the same time citizens had come to expect much more from their governments in terms of economic management and social policy than had been the case before 1914. The attempts of governments to deal with these challenges will be described below, but it is first necessary to consider the growth in the role of government and the immediate problems of coping with the costs of the war.

First World War and the Economic Role of Government

Given the scale of the First World War, governments had been forced to abandon the generally laissez-faire approaches characteristic of the nineteenth century and, though government intervention in the economy was intended at the time to be temporary, it proved impossible to completely turn back the clock. Governments during the interwar period (1919–1939) controlled a much larger proportion of GDP than before the war and were held responsible by their citizens for solving economic and social problems.

During the war itself the state had become heavily involved in managing food supplies, industrial production, and war financing. As a result of Allied blockades, food shortages became acute in Germany and Austria by 1915, and by 1917 the United Kingdom was also experiencing food shortages as a result of Germany's use of U-boats to sink ships going to and from Britain. These food shortages led not only to a rise in food prices but also to government economic intervention in the form of rationing.

There was also a new interest in supporting research into developing substitutes for specific products in short supply. Economic management by the state was also a feature of manufacturing, which had to be quickly redirected from peacetime production to the supplying of goods vital to the war effort, such as munitions, motor vehicles, and ships. This involved government direction of the labor force to a substantial degree and detailed regulations with respect to wage rates and industrial standards. In addition, of course, a large proportion of the adult male population was conscripted into the armed forces.

A further area of government responsibility involved the financing of the war. Higher taxes were needed to finance massive increases in government expenditure and to dampen down spending in the private sector as a measure to prevent inflation. Consequently, income taxes were either introduced for the first time or substantially increased in those countries where they already existed. As it turned out, higher taxes were not able to deal fully with either of the problems at which they were directed. Inflation developed and tax revenues were insufficient to cover war expenditures. Wage and price controls were adopted to suppress inflation, but these were only temporarily successful, and inflation was to appear to devastating effect after the war. Since large increases in government borrowing were required to supplement tax revenues, the war left a legacy of debt. Part of the borrowing—15 percent of war spending in the case of the Allies—was covered by external lending. During the course of the war, the United States and the United Kingdom each lent $7 billion to allied countries, while France lent $2.2 billion. The question of repayment of these loans was to cause great difficulties after the war.

Immediate Costs of the War

The costs of the war can be indicated under three headings: (1) population losses, (2) physical destruction, and (3) financial effects. Each will be considered in turn.

Population Losses

The most easily quantifiable population losses were direct military casualties. During the First World War about 9.5 million men were killed in active service, which accounts for about 13 percent of those who served in the military.

In addition to those killed in combat, about 7 million men were permanently disabled and 15 million otherwise wounded. Civilian deaths also occurred, mainly as a result of disease and famine, though these are harder to quantify. We could add to the list deaths that occurred after the war ended but were a consequence of it. Russia suffered almost 6.5 million casualties (killed, missing, wounded) during the civil war of 1918–1922, which was a direct consequence of the overthrow of the Tsarist regime during the First World War. Finally, account should also be taken of the birth deficit (reductions in births) as a result of the deaths of so many young men. Aldcroft (1978) estimates that when combat deaths, civilian deaths, and the birth deficit are taken into account the European population deficit amounted to between 22 and 24 million people, or about 7 percent of Europe's prewar population. This gives a reasonable picture of the population cost of the war for although there were also birth deficits in other parts of the world, the casualties of the First World War were more heavily concentrated in Europe than was the case in the Second World War.

Physical Destruction

Physical destruction due to the war was substantial but is difficult to quantify. The occupied countries suffered the most. Destruction of farms, houses, and industrial infrastructure was greatest in France and Belgium, since much of the fighting occurred on their land, but other countries also fared badly, notably Russia and Italy. In terms of physical destruction, Belgium suffered more than any other country, losing about 6 percent of its housing stock, half of its steel mills, and three-quarters of its railway rolling stock. Britain did not suffer significant aerial bombardment, as it was to do in World War II, but it did suffer heavily in terms of destruction of its merchant fleet, losing almost 8 million tons of shipping. During the war the total losses to world shipping were more than 15 million tons, most of these losses being on the Allied side. In addition, a significant proportion of the capital stock had worn out during the war and not been replaced because savings had been diverted to military uses. The overall physical destruction due to the First World War was estimated in 1930 by the British statistician A.L. Bowley at £2,000 million at prewar prices, which amounted to about 3.6 percent of the total value of capital of all European countries, including Russia. Clearly there was an immense task to be undertaken in reconstruction and in shifting industry back from serving military purposes to serving civilian needs.

Since governments had played such a major role in economic management during the war, citizens now held governments responsible for bringing back the relative prosperity of the prewar period. Unfortunately, however, the war had left governments with severe financial difficulties that hindered their ability to cope with the needs of postwar reconstruction. It was not until the mid-1920s that production in Western Europe returned to the levels of 1913.

Medieval cloth hall of Ypres, Belgium, in flames as a result of artillery fire.

Financial Effects

The direct costs of the war obviously entailed huge expenditures and, since all participants in the war relied primarily on borrowing to finance the war, one of its legacies was a huge increase in government debt. Table 3.1 shows government expenditures by the major warring countries between 1914 and 1918, while Table 3.2 shows how government budgets moved

TABLE 3.1. Total Expenditures, 1914–1918 (millions of dollars)

Germany	Britain	France	Russia	Italy	United States
$32,388	$45,307	$30,009	$11,778	$12,892	$35,731

Source: Niall Ferguson. (1998). Table 36 in *The Pity of War.* London: Allen Lane.
Copyright © March 3, 2000 Niall Ferguson. Reprinted by permission of Basic Books, a member of the Perseus Books Group.

TABLE 3.2. Government Budget Balances as a Proportion of Total Expenditures (%)

	Germany	Britain	France	Russia	Italy	USA
1913	−40.5	+3.1	+0.5	+0.1	−19.4	
1914	−73.5	−61.3	−54.8	−57.0	−6.1	−0.1
1918	−93.8	−69.2	−80.0	n/a	−70.2	−71.2

Source: Niall Ferguson. (1998). Table 37 in *The Pity of War.* London: Allen Lane.
Copyright © March 3, 2000 Niall Ferguson. Reprinted by permission of Basic Books, a member of the Perseus Books Group.

sharply into deficit. Government debt did not decrease once the war was over but continued to grow in the immediate postwar years as governments struggled to cope with the aftermath of the conflict. Once the armistice had been signed, the most urgent problem was the relief of poverty and hunger, food being in very short supply, particularly in Central and Eastern Europe. Between February and August 1919 the American Relief Administration delivered to Europe food worth about $1,250 million. This fell, however, far short of the needs of the time, was sharply reduced in mid-1919, and was far less generous than might appear at first sight. The United States had a large surplus of farm produce at the end of the war, and less than 10 percent of the food was provided as outright gifts. The remainder was provided either for cash payments or on credit, which added to the debt burden of the recipient countries. Financial obligations to the United States made the victorious European countries even more determined than they otherwise would have been to make Germany compensate them for the costs of the war, while high levels of debt reduced Germany's ability to pay.

The Postwar Boom and Slump

Though many countries had to deal with poverty and famine immediately after the war, others enjoyed a spectacular boom, though this was followed quickly by an equally dramatic slump. The boom, which was particularly pronounced in the United States, the United Kingdom, and Japan, had not been expected. Instead a recession had been anticipated as soldiers and sailors were demobilized and military orders from industry were cancelled. There was in fact a mild, short-lived recession in early 1919, but this soon gave way to a strong boom as a result of pent-up demand for commodities with a resulting demand for labor, which soaked up the demobilized men.

An unfortunate consequence of this boom was a sharp rise in inflation since stocks of goods were in short supply and industry was only beginning to return to peacetime production. Things were made worse by the fact that governments quickly abandoned the wartime economic controls in their haste to return to peacetime conditions. In addition, monetary policy was lax and government spending was only slowly reduced from its high wartime levels.

In early 1920 the bubble burst and a severe slump began. For Britain and Sweden incomes and production fell more sharply in 1920–1921 than they were to fall in 1929, and on a monthly basis the decrease in output for the United States was greater than during the Great Depression. Fortunately, the postwar slump, while severe, was of much shorter duration than the later slump of the 1930s. There were three major reasons for this sudden and dramatic switch from postwar boom to postwar slump. The first reason is that the boom inevitably came to an end as output caught up with demand, and overseas supplies of commodities resumed

A tenant farmer on relief.

after production and shipping adjusted to peacetime conditions. A second reason was that inflation resulted in falls of real wages as money wages lagged behind prices, and this caused a decline in consumer spending. The third reason for the bursting of the bubble was that governments and central banks belatedly reacted to inflation with sharply contractionary policies. Some monetary and fiscal contraction was undoubtedly necessary to control the boom but the policies followed were too severe and were persisted in for too long.

The slump made worse an already difficult situation for countries seeking to return to normal peacetime economic conditions. Some countries, however, were to experience far worse troubles. Germany largely missed out on both the boom and the slump and in fact experienced an increase in industrial production in 1921, while other countries were suffering very sharp decreases in production. But hyperinflation was soon to have far more disastrous consequences for Germany than the postwar slump had for Britain or the United States.

Hyperinflation

All the war economies experienced varying degrees of inflation, but in a number of countries this inflation developed into hyperinflation. Hyperinflation is easier to recognize than to define. It has been described simply as inflation that is "very high" or "out of control." More specifically it is characterized by an unchecked increase in the money supply and in prices to the point that the population begins refusing to hold money or accept it in payment. In a pioneering study of hyperinflation in 1956, Phillip Cagan defined hyperinflation as a monthly inflation rate of at least 50 percent, though hyperinflations often have a much higher rate of price increase than that. In Germany in 1923, prices were, at one point, increasing at a rate of about 30 percent per day. In the 1920s hyperinflations occurred in Austria (1922–1923), the Free City of Danzig (1923),[1] Hungary (1922–1924), Poland (1921–1924), Russia (1921–1922), and, most famously, in Germany (1921–1923). It is the German hyperinflation, the one that had the most serious international consequences, that is the next topic.

During the First World War in Germany, as with all combatant countries, the money supply increased rapidly, but inflation was suppressed through price controls and rationing. In Germany's case, banknotes in circulation increased by 464 percent in nominal terms between 1914 and 1918, but the consumer price index rose by only 140 percent. This meant that large holdings of money balances were accumulating and ready to fuel inflation once controls were lifted. In this respect Germany was not exceptional, but there were also other dangers facing Germany's newly created Weimar Republic.[2] In its early years, the republic was threatened by extremists of both the Left and the Right, and by independent paramilitaries and

---
[1] Previously part of Germany; now Gdansk in Poland.
[2] The term *Weimar Republic* refers to the republic established in 1919, after the overthrow of the monarchy at the end of the First World War, and was named after Weimar, the city in which its constitution was drafted. The Weimar Republic lasted until Hitler came to power in 1933.

Legacy of the First World War   35

militias. The government, struggling to merely survive, was in no position to exert the kind of strong leadership that would be needed to keep inflation under control.

In addition, the immediate postwar years were overshadowed by expectations of reparations payments. The Treaty of Versailles, which officially ended the state of war between Germany and the Allied Powers in 1919, forced Germany to accept responsibility for causing the war and specified that it would have to pay reparations to the Allies in compensation. The actual sum was not specified when the treaty was signed. It was to be determined by an Inter-Allied Reparations Commission, which did not report until January 1921. At that time the amount was set at 269 billion gold marks ($64 billion) but was almost immediately reduced to 132 billion gold marks ($31.4 billion). This may seem to be a very large amount of money but Niall Ferguson and others have argued that the sums paid in reparations were much less significant than was claimed by Germany at the time. Reparations were to be paid not in one lump sum but rather in annual payments of 2 billion gold marks plus 26 percent of German export receipts, which amounted to about 4 to 7 percent of Germany's national income. After the Franco-Prussian War of 1871 Germany had forced France to pay over 25 percent of its national income in reparations over a three-year period, which France was able to do without being driven into national bankruptcy. In fact, while Germany paid 19 billion gold marks ($4.5 billion) in reparations between 1921 and 1931, it borrowed from the United States in this same period a total of 27 billion marks ($6.4 billion), on which it defaulted in 1932. The problem was not that the reparations payments were unaffordable but that they created a climate of uncertainty and caused considerable resentment among Germans, who did not believe they were responsible for starting the war. Nor did they believe that they had been defeated militarily. It was much more comforting to blame Germany's failure to achieve victory on a "stab in the back" by cowardly politicians than to face the fact that the German armies had been defeated in the field.

Once the war was over, inflation took off. Between January 1919 and January 1920 the consumer price index rose almost fivefold. This was almost twice the rate at which the money supply was growing. The increase was due mainly to the fact that billions of hoarded marks were now entering the economy, though the depreciation of the mark against foreign currencies as a result of uncertainty about the size of the reparations bill also played a role. Inflation then died down and prices were fairly stable for 15 months, but it then resumed and the price level rose by about 600 percent between July 1921 and July 1922. This return of inflation was associated with reparations. As indicated, the Reparations Commission reported in January 1921 and required Germany to make annual payments of 2 billion gold marks plus 26 percent of export receipts. These payments were actually met in early 1922, but the German government claimed it was unable to continue meeting these terms and in June 1922 suspended all payments.

It was at this point, in July 1922, that the hyperinflation began. Things got worse after French and Belgium troops occupied the Ruhr region in January 1923, in retaliation for Germany's refusal to pay reparations. When the local population engaged in passive resistance toward the occupiers, they were financially supported by the German government, which added to the already massive budget deficits. An idea of the scale of the problem can be gained from Table 3.3, which shows the wholesale price index between July 1914 and December 1923.

TABLE 3.3. German Wholesale Price Index, 1914–1923 (July 1922 = 100)

1914, July	1	1923, August	944,000
1919, April	3	1923, September	23,900,000
1922, January	70	1923, October	7,100,000,000
1922, December	1,475	1923, November	726,000,000,000
1923, January	19,835	1923, December	1,300,000,000,000

The hyperinflation is associated with many colourful anecdotes, of which some are probably true. The most famous story is of people taking wheelbarrows full of money to market to buy baskets of goods, but there are many others. It was said that people would order two beers at a time because the price would have risen by the time the first beer was finished and that taxis were preferred to trams because the taxi fare was paid at the beginning of the trip, while the tram fare was paid at the end. There were stories of shoppers finding that the thieves who stole the baskets in which they carried their money had left the worthless money itself on the ground. By mid-1923 workers were being paid as often as three times a day, with time off to rush out and spend the money before it lost its value. By this stage, farmers were refusing to sell food for worthless paper and food riots began to break out in the cities.

A Berlin woman burns money to keep warm.

Cause of the Hyperinflation

The obvious question is how did such a situation occur? Most explanations are variants of two general approaches. The first approach, accepted by the majority of economists, emphasizes German fiscal and monetary policy. In this view the hyperinflation was a result of excessive government budget deficits, financed through money creation. In the turbulent years at the beginning of the Weimar Republic successive German governments found it impossible to either raise taxes or cut spending sufficiently to get the budget close to balance. In 1918–1923 taxes covered only 15 percent of expenditures. At first governments were able to finance deficits by borrowing but the public soon refused to buy more government securities, at which point the authorities were forced to issue Treasury bills financed by the central bank. This added to the money supply and stimulated inflation. A vicious circle developed in which rising prices increased the budget deficit, which resulted in the creation of more money and even faster-rising prices. There were suspicions on the part of the Allied Powers that Germany deliberately

Legacy of the First World War **37**

encouraged inflation through money creation to demonstrate the country's inability to pay reparations. Whether or not this was true, the disastrous decision of the German government to financially support passive resistance to French and Belgian occupation of the Ruhr certainly gave a strong impetus to inflation.

The alternative approach emphasizes balance of payment imbalances as the cause of the hyperinflation. In this view balance of payment deficits caused exchange rate depreciation, which increased the cost of Germany's imports and triggered inflation. Reparations payments can fit neatly into this explanation as the cause of the balance of payment deficits. The view that reparations payments were the cause of the hyperinflation was a popular one with German nationalists since it placed responsibility for the catastrophe on the Allies rather than the Germans. Problems with this particular argument are, firstly, as indicated above, the reparations payments were not beyond the capacity of Germany to pay and, secondly, payments were suspended in June, just before the start of the hyperinflation. Nevertheless, reparations played a role in the run-up to inflation by creating uncertainty, even if they were not the principal cause of the economic crisis.

The End of the Hyperinflation

By mid-1923 the economy was on the verge of collapse. As indicated, farmers were refusing to sell their produce for worthless paper money and food riots were beginning to break out. At this point the political will needed to end inflation finally emerged. The first step toward restoring economic stability was the successful issue of a 500 million gold mark loan in August 1923. Such was the desire for an alternative to paper marks that the loan was taken up and the gold mark bonds came to be accepted as a form of hard currency. October of the same year saw the end of the policy of supporting passive resistance in the Ruhr and the introduction of a comprehensive stabilization policy. There were two essential elements of this policy.

1. The Rentenbank was set up in mid-October. It was backed by fictitious claims on industry and land. This was essentially a confidence trick since there was no way of realizing these claims, but the trick worked and the public gave its confidence to the new institution. The Rentenbank was authorized to issue the rentenmark, which was linked to the successful gold mark loan. Five hundred rentenmarks could be converted, upon demand, into a bond having a nominal value of 500 gold marks. Each rentenmark was valued at 1 trillion paper marks.

2. Paper marks remained, for the moment, legal tender but the Reichsbank was no longer allowed to discount government bills, and Reichsbank notes had to be backed at least one-third by gold.

Within a month of the first issue of rentenmarks in November 1923 the hyperinflation was over. In August 1924 the old paper marks were replaced by a new Reichsmark equal in value to the rentenmark. The introduction of a new currency worth 1 trillion old marks would not by itself, of course, end hyperinflation. So why did the hyperinflation come to an end? There is no single explanation as to why stabilization succeeded at this stage but rather a combination of the following factors.

38   Chapter 3

1. *A restoration of confidence in the currency.* This was achieved by the bogus backing of the Rentenbank with land. Acceptance of the new currency was also due to the fact that in spite of the rate at which nominal money was being created, there was actually a severe shortage of money in 1923. Because of a phenomenon known as the "paradox of inflation," prices were increasing even faster than the money supply as people tried to unload their money as quickly as possible. As a result, in late 1923, the quantity of money circulating was equivalent in real terms (or purchasing power) to only 168 million prewar gold marks. This meant that there was a thirst for a new money in which the public could have confidence. In a sense the public was willing to suspend disbelief.

2. *Monetary stabilization.* This was achieved by the imposition of strict limits on the quantity of marks that could be issued by the Rentenbank and then by the Reichsbank.

3. *Fiscal stabilization.* New taxes were introduced and severe spending cuts imposed to bring the budget into balance. The hyperinflation, at this stage, actually made it easier to balance the budget since, despite its otherwise disastrous impact, it had the positive effect of almost wiping out long-term government debt. At the end of the war debt servicing accounted for more than half of government expenditure, but by 1924 it accounted for less than 3 percent of expenditure.

4. *Exchange rate stabilization.* The Allied Powers were persuaded that Germany needed some relief in terms of reparations payments. A committee was set up under the chairmanship of Charles G. Dawes, an American banker (and future U.S. vice president). Under the Dawes Plan of 1924 Germany received a loan of 800 million gold marks (equivalent to £40 million) and reparations payments were rescheduled. The Reparations Commission in 1921 had required Germany to make annual payments of 2 billion gold marks plus 26 percent of export receipts. These were now reduced to payments of 1 billion in the first year, increasing to 2.5 billion marks annually after five years. The currency stabilization and the Dawes Plan enabled Germany to return to the gold standard in 1924 with a new currency (the reichsmark) at the prewar parity of 23.8 cents (U.S.).

The immediate aftermath of stabilization was a short but severe recession. Capital goods industries had overexpanded during the hyperinflation, counting on it to wipe out the real value of their debts. They now found themselves weighed with debts that would have to be repaid in real money. While there had been only 263 bankruptcies in 1923, there were 6,033 in 1924. Subsequently the German economy recovered and experienced three years of prosperity before the onset of the Great Depression. This recovery was, however, due to a large extent to inflows of American capital, a fact that had adverse effects. Eichengreen (1992) has pointed out that U.S. lending to Germany in the mid-1920s enabled the country to avoid fully adjusting to the structural changes that had occurred in its economy, though this was not necessarily apparent to observers at the time. Klug found that in 1925–1929 Germany had an annual growth rate of real net national product of 2.4 percent and a growth rate in real consumption of 3.1 percent.[3]

---

[3] Klug, quoted in Barry Eichengreen (1992). The Origins and Nature of the Great Slump Revisited. *Economic History Review* XLV, p. 220.

Legacy of the First World War   **39**

Gainers and Losers

Overall, the hyperinflation was obviously a catastrophe, but there were some who benefitted from it, at least in the short run. The major beneficiaries were the following:

1. Large corporations could borrow to buy stocks of materials and then watch as inflation wiped out their debts. During the hyperinflation there were very few bankruptcies. In 1913 there had been an average of 815 bankruptcies per month; in late 1923 there were only 10 per month. Big businesses also benefitted from the fact that the money wages of their employees lagged behind the price increases of their products. One of the lasting effects of the inflation was an increase in the concentration of industry. Another effect was an expansion in capital goods industries.

2. Speculators who traded in foreign exchange often benefitted and some substantial, though usually short-lived, fortunes were acquired at this time. The industrialist Hugo Stinnes was able to build up a giant industrial empire during the hyperinflation. Using his access to foreign currency as collateral, he borrowed large sums in reichsmarks and repaid them in worthless paper. Because of his success in exploiting inflation he came to be known as the *Inflationskönig* (inflation king). His empire, however, collapsed soon after the stabilization of the mark.

3. It is arguable that the German government benefitted to some degree from the inflation since it seemed to prove that the country could not afford to pay reparations, though it is unlikely that the government actually anticipated or planned for the degree of inflation that eventually occurred. The government also benefitted from the fact that, as seen above, hyperinflation largely eliminated its debt.

While some may have gained from hyperinflation, however, the losers far exceeded the gainers in number. Among those hardest hit were the following:

1. The consumer goods industries, such as textiles and food. Their sales suffered as a result of the fall in real wages, which had the effect of reducing consumer spending.

2. Small businesses, which found it much harder to obtain credit than large corporations.

3. Wage earners, whose wages lagged behind prices.

4. Those on fixed incomes, who were the most severely affected of all. In 1914 a nest egg of 68,000 marks would have been worth $16,000, which was then enough to support a comfortable retirement. In 1923 such a sum would have been insufficient to buy a postage stamp. There was some restitution made to holders of financial assets after the stabilization of the mark, but this fell far short of what was needed to restore the real wealth of people on fixed incomes. Those still holding bank deposits denominated in marks were repaid between 15 and 25 percent of their original deposit value and bondholders received 2.5 percent of the original bond values. Most people, however, had already liquidated their bonds and emptied their bank accounts in the desperate struggle to survive the hyperinflation. They received nothing.

40   Chapter 3

Restoration of the Gold Standard

Once the immediate postwar chaos was ended, political leaders and their economic advisors could turn their attention to more long-term problems. The first of these to be addressed was the restoration of an international system of multilateral payments. The gold standard had effectively been suspended in World War I when convertibility between paper money and gold and the free export of gold were halted. It was taken for granted that once the war was over the gold standard would be restored and the prosperity of the prewar years would return. Unfortunately, little thought was given as to what the rates of exchange between the various national currencies and gold should be. There seems to have been a general assumption that the prewar parities would simply be resumed but this assumption took insufficient account of the price inflation, which had occurred since the suspension of gold payments in 1914. Some countries, such as Britain, which had experienced relatively mild inflation during the war, chose to undergo deflation and return to gold at prewar parities, while other countries which had experienced higher rates of inflation, such as France, preferred to return to gold at much less than prewar parities rather than undergo the severe deflation that would otherwise have been necessary. Even Britain, however, although it had suffered less from inflation than Germany or France had experienced higher inflation than the United States. The result was that the pound was seriously overvalued relative to the dollar, while the franc was undervalued.

A more general problem was that after the war, price levels were higher than before 1914, but the world's gold stock had hardly changed. There was now too little gold to support the world's currencies at anything like prewar parities. Consequently, the gold exchange standard was adopted as a compromise. Many countries held "key currencies," mainly pounds or dollars, as substitutes for gold. While this was not a totally new phenomenon, the share of foreign exchange in international reserves increased by more than 50 percent between 1913 and 1928. This could create problems if these countries converted their holdings of the "key currencies" into gold. Until 1931 this was not a serious problem for the United States, which had half of the world's gold reserves with which to convert dollars into gold. But from the beginning it

TABLE 3.4. Gold Reserves of Selected Countries as a Proportion of Total World Gold Reserves (%)

	1920	1925	1930	1935
United States	32.6%	43.2%	38.6%	44.6%
United Kingdom	7.6	7.5	6.6	7.3
Japan	7.4	6.2	3.8	1.9
France	14.4	8.6	19.2	19.4
Germany	3.5	3.1	4.8	0.3
Italy	2.7	3.6	2.6	1.2

Legacy of the First World War   **41**

represented a serious threat to Britain since the pound was seriously overvalued relative to most currencies and the United Kingdom had relatively modest gold reserves.

Even with adequate gold reserves and more appropriate exchange rates it is unlikely that the international monetary system would have functioned well. A major problem, not generally understood at the time, was that the conditions which had allowed the prewar gold standard to function smoothly no longer operated. The following major changes had occurred in the nature of international investment.

1. The United Kingdom was no longer the principal international investor. This position had passed to the United States, which had implications for the stability of the international financial system. Before 1913 British capital had gone predominantly to countries that supplied Britain with food and raw materials and were complementary to the European producers of manufactured goods. American investment after 1919, in contrast, tended to go to European countries that were competitive to the United States. These countries had export surpluses with countries that depended on selling primary products to the United States. But the European countries themselves had trade deficits with the United States, so their ability to service their American debts depended on a more roundabout flow of goods and finance. More specifically, this meant that if there was a drastic decline in American imports from primary producing countries, this would reduce their ability to import European goods and therefore affect the ability of those countries to service their U.S. debts. The international economy was also vulnerable to a drastic reduction in U.S. investment abroad as this would reduce the ability of European countries to import American goods. When, in the early 1930s, both American import demand and American foreign lending dried up, an international economic crisis was inevitable.

2. Before 1914, financial transactions had been centralized in London. After the war, New York and Paris competed with London, which made it easier for destabilizing funds to move internationally from one center to another. Large and unstable movements of short-term capital were characteristic of the 1920s. French foreign investment, in particular, was largely short term and often took the form of capital flight and repatriation, which were motivated by instability in the economy of France rather than the needs of the international economy.

3. The New York market was less responsive to changes in the balance of payments than the London market. Only a small fraction of U.S. financial transactions and production was accounted for by the international economy, a fact that prevented a close connection between the U.S. balance of payments and the U.S. level of foreign lending.

4. Many central banks adopted policies of neutralizing the domestic monetary effects of gold inflows and outflows. This was not a totally new development, but it became much more widespread in the 1920s. Policies were adopted to insulate domestic output and employment from external disturbances (a practice referred to as violating "the rules of the game"). Rather than risk inflation as a result of gold inflows, surplus

countries, notably France and the United States, raised interest rates and restricted domestic credit, forcing other countries to do the same or lose gold reserves. These actions obstructed the adjustment mechanism of the gold standard and introduced a deflationary bias into the international monetary system.

The Chain of Debt

The survival of the restored gold standard depended crucially on the international flow of credit. As a result of the Dawes plan and the end of hyperinflation, Germany was able to return to the gold standard, but the hyperinflation had seriously weakened the country's economy by wiping out the value of savings and bank reserves. As a result, German governments, banks, and corporations in the 1920s had to borrow heavily from U.S. investors not only to pay reparations but also to finance domestic investment. This made the international debt situation worse than it otherwise would have been.

The international financial system was able to function only as long as there was a continuous flow of credit. America's European allies argued that there should be a general forgiveness or at least a reduction of war debts once peace was restored, and they did in fact grant some debt forgiveness to wartime allies that owed them money. They considered American loans as a part of the American contribution to the war, especially since the United States entered the war late and relatively few American soldiers were killed. The United States, however, did not see things this way and insisted in being repaid in full with interest, while urging its European associates to be lenient toward Germany in regard to reparations. It seemed, in fact, as though the Americans were much harsher toward their recent allies than they were toward their defeated enemies. As a result, Britain, France, and Belgium felt they had no choice but to insist on reparations from Germany. The question then arose as to how Germany was to obtain the gold or dollars needed to pay reparations. Since the United States continued the policy of high tariffs that it had adopted since the mid-nineteenth century, it was difficult for Germany to obtain gold or dollars by exporting to the United States. In fact, U.S. tariffs were substantially raised in 1922 and 1923.

Fortunately, the system was able to function for the time being because of the willingness of American investors to lend to Germany. About $6.4 billion in American investment entered Germany between 1921 and 1931. During the same period, Germany's reparations payments totaled about $4.5 billion. As long as this situation continued there seemed to be no problem. The Americans lent the Germans more than sufficient

Cartoon expressing German resentment of reparations.

Legacy of the First World War **43**

funds for them to pay reparations, which Britain and France then used to service their debts to the Americans. The true problem was that this situation could not continue. Once U.S. credit dried up, the system was almost bound to collapse. This became apparent in 1928, when American investors began cutting back on foreign investment when they found they could get much larger returns from speculating on the New York stock market. Germany began to move into recession more than a year before the Wall Street crash of October 1929 signaled the start of the global Great Depression.

Changing Patterns of Production and Demand

The problems of the international economy were not limited to postwar reconstruction and deficiencies in international finance. The war had severely disrupted agricultural trade. As a result of blockades, countries such as the United Kingdom and Germany, which had previously imported a large proportion of their food, had to greatly increase their agricultural production. After the war, previous sources of supply were once again available, but the new producers continued to produce. As a result there was global overproduction of agricultural products, and prices were stagnant or falling through much of the 1920s. The rapid spread of improved agricultural technology at this time only made the overproduction worse.

For the United States, the effect of falling prices on farmers was made more severe by the fact that they had borrowed during the war to take advantage of the then-high prices. They had also expanded into marginal lands, which subsequently resulted in erosion. For the world in general problems were not evenly spread either across agricultural industries or between farmers within each agricultural industry. Large-scale farmers were better able to take advantage of advances in technology than were small farmers. Rising urban standards of living in some countries, such as the United States and Canada, led to a shift in consumption away from cereals and toward more income-elastic foodstuffs such as dairy products and fruits. The result was that primary producers, particularly small producers who concentrated on cereals, fared badly, while other primary producers did quite well. Farmers in Australia and Argentina, who concentrated on meat or dairy products, actually flourished during the 1920s.

It was not only the primary sector that went through a difficult adjustment period. Parts of the manufacturing sector also faced problems. This was due partly to a growth in production by new industrial producers and partly to diffusion of new technology. Even before the First World War the United States and Japan had been competing increasingly with the older manufacturing countries in Western Europe. The war enabled them to gain market share at the expense of the Europeans, who were preoccupied with military conflict. Other countries, such as Canada, which had imported manufactured goods were now driven by war shortages to produce their own. Once the war was over the traditional exporters of manufactures, such as Britain, found it difficult to recover the markets lost during the war.

As with agriculture, not all industries in the manufacturing sector suffered equally. This was a consequence of the growth of new industries and the decline of old ones. The interwar period is sometimes cited as one that lacked epoch-making new inventions, in comparison to the decades before the First World War or after the Second World War, but it was a period in which innovations were more widely adopted and existing technology was improved. The

44   Chapter 3

automobile had been invented in the nineteenth century, but it was in the early twentieth century that the assembly line was developed in car production and cars became widely available. There were also major improvements in communications, wider use of electricity, and continuing improvements in the chemicals industries, including the development of synthetic fibers. These developments had been considerably accelerated by the war. A consequence was declining demand for the products of the old industrial economies, such as the coal and cotton industries in the United Kingdom, while producers in the newer industries prospered.

When we add to the above problems of agriculture and manufacturing the difficulties of adjusting from war to peacetime production, we get a world economy that performed poorly throughout the period between the two world wars. Certainly the decade of the 1920s was much better than the Depression decade of the 1930s, but even in the 1920s conditions were very difficult for large parts of the world's population. This was generally a prosperous decade for urban populations in North America, but the European countries fared much worse than Canada or the United States. Even in North America many farmers faced difficulties as a result of low agricultural prices. Only Japan did unambiguously well in the 1920s.

International Trade

The changes in production and demand were reflected in international trade. Two important developments in world trade during the interwar period were the decline in international trade both absolutely and as a proportion of world production, and a decline in the trade share of Europe. Trade, not surprisingly, fell during the Depression, which saw a breakdown in the international economy. But a decrease in international trade relative to world production was also a feature of the 1920s. This is all the more striking because there were more countries in existence after the First World War than before so that a good deal of what had previously been recorded as domestic trade was now international trade. A major cause of the shrinkage in trade was an increase in protectionism fueled by nationalist rivalries that were worsened rather than moderated in the period after the war. This growth in protectionism will be described in the next section.

Also important was the shift in national shares of world trade and changes in its composition. There was a significant decline in Europe's dominance in world trade between 1913 and 1938, as shown in Table 3.5. During the war, the United States and Japan increased their market share in Latin America, Asia, and Australasia at the expense of the warring European powers. Those powers were subsequently unable to fully recover their prewar shares. Europe's share in the export of manufactures fell from 81.5 percent in 1913 to 67.1 percent in 1937, while the shares of the United States and Japan correspondingly increased. Other factors associated with a decline in Europe's share of international trade were the fall of Tsarist Russia and a decline in intra-European trade. Tsarist Russia had accounted for 4 percent of world trade, while the Soviet Union, which replaced it, accounted for only 1 percent of trade in 1937, partly as a result of its own pursuit of self-sufficiency and partly because of the enmity of other countries to what was then the world's only socialist state. As for intra-European trade, 40 percent of imports into European countries in 1913 came from within Europe, while the proportion had fallen to 29 percent by 1938. The problem was not so much that these changes occurred—a

Legacy of the First World War

TABLE 3.5. Share of World Trade (Exports plus Imports) (Percent)

	1913	1937
Europe	62.0	51.5
North America (Canada and the United States)	13.0	15.5
Asia	11.0	15.5

decrease in Europe's share of world trade was inevitable. The accelerated pace at which the changes occurred, however, created serious structural adjustment problems.

As well as regional shifts, there were also changes in the composition of trade. In the nineteenth century, trade largely followed the pattern predicted by comparative advantage. Industrialized countries exported manufactured goods and imported primary products, while the opposite was true of less-developed countries. This pattern remained broadly true during the interwar period. In fact, trade in manufactured goods between industrialized countries actually declined and there was an increase in the share of trade consisting of exports of manufactures by industrialized to nonindustrialized countries, the opposite of the pattern which was to develop after the Second World War. This was partly due to protectionism in industrialized countries and partly due to the changing composition of manufactured exports. There was a decrease in trade in consumer goods, such as textiles, which were imported by the industrial countries, and increased trade in capital goods, such as iron and steel, which were imported by the less-developed countries.

There were also changes in the composition of primary product exports. The share of food in exports of primary products fell relative to the share of minerals, but equally significant were changes within the food groups. Exports of tropical foodstuffs, such as cocoa, coffee, and bananas, grew, while exports of cereals fell, reflecting the overproduction of basic food staples as a result of the drive for self-sufficiency in food during the war. One consequence of the shift in the composition of food exports was an increase in the importance of Africa in world trade. This decline in the overall share of food in primary product exports was matched by a rise in the share of minerals, largely due to the increased importance of oil. Though coal was still the most important source of energy during the interwar period, oil was needed by the growing automobile and petrochemical industries.

Demographic Changes

A contributing factor in the slower growth of production and trade during the period was the slowing down of population growth in the industrialized countries. During the nineteenth century, improvements in hygiene and medicine had sharply reduced infant mortality rates in the high-income countries. Since birth rates remained high, the decreased infant mortality rates had led to accelerated population growth in Europe and areas of European settlement, including the United States, Canada, and Australia. The rate of population growth had already begun to slow in Europe in the late nineteenth century as birth rates responded belatedly to higher survival rates. The high death rate among young men during the First World War, however, drastically reduced the rate of population growth within a very short time period. The

46   Chapter 3

rate of population growth also slowed in the United States, but this was due at least as much to tighter immigration controls as to a lower birth rate. Laws were passed in 1917, 1921, and 1924, successively tightening controls over immigration. These laws were motivated partly by fear of the elites that immigrants would bring socialism and communism into the United States and partly by fear on the part of labor unions that American wages would be forced down by floods of immigrants from economically depressed parts of Europe. At the same time as population growth was slowing down in the industrialized countries, population was beginning to increase in some of the poorer countries of the world. The population explosion of the less-developed countries was a phenomenon of the decades after the Second World War.

Protectionism

One reaction to the loss of foreign markets in the 1920s was increased protectionism. Farmers, faced with falling international agricultural prices, sought to defend their livelihoods by pressuring their governments to protect the home market from foreign competition. There was also pressure for protection from producers in the industrial sector. The old industrial countries sought to protect their declining manufacturing industries, while formerly nonindustrial countries whose manufacturing sectors had developed during the war wanted to protect their new industries from renewed import competition. Another factor was nationalism. There were new countries on the map as a result of the breakup of old empires. Deeply suspicious of their neighbors they tried to be as independent as possible and believed that this would be best accomplished through keeping imports to a minimum.

Restrictions on imports were not limited to new countries. As previously indicated, protectionism in the United States created difficulties in making international payments. Before 1914 the United Kingdom had been the world's leading creditor nation and had maintained a free trade policy. Since the adoption of the McKenna Duties of 1915, Britain had adopted increasingly protectionist policies and in any event was no longer in a position to fulfill the role of the principal world creditor. The United States was now the leading creditor nation and not only maintained its traditional protectionist stance but became even more protectionist than before. This created special difficulties for other countries because of its role as world creditor. The U.S. government and American financial institutions insisted on repayment of debts in gold or convertible currency, preferably U.S. dollars. The United States, however, had accumulated half of the world gold reserves, which made it difficult for other countries to acquire dollars through exporting. For the time being the international payments system was able to function because of the willingness of Americans to invest abroad, but the crunch came when they cut back on foreign investment.

The fundamental problem of the time was insufficient recognition of the need for economic coordination between countries. Many countries, including the United States and France, frequently acted in isolation for their short-term self-interest. This can be explained, if not justified, by the general belief that once the gold standard was reintroduced, it would automatically provide coordination, as it was believed to have done before the First World War. As already shown, this view failed to recognize that the prosperity of the decades immediately prior to 1914 was due not just to the gold standard but to very special and fortuitous circumstances.

Diminishing Trade

In the face of the decline in international trade as a proportion of world production and the growth of protectionism, many economists of the interwar period believed that international trade would continue to decline for the foreseeable future. This hypothesis of diminishing trade had been proposed by Robert Torrens as early as 1821, when he stated, "As the several nations of the world advance in wealth and population, the commercial intercourse between them must gradually become less important and beneficial."[4] The hypothesis, which was stated more fully by Dennis Robertson in 1938, was based on the premises that differences in comparative advantage between countries would diminish over time and that countries would continue to adopt protectionist policies. More specifically, trade as a proportion of production would diminish over time for the following reasons, all of which seemed to be consistent with experience between the two world wars.

1. *Technological progress.* In the industrial countries, synthetic materials, such as nylon, which were manufactured, were replacing natural products, such as cotton, which were imported from less-developed countries. Similarly, the less-developed countries would industrialize over time and have less need to import manufactured goods.

2. *Rising real incomes.* Engel's law, named after the nineteenth-century German statistician Ernst Engel, states that as incomes increase, a declining proportion of household incomes is spent on food and a larger proportion is spent on manufactured goods. In economic terminology, food is "income inelastic." Engel's law was based on the observation that the poor have to spend most of their incomes on basic necessities of life and there is no necessity more basic than food. As incomes increase, however, there is a surplus available to be spent on manufactures. A later corollary of Engel's law is that as incomes continue to rise still further, an increasing proportion of income will be spent on services. Since a large proportion of food is imported and services are mostly domestically produced, international trade would diminish.

3. *Economic instability* was growing during the interwar period and this was leading to greater political pressure for protectionism.

All of the above arguments appeared to be plausible at the time. Since the Second World War, however, international trade has grown at a faster rate than world production. Where did the hypothesis go wrong? One respect in which it obviously proved to be inaccurate was in its assumption that protectionism would continue. In fact, the decades since the Second World War have seen a reduction in barriers to trade. In other respects, however, the hypothesis is correct. The traditional pattern of trade based on comparative advantage, in which industrialized countries export manufactures and import mainly primary products, has become less significant. An increasing proportion of incomes in wealthy countries is spent on services and, though international trade in services is growing, services are still less likely to be internationally traded than manufactures or primary products. What the hypothesis did not predict was the growth in imports of manufactures by industrialized countries, often from other

---

[4] Robert Torrens. (1821). *An Essay on the Production of Wealth.*

48   Chapter 3

industrialized countries, which now accounts for the bulk of international trade. The fastest growing variant of international trade since the Second World War has involved countries importing the same type of goods as those that they export. For example, the United States exports and imports cars to and from Canada. The two countries specialize in terms of brands, and this type of pattern is repeated across the industrialized world.

References

Books

Ferguson, Niall. (1998). *The pity of war.* London: Allen Lane.

Kenwood, A. G., and Lougheed, A. L. (1999). *The growth of the international economy 1820-1990* (4th edition). London: Routledge.

Mitchell, B. R. (1978). *European historical statistics 1750–1970.* New York: Columbia University Press.

Rider, Christine. (1995). *An introduction to economic history.* Cincinnati, OH: South-Western College Publishing.

Smiley, Gene. (2002). *Rethinking the great depression.* Chicago: Ivan R. Dee.

Stevenson, David. (2004). *Cataclysm: The first world war as political tragedy.* New York: Basic Books.

Articles

Cagan, Phillip. (1956). The monetary dynamics of hyperinflation. In Milton Friedman (Ed.), *Studies in the quantity theory of money.* Chicago: University of Chicago Press.

Dornbusch, Rudiger. (1985). Stopping hyperinflation: Lessons from the German inflation experience of the 1920s. *NBER Working Paper 1675.*

Eichengreen, Barry. (1992). The origins and nature of the great slump revisited. *Economic History Review, XLV.*

Green, Timothy. (1999). Central bank gold reserves: An historical perspective since 1845. London: Centre for Policy Studies, World Gold Council.

Kosares, Michael J. (2004). The nightmare German inflation: Hyperinflation in 1923 Germany. *Gold classics Series.* Denver, CO: USAGold/Centennial Precious Metals.

Robertson, Dennis. (1938). The future of international trade. *Economic Journal, 48*(189).

Temin, Peter. (1994). The great depression. *NBER Working Paper Series on Historical Factors in Long Run Growth,* 62.

Chapter 4

The Great Depression

Introduction

The Great Depression of the 1930s was the greatest economic catastrophe of modern times. By 1933 about 25 percent of the American labor force was out of work, and about 20 percent were still out of work in 1938. The Depression also caused severe price deflation in almost every country.

A downturn in the American economy was not unexpected. By mid-1929 weaknesses were appearing in both the American and international economies. Primary producers were facing financial difficulties, largely as a result of rising interest rates in the United States in 1928 and 1929 and the repatriation of French capital following the stabilization of the franc in 1928. These developments led to a flood of agricultural products on world markets and a collapse in agricultural prices. A number of European countries reacted by restricting imports to protect domestic producers, which only worsened the situation of agricultural exporters.

Producers of manufactured goods were also affected by the deteriorating situation in agriculture, because it reduced the ability of primary producers to buy their goods. Indexes of industrial activity and factory production in the United States began decreasing in June 1929, though it was not until October that other indicators, such as factory payrolls and department store sales, also turned down. A downturn in economic activity was clearly to be expected. The big question is why the downturn became so long and so severe.

A great deal of the responsibility lies at the door of the U.S. Federal Reserve, the monetary authority of the United States, which was tightening monetary policy in the late 1920s in order to dampen down anticipated inflationary pressures arising from speculation on the stock market and in real estate. Eichengreen (1992) suggests that a relatively brief financial crisis in 1920–1921 led the Federal Reserve to believe that the economy could be deflated without a severe cost in terms of reduced output. The successful deflation of 1920–1921, however, was due to the special circumstances of the time. In 1920–1921, American exports were facing little competition from the European economies, which were still recovering from the First World War and, since the gold standard had not yet been restored, the European countries were not forced to match the U.S. deflation.

While the slump in production was particularly severe in the United States, no major economy escaped unscathed, with the exception of the centrally planned economy of the Soviet Union. Table 4.1 indicates the changes in industrial production for the major industrial economies between 1929 and 1935. The fall in industrial production between 1929 and 1932 was most severe for the United States, with industrial production in 1932 at only 55 percent of its 1929 level and for Germany, with production at 59 percent of its 1929 level. All the

TABLE 4.1. Indices of Total Industrial Production, 1929–1939 (1929 = 100)

	1929	1931	1933	1935	1937	1939
Britain	100	90	95	113	130	--
France	100	85	80	72	81	--
Germany	100	71	68	100	127	147
Italy	100	86	91	91	111	121
United States	100	71	63	82	104	102

Sources: For the four European countries: calculated from data in Table D1 of Mitchell (1978); for the United States: calculated from data in Series P 40-57 of *Historical Statistics of the United States* (1975).

countries shown, however, saw some decline in industrial output during this period and only two of the eight countries shown had regained their pre-Depression production levels by 1935.

This chapter will begin by considering alternative explanations for the onset and severity of the Great Depression in the United States and will then describe how it spread to other countries. The brief but severe recession of 1937–1938 will also be described. Chapter discussion continues with some international aspects of the Depression and its aftermath, and ends with similarities and differences between the Great Depression of the 1930s and the "Great Recession" of 2008–2009.

The Depression in the United States

Although signs of economic weakness appeared in some countries, notably Germany, before they were apparent in the United States, it is clear that the economic catastrophe owed its origin to developments in the American economy. Since the United States was the world's largest economy and the leading international creditor, any economic problems it experienced could not fail to have a major international impact, although the weaknesses of the gold standard also played an important part. The transmission of the economic collapse from country to country would have been slower and less complete if the gold standard had not been in force.

Unemployed men queued outside a soup kitchen opened in Chicago by Al Capone.

The cause of the U.S. economic slump, however, is still the subject of debate. The major competing explanations at the time were those of the classical school, the Austrian school,

The Great Depression   51

and the Liquidationists. Subsequently, a variety of explanations have emphasized monetary and nonmonetary factors.

Contemporary Explanations

The following three explanations for the economic collapse were commonly proposed at the time and soon afterwards.

1. The classical approach stressed Say's law and the self-equilibrating powers of the market. Say's law, named after the early French economist Jean-Baptiste Say (1767–1832), saw market forces as working quickly, through price adjustments, to eliminate any gluts that might emerge in labor or product markets. In this view, wages and prices would quickly adjust sufficiently for the economy to return to full employment. Unanswered questions were why the economic slump was so severe and why it took so long for full employment to be restored.

2. The Austrian school, as exemplified by Ludwig von Mises and Friedrich Hayek, argued that the economic collapse was a result of overinvestment during the 1920s as a result of the overexpansion of credit. The best solution was to let the Depression run its course in order to eliminate the effects of overexpansion. Government intervention to prevent a decrease in output would not cure the problem but would simply prolong the agony.

3. "Liquidationists," such as Herbert Hoover's then-secretary of the treasury Andrew Mellon viewed the Depression as the punishment for the speculative excesses of the 1920s. Mellon famously advised Hoover to "liquidate labour, liquidate stocks, liquidate the farmers, liquidate real estate" since this would "purge the rottenness out of the system." Unlike the Austrians, the Liquidationists sought not just to allow the Depression to run its course but to actively encourage deflation.

Nonmonetary Factors and the U.S. Depression

Since the 1930s a number of economists and economic historians have emphasized the following weaknesses of the U.S. economy between the two world wars.

1. *The distribution of wealth and income.* John Kenneth Galbraith emphasized the unequal distribution of income and wealth as a contributing factor. Throughout the 1920s, production and productivity rose steadily but wages, salaries, and prices were relatively stable. This resulted in an increase in the income share of profits, as a result of which the economy became dependent on capital investment and luxury consumer spending, which was more erratic than spending on necessities. There is some question, however, as to whether the shift in income distribution, which undoubtedly occurred in the 1920s, was sufficient to explain the Great Depression. Temin (1976) observes that the rise in the share of profit amounted to about 5 percent of national income, which he believes was insufficient to have a massive effect. It is probable, however, that the shift in income distribution, in combination with increased purchases

52   Chapter 4

of consumer durables, contributed to the increase in consumer debt during the 1920s. This, in turn, contributed to the decline in consumption at the start of the 1930s. Olney (1999) suggests that the decline in consumption was the result of high levels of consumer debt. In this view the fear of repossession by creditors in 1930 caused households to cut consumption rather than risk having to default.

2. *The corporate structure.* Galbraith pointed out that the 1920s saw a growth in the importance of holding companies and investment trusts, which increased the danger of reverse leverage. Dividends from operating companies paid the interest on the bonds of holding companies so that there was a temptation to cut back on investment in operating plants in order to continue dividend payments.

3. *Problems with the external balance.* Before World War I, when the United States was a debtor nation, protectionist policies encouraged a balance of trade surplus, which was used to pay foreign creditors. After the war the United States was a creditor nation, but it continued to maintain protectionist policies. This meant that debtor countries could not export enough to earn the necessary sums they needed to meet their debt obligations to the United States with payments in gold or dollars. Instead they became reliant on private loans from the United States to other countries (mainly national, state, and municipal levels of foreign governments). This rendered the international economy vulnerable to any stoppage in U.S. foreign lending. It is in this context that blame for the Depression has often been attached to the Smoot-Hawley Tariff of 1930, which is alleged to have caused a collapse in international trade. A problem with this argument, however, is that, by itself, a tariff would be expenditure switching rather than expenditure reducing. This might cause a reduction in efficiency and world welfare. Only if it provoked retaliation, leading to a reduction in exports, would a tariff such as the Smoot-Hawley Tariff reduce aggregate demand in the United States. There was retaliation, and exports fell by 1.5 percent of GDP over the next two years. But this is insufficient to explain the overall fall in real GDP of more than 15 percent during this period.

4. *Economic orthodoxy.* Macroeconomic analysis between the two world wars emphasized the need to balance budgets at all costs, preserve the gold standard, and remain in a state of constant vigilance toward inflation (even at a time of deflation). These views acted as an obstacle against any affirmative economic policy.

5. *Composition of production.* Eichengreen (1992) emphasizes changes in the composition of production. Although earlier economic historians had argued that the rapid pace of structural change in the 1920s caused high levels of unemployment, this was seemingly contradicted by recent research which suggests that, in general, the pace of structural change between the wars was not especially rapid. Structural change was, however, important in certain sectors. During the 1920s there was a significant increase in the relative importance of consumer durables (such as motor vehicles) in the United States, though this was less apparent in other countries. Consumer durables were expensive items, usually purchased on credit, and they increased the

vulnerability of the economy to contractions in the availability of credit, which may explain why the depression was especially severe in the United States.

6. *Agriculture.* Changes in primary production also played a significant role. The disruptions of the First World War caused an expansion in primary production in those countries that had previously been major food importers. After the war, European grain supplies came back on stream, while the higher levels of production in importing countries persisted. The result was a fall in commodity prices and a collapse in land prices. Though there was some recovery in the mid-1920s, the agricultural sector continued to experience problems throughout the decade. The effects of falling prices on American farmers was made worse by the fact that they had borrowed during the war to take advantage of the then high prices. They had also expanded into marginal lands, which subsequently resulted in erosion. Not all farmers suffered equally, however, since large-scale farmers were better able to take advantage of advances in technology than were small farmers.

Military police at a farm foreclosure sale in Iowa.

7. *A collapse in housing construction.* There was a decline in construction after 1925 as a result of slower population growth owing to a falling birth rate and tighter immigration controls.

8. *Alvin Hansen* (1939) proposed a more long-term explanation for the Depression. He believed that the success of the United States during the nineteenth century was due to an expanding population (so that demand for goods was continually growing) and an expanding geographical frontier (which provided opportunities for investment). By the 1930s, population growth had slowed and the frontier had vanished. Hansen's conclusion was that the United States would experience recurring depressions unless government spending was used to expand demand.

The aforementioned developments in combination may have been responsible for the economic downturn, though none are sufficient on their own to explain the severity or duration of the Great Depression. The best known alternative explanation of the slump attributes its duration and severity to monetary factors.

54 Chapter 4

SIDE BAR II

THE PROCESS OF MONEY CREATION

In order to understand the monetarist explanation it is necessary to review the process of money creation. In a modern economy most of the money supply consists of bank deposits created when banks make loans to their customers. The ability and willingness of banks to create money in this way depends on the level of their reserves (approximately equal to the "monetary base" or the quantity of "high-powered money").[1] Bank reserves consist mainly of deposits of commercial banks in their accounts at the central bank, which in the case of the United States is the U.S. Federal Reserve (generally known as "the Fed"). The profits of banks depend on the interest they charge on their loans so that profit considerations alone would encourage banks to lend as much as possible and keep no reserves. The reason they do hold reserves is because they need to satisfy the demands of their depositors to make withdrawals from time to time. Inability to satisfy demands by depositors to withdraw their money would result in the bank failing (being forced into bankruptcy). From long experience the banks know that only a fraction of their deposits are likely to be withdrawn within a limited time frame, so they seek to keep a proportion of their deposits on reserve. This determines the reserve–deposit ratio (also known as the "desired reserve ratio"), which may vary according to how banks view the state of the economy. The banks also need to take account of the fact that whenever they make loans and create deposits, some proportion of those deposits will be withdrawn by members of the public in the form of currency (coins and bank notes). This proportion is the currency–deposit, or currency drain, ratio. Therefore, the quantity of money that banks will create increases with the monetary base or quantity of high-powered money, H, and decreases with the reserve–deposit ratio, R, and the currency–deposit ratio, C.

The relationship between these variables and the quantity of money, M, is shown by the monetary equation

$$M = H (1 + C) / (C + R)$$

so that, individually or in combination, a decrease in H, an increase in C, or an increase in R will bring about decreases in the quantity of money in the economy. On several occasions between 1929 and 1933, changes in these ratios, either individually or collectively, caused falls in the money supply.

Monetarism and Wage Rigidity

The Monetarist Explanation of the Great Depression

The monetarist explanation has been most fully described by Friedman and Schwartz in their *Monetary History of the United States*. They focus on the policies of the U.S. Federal Reserve (the "Fed") and on a series of bank failures between 1930 and 1933.

The American economy began cooling off in the summer of 1929 as a result of the Federal Reserve's contractionary monetary policy in 1928. In order to tighten monetary

---

[1] High-powered money includes coins and bank notes held by members of the public as well as bank reserves.

policy the Fed had begun open market sales of securities in January 1928, but there had been little immediate decline in the money supply because the stock market boom increased the demand for loans and made it profitable for banks to borrow reserves despite the increase in the cost of doing so.[2] The combination of open market sales by the Fed and an increased demand for money caused an increase in both nominal and real interest rates.[3] In contrast to the situation after 1931, when U.S. gold reserves came under pressure, the major motivation behind the decision to tighten monetary policy seems to have been to dampen down stock market speculation rather than protect U.S. gold reserves. The tight monetary policy continued to be imposed in 1929 even while gold was flowing into the United States.

More surprisingly, monetary policy remained tight even after the onset of the Depression. Overall, the period between August 1929 and March 1933 saw a decline of 31 percent in the stock of money in the United States. This was due to increases in the currency deposit and reserve ratios. The quantity of high-powered money actually increased in this period but obviously not sufficiently. When the stock market crash occurred, the banks and other holders of securities tried to liquidate them (convert them into cash), which caused a fall in the price of securities. Initially the situation was eased by the willingness of the New York banks to increase their lending. To do this they needed additional reserves. The New York Reserve Bank supplied these on its own initiative by purchasing securities to provide cash to the New York banks during and immediately after the stock market crash, but this support soon ceased. In the month following the crash, the quantity of high-powered money declined and, in conjunction with an increase in the currency–deposit ratio, this caused the money supply to decline. Although the money supply declined between August 1929 and August 1931, the authorities failed to understand the need for an easing of monetary policy. In fact, since the discount rate was low and excess reserves held by the banks had grown, Federal Reserve officials seem to have thought that monetary policy was already easy. In holding this view they failed to distinguish between nominal and real discount rates. Since short-term interest rates had fallen at least as much as the discount rate, the banks had no incentive to borrow funds from the Fed in order to lend to firms. Eichengreen (1992) also points to the role played by price deflation in misleading the monetary authorities. At the time it was not obvious to the Fed that monetary policy was tightening since nominal interest rates were low. Real interest rates, however, were in fact higher than nominal rates since deflationary expectations had developed by September 1931, if not earlier.[4]

Bank Failures

Friedman and Schwartz, in their analysis of the economic collapse of the early 1930s, describe the economic effects of successive banking crises. The first of these occurred in October 1930.

---

[2] See chapter 3 for an account of the monetary effect of open market sales.

[3] Nominal interest rates are the stated interest rates, without adjustment for inflation. Real interest rates are the nominal rates minus the expected rate of price inflation and are more accurate indicators of the cost of borrowing money.

[4] The real interest rate, r, is related to the nominal rate, i, according to the formula $r = i + P^e$, where P^e is the expected rate of price inflation. Since P^e is negative in times of expected deflation, r was greater than i.

56   Chapter 4

On that occasion the quantity of high-powered money actually rose as a result of both an inflow of gold and a rise in Federal Reserve credit, but this increase was only small and not sufficient to counterbalance simultaneous increases in the two deposit ratios.

The second crisis began in March 1931. As with the first crisis, the effect of increases in the deposit ratios was partially offset by a rise in the quantity of high-powered money, but this time the rise was due almost entirely to gold inflows. Subsequently, an increasing preference on the part of the public for currency, as opposed to bank deposits, caused the money supply to decrease. This preference for currency was understandable given the rate of bank failures.

Subsequently, when the United Kingdom went off gold in August 1931, there was a sharp outflow of gold from the United States. The quantity of high-powered money nevertheless rose because of a sharp rise in Federal Reserve credit as banks borrowed to cope with a rise in the currency-deposit ratio. As a result, the quantity of high-powered money increased by $330 million between August 1931 and January 1932. This was, however, insufficient to match the increase of $720 million in currency held by the public. Bank reserves therefore fell and there was a multiple contraction of deposits. In April 1932 the Fed engaged in large-scale open market purchases, but there was no increase in the stock of money because (1) the purchases were partly offset by an outflow of gold, mainly to France, (2) a wave of bank failures in June produced a further decline in the deposit–currency ratio, and (3) the banks began to hold reserves in excess of the legal requirement.

The third and final banking crisis came with the panic of 1933 and was the most drastic of all the crises. The main difference between this and the earlier crises was that the internal drain included an increased demand for gold coin and certificates, reflecting a widespread fear of devaluation. The net effect of the banking crises was that by 1933, one-fifth of the banks in existence at the start of 1930 had failed.

The interesting question which then arises is, who has responsibility for the failure of so many banks during the Depression years? Though there were undoubtedly weaknesses in the banking sector in the 1920s, the bank failures were due mainly to developments of the early 1930s. The quality of loans may have deteriorated in the late 1920s, but in 1928 and 1929 the banks faced tight reserves, which limited their ability to engage in reckless lending. It was the inability of the banking system to acquire sufficient high-powered money in the early 1930s that caused bank failures. The Fed's complacency about these bank failures was due to a failure to fully understand the connection between bank failures and the availability of credit. The monetary authorities thought that bank failures were a problem of bank management and not the responsibility of the Federal Reserve System.

The subsequent worsening of the U.S. economy in 1931 and 1932 was due to the banking panics. These directly reduced the money supply. As depositors became nervous about the safety of banks, the ratio of deposits to currency fell dramatically, which reduced the money multiplier. Since the Federal Reserve did little or nothing to increase the stock of high-powered money, the money supply declined sharply. This had international implications since the gold standard ensured that deflation, which began in the United States, would be forced on other countries. The situation was made worse by the fact that the United States did not follow the gold standard rules. Even as gold stocks increased between August 1929 and August 1931, the money stock decreased.

Understanding the conduct of the Federal Reserve in this period requires a closer look at the structure of the organization between 1929 and 1933. Friedman and Schwartz attribute the ineptitude in the conduct of American monetary policy in the 1930s to a shift in power within the Federal Reserve System. They argue that the inaction of the Federal Reserve was partly due to the death of Benjamin Strong, governor of the Federal Reserve Bank of New York. Strong had understood the importance of limiting panics, and his death left power at the Federal Reserve in the hands of less capable leaders. In short, part of the problem was a shift in power within the Federal Reserve system from New York to Washington. At the beginning of the stock market crash the New York Reserve Bank acted decisively and independently, while meeting resistance from the governors of the other reserve banks and from the Federal Reserve Board in Washington. This division between the governors was, however, temporary. When Britain went off gold there was a consensus about the appropriate response. It was agreed that the preservation of the gold standard and international stability should take precedence over internal stability.

United States Federal Reserve Building.

After Britain left the gold standard in September 1931 the United States experienced serious outflows of gold because of speculation that it would soon be forced to devalue as well. Eichengreen has argued that under these circumstances the U.S. Federal Reserve had no choice but to raise interest rates to stem the gold drain. This view was not shared by Friedman and Schwartz, who pointed out that the Fed still had large gold reserves. Regardless of the situation in 1931, however, the Fed could certainly have done more to counter the first wave of bank panics in 1930.

The question then remains as to why the United States was so prone to financial panics in the first place. Economists and economic historians generally explain this by referring to the large number of small banks in the United States and the big expansion in agricultural lending during the First World War, which left American farmers heavily in debt. With the onset of the depression many of these farmers defaulted on their loans. Small banks with only one or two branches are much more vulnerable to panic withdrawals by depositors than are large banks with numerous branches across which the risk of panic can be spread. This was particularly true in the 1920s, before the availability of deposit insurance.

The Effect of the Gold Standard

The Fed had maintained a largely passive stance in the early stages of the Depression but this changed to an active policy of contraction in 1931, in response to the run on the dollar after Britain and Germany left gold. After September 1931 monetary policy seems to have been

58 Chapter 4

driven by the perceived imperative to preserve the gold standard more than by shifts within the power structure of the Fed.

After Great Britain left the gold standard the Fed had to raise the discount rate, which pushed up short- and long-term interest rates. In Eichengreen's view it had no alternative while the United States was still on the Gold standard since only the president and Congress could make the decision to take the country off gold. The effect of rising interest rates was to reduce bond prices, which worsened the financial position of the banks holding bonds and led to a sharp increase in bank failures in 1931–1932. Economic recovery began in 1933. Only then did monetary policy ease and deflationary expectations end. This was the result of a clear signal from the government that deflationary policies to protect the gold standard were being abandoned.

Criticisms of the Monetary Explanation

While it is generally agreed that the monetary policy of the Federal Reserve was unsound, various criticisms have been made of Friedman and Schwartz's monetary explanation of the Great Depression. Some scholars believe that the monetary contraction was insufficient to explain the severity of the Depression, while others emphasize that it operated in conjunction with additional factors rather than in isolation.

Samuelson (1986) doubted that monetary policy was all that tight, pointing out that the monetary base did not actually fall during the Depression, although the money supply obviously did. Romer (1993) accepts that a tightening of monetary policy may explain why the United States was entering a recession by mid-1929 but believes that the monetary contraction was not large by historical standards and was certainly not sufficient to explain the collapse in demand that followed the stock market crash of October 1929. In the view of Moses Abramovitz, the fall in the money supply that did occur in the 1930s may have been a result of declining economic activity rather than the cause of the decline.[5]

Bernanke (1983) observes not only that the changes in the money supply in the 1930s were quantitatively insufficient to explain the depth of the decline in output but also that the monetary hypothesis does not explain how decreases in the money supply caused output to keep falling over many years. In the long run, changes in the supply of money should affect only prices and nominal income, not real output. This leads to the question of why, in the face of very high unemployment, prices and wages did not fall to bring about a rapid recovery in consumption and employment. Any attempt to answer that question requires a consideration of the aggregate demand–aggregate supply model of the economy.

---

[5] Interview with Randall Parker, cited in Parker (2002).

SIDE BAR III
AGGREGATE DEMAND–AGGREGATE SUPPLY AND WAGE AND PRICE RIGIDITY

In the aggregate demand–aggregate supply framework, aggregate supply is the total quantity of real output (gross domestic product [GDP]) that producers in an economy wish to supply during a given period (usually one year). Real output is defined as output measured in terms of the prices of a given year, known as the "base year." In the long run, aggregate supply is determined by the productive capacity of the economy and becomes equal to "potential" GDP. It is independent of the price level or average level of prices in the economy. Diagramatically, it is represented by a vertical line (LAS), as in Figure 4.1. In the short run (which may be months or even years), however, aggregate supply increases with the price level, because in the short run not all prices adjust or adjust equally. Wage rates, in particular, may adjust more slowly than prices of products sold by firms. This means that, temporarily, an increase in product prices may result in increased profits for firms since wage costs lag behind other prices. Firms, therefore, will increase the quantity of goods they wish to supply when the average price level increases. The process works equally in reverse. A fall in prices will result in temporary falls in output and employment. Diagrammatically, when aggregate supply is graphed against the price level, it is represented by the upward sloping curve (SAS) in Figure 4.1.

Aggregate demand is the total quantity of goods and services produced in a country during a given time period that consumers, businesses, government, and foreign residents wish to buy. The quantity of GDP demanded will decrease as the average price level increases for a number of reasons, the most important being the "wealth effect." The wealth effect results from the fact that as the price level increases, the purchasing power of the money held by members of the public decreases. A given quantity of money will now buy fewer goods than before. To restore the purchasing power of their money holdings, people save more and spend less. Diagramatically, when aggregate demand is graphed against the price level it is represented by a downward sloping curve (AD). "Equilibrium" in the economy occurs at the real GDP level and price level where aggregate demand equals aggregate supply.

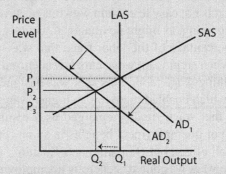

FIGURE 4.1. Aggregate Demand and Aggregate Supply

60   Chapter 4

Wage Rigidity

In Christina Romer's analysis, the aggregate demand curve for the U.S. economy declined several times between 1929 and 1933, causing decreases in both real GDP and the price level so that the economy simultaneously experienced rising unemployment (as a result of falling production) and price deflation. This result depends on the existence of an upward-sloping aggregate supply curve. If the aggregate supply curve were independent of the price level, in the short run as well as the long run, it would be represented by a vertical line (the LAS curve in Figure 4.1). With such an aggregate supply curve, shifts in aggregate demand would affect the price level but not the output or employment because even if prices fell firms would be able to maintain their profits by cutting wage rates at an equal rate. In earlier contractions, such as that of 1920–1921, falls in aggregate demand had affected prices much more than output or employment but by 1929 wage rigidity had emerged and the upward sloping aggregate supply curve had come into being.

As indicated, the classical economists believed that the market was self-equilibrating. Adjustments in wages and prices were expected to quickly restore the economy to full employment equilibrium but, as it turned out, the necessary adjustments occurred very slowly, if at all, during the Great Depression. In Romer's analysis a series of shocks caused aggregate demand to decline repeatedly in the United States between 1929 and 1933, moving the economy down along an upward-sloping aggregate supply curve. The result was a progressive worsening of unemployment in combination with price deflation. The question then becomes when and why did the U.S. aggregate supply curve become upward sloping? While there is disagreement over the answers to these questions, almost all economists agree that wages and prices were far from perfectly flexible in the 1920s and 1930s. Consequently, changes in aggregate demand had real effects.

The contraction of 1929 was certainly different from earlier contractions. In 1920–1921 there had been a rapid and sharp decline in prices and wage rates, causing a severe but short-lived downturn. In 1929–1931 prices fell, but the larger firms laid off employees rather than cut wages or profits. Falling prices and steady nominal wages meant rising real wages in a time of falling demand, but it is not easy to explain why this occurred. It was evidently not due to aggressive collective bargaining, as might be imagined. Unions, of course, are never happy about wage cuts, but the percentage of the labor force that was unionized had fallen by 50 percent since 1920–1921, when significant wage cuts *had* occurred.[6] The Smoot-Hawley tariff also played a role in preventing wage reductions as it was designed to protect manufacturers from foreign competition, which enabled them to pay higher wages.

It has been suggested that wage rigidity emerged as a result of more generous social programs. The introduction of unemployment benefits in some countries during the interwar period may have had a small effect, but Benjamin and Kochin's argument that most British unemployment between the wars was due to generous unemployment insurance benefits has been largely discredited. In any case this argument would not apply to the United States, where such policies did not exist at that time. For the United States, the use of personnel

---

[6] According to Smiley, the major difference between 1920 and 1929 was the conversion of government and business leaders to a "high wage" policy in the belief that if firms paid high wages their workers would be able to buy the goods being produced.

departments in large enterprises and the resulting bureaucratization of wage bargaining may help to explain wage rigidity in that country. But this does not apply to other countries, where personnel departments were not yet common. Perhaps the most plausible explanation for the emergence of wage rigidity is that of Smiley (2002), who argues that the major difference between 1920 and 1929 was the conversion of government and business leaders to a "high wage" policy in the belief that if firms paid high wages their workers would be able to buy the goods being produced.

Other Explanations of the Depression in the United States

A number of other explanations have been put forward for the U.S. Depression. These include Bernanke's credit hypothesis, Temin's view that the gold standard engendered deflationary expectations, and a renewed emphasis on the stock market crash of 1929.

Credit Hypothesis

Bernanke (1983), while emphasizing the importance of bank failures, has argued that they affected the American economy through different channels than those suggested by Friedman and Schwartz. Building upon Fisher's debt deflation hypothesis of 1933 he developed the "credit view." Fisher had argued that the combination of price deflation and declining nominal income in the years following 1929 increased the real debt burdens of households. This caused an increase in debtor insolvency, which reduced aggregate demand and caused further deflation. There thus developed a vicious circle of deflation–debt–further deflation. Bernanke focused on the effect that this deflation had on the banks. In his view deflation in the price of assets foreclosed on by the banks caused a reduction in the nominal value of the assets held in bank balance sheets so that fear of insolvency forced the banks to cut back on lending and focus on safer investments, such as government securities. As a result, other borrowers were unable to obtain funds. This kind of debt deflation is likely to occur if there has been a substantial buildup of debt as was the case immediately prior to the Depression.

Ben Bernanke.

In addition, financial panics, such as those of the 1930s, hinder the credit allocation mechanism since the process of credit intermediation requires the substantial gathering of information, which is lost when banks fail. Banks are a major source of funds for small businesses and, when a bank fails, all the long-term relationships and information acquired by that bank are lost. Other banks will be reluctant to lend to the failed bank's customers because they will need time to learn which customers are reliable and which are not. Bernanke describes this situation as a rise in the "cost of credit intermediation" and argues that it explains much of the deepening of the Depression in 1931 and 1932.

Deflationary Expectations

Between 1929 and 1933 the U.S. wholesale price index decreased by 33 percent. Temin (1994) argues that the gold standard, by mandating deflation, bore the major responsibility for the slump. There are potentially two major effects of a general deflation.

1. *The static effect,* sometimes called the *Keynes effect,* is expansionary. It describes the effect of the increase in real money balances that occurs when the price level falls with a given nominal stock of money. The increase in purchasing power of a given level of nominal money balances as a result of falling prices has an expansionary effect on consumption.

2. The *dynamic effect,* sometimes called the *Mundell effect,* is contractionary and is based on expectations about future prices. If people expect deflation to continue they will postpone purchases.

Temin believes that expectations about prices began to change at the start of 1931 and that, at this time, the Keynes effect was overwhelmed by the Mundell effect, preventing economic recovery.

The Stock Market Crash

Stock ticker.

The Wall Street crash of 1929 has achieved a legendary status as marking the start of the slump, but this has long been dismissed by economic historians as the major cause of the Depression. During the 1920s there was a huge increase in stock market trading. In 1923, 236 million shares were sold and in 1928, the number had increased to 1,125 million. As a result of the increase in demand for stocks, share prices rose far above the level justified by the performance of the relevant companies. A speculative bubble was built up with the Dow Jones Industrial Average increasing by 500 percent in six years. As the economy slowed down at the end of the decade, however, confidence in the stock market declined. The lack of confidence turned into panic on "Black Thursday" (October 24, 1929) when 12.9 million shares were traded on one day, a record up to that time. A group of Wall Street bankers attempted to stop the slide in share prices by bidding for stocks and were largely, though temporarily, successful. The Dow Jones Industrial Average closed down only 6.38 points on that day. A few days later, however, another slide began, culminating in "Black Tuesday" (October 29), when about 16 million shares were sold and the market lost over $14 billion, bringing the loss for the week to $30 billion. Over the next three years the market experienced periods of recovery, but overall, the trend was downwards. In 1932, the Dow reached 41.22, a decline of 89 percent from its peak.

The crash reduced private wealth by about 10 percent, but the decline in consumption that occurred in 1930 seems too large to be explained exclusively or mainly by the crash. A number of economists and economic historians have suggested, however, that in the peculiar circumstances of the 1920s, the stock market crash had a much larger impact than would have been the case in more normal times. Galbraith argued that the crash had a disastrous impact. The stock market crash was made possible by the speculative orgy of 1928 and 1929. This was not owing to easy credit because money was actually tight in the late 1920s, but was the result of a climate of optimism that followed a period of widespread, though not universal, prosperity. In Galbraith's view the crash played a significant part in causing the Depression. Although it is true that the collapse in the value of securities in 1929 affected mostly a small part of the population, namely the wealthy, this was a vitally important section of the population, given the unequal distribution of wealth at the time. The effect of the crash was also magnified by the corporate structure of the 1920s and the pattern of international payments. As has already been noted, holding companies and investment trusts had grown in importance, and operating companies were forced by the crash to retrench so they could maintain dividend payments to their holding companies. As far as international payments were concerned, the crash effectively brought an end to the foreign lending that had allowed international accounts to be balanced.

More recently, Romer and others have also emphasized the role of the stock market crash in starting or prolonging the Great Depression. Romer argues that while a tightening of monetary policy may explain why the United States was entering a recession by mid-1929, the monetary contraction was not large by historical standards and certainly not sufficient to explain the collapse in demand that followed the stock market crash of October 1929. Rather the Great Depression was the result of a collapse in domestic consumption, which was caused by the stock market crash itself. Romer believes that the crash affected aggregate demand by generating uncertainty about future incomes, as a result of which consumers and producers cut their spending on consumer durables. The crash may additionally have depressed consumer spending by decreasing wealth levels.

Recovery and the Recession of 1937–1938

In 1933, the United States began a period of rapid recovery in output. Excluding the severe recession of 1937–1938, the GNP growth rate averaged about 10 percent between 1933 and 1941, though unemployment remained close to or above 10 percent until 1940. Real GNP did not catch up to its pre-Depression secular trend until 1942. Once the United States entered the Second World War in December 1941 the unemployment rate quickly plummeted. It is for this reason that it is often stated that the Depression was ended by the war.

Expansionary fiscal policy contributed little to this recovery since it was not actually tried, though contractionary fiscal policy played a part in temporarily reversing the recovery in 1937–1938. Although Roosevelt's New Deal established a number of programs aimed at promoting recovery, the actual increases in spending were small compared to the size of the economy. The recovery after 1933 was due, rather, to the abandonment of the gold standard and the expansionary effect this had on the money supply. This did not reflect any newfound

64   Chapter 4

faith in monetary expansion on the part of the U.S. Federal Reserve, which, as Friedman and Schwartz point out, was largely passive after 1933. Rather it was the Treasury that increased the monetary base by issuing gold certificates equal to gold reserve inflows and depositing them with the Fed. When the government spent money, the Treasury swapped the gold certificates for Federal Reserve notes, which were a component of the monetary base.

The rapid recovery of the American economy between 1933 and 1937 was halted by a severe recession in 1937–1938. Between 1933 and 1937, annual growth of real GDP averaged 9 percent and unemployment fell from 25 to 14 percent. In 1937–1938, however, unemployment climbed again to 19 percent. This recession was due to unintentional contractions in both fiscal and monetary policy. The year 1936 had seen the payment of a large bonus for veterans of the First World War. This stimulus disappeared in 1937, while in that same year Social Security taxes were collected for the first time. The combined effect of these factors was a reduction in the budget deficit by approximately 2.5 percent of GDP.

Also important was a switch to a contractionary monetary policy. By 1936, the Federal Reserve was beginning to be concerned about possible future inflation or speculation on Wall Street. Since the commercial banks were holding reserves in excess of the legislated requirements, the Fed feared that these excess reserves would make it difficult to tighten monetary policy in the near future. Seeking to reduce excess reserve holdings the Fed doubled reserve requirements, believing this would have little or no effect on bank lending. It turned out, however, that the banks, given their experience of the early 1939s, wanted to hold excess reserves as a cushion. When the Fed converted their excess reserves into required reserves by increasing the required reserve ratio, the banks maintained their cushion of excess reserves by reducing their lending.

The experience of 1937–1938 clearly indicates that it is dangerous to abandon an economic stimulus before the economy is again approaching full employment. To switch to austerity prematurely can set back recovery from an economic crisis.

International Aspects of the Depression

Although the Depression was in part due to developments in the United States, it was a worldwide phenomenon, and weaknesses in the international economy were also important. Economists and economic historians who emphasize international factors have focused on protectionism, failures of international leadership, and the weaknesses of the gold standard.

Protectionism

Protectionism in both the United States and elsewhere was later to receive much of the blame for the rapid spread of the economic slump from country to country. The Smoot-Hawley tariff, in particular, was singled out for criticism. Protectionism was certainly not helpful and by aggravating the balance of payments problems of debtor countries it undermined the gold standard, but it played only a secondary role in the international transmission of the slump.

In the absence of international coordination, individual countries could reflate unilaterally and protect their balances of payments from the consequences by either depreciating their currencies or implementing trade restrictions. Historians of the Great Depression have often emphasized the macroeconomic effects of trade restrictions at this time. Although they could have important microeconomic effects since some industries were adversely affected by tariffs while others benefitted, tariffs by themselves are expenditure switching rather than expenditure reducing. This might cause a reduction in efficiency and world welfare, but only if it provoked retaliation, leading to a reduction in exports, would a tariff such as the Smoot-Hawley tariff reduce world or U.S. aggregate demand. There was in fact retaliation, and U.S. exports fell by 1.5 percent of GDP over the next two years, but this is insufficient to explain the overall fall in real GDP in the United States of more than 15 percent during this period.

Senator Reed Smoot.

Kindleberger's Financial Leadership Model

While Friedman and Schwartz stressed the importance of a shift in monetary leadership from New York to Washington, Kindleberger (1973) emphasized a shift in world economic leadership from London to Washington. In his view, the Depression was able to spread from the United States to the other major economies partly through the mechanism of the gold standard, which imposed a deflationary bias, and partly through the inability or unwillingness of the United States to provide the economic leadership which had previously come from Britain.

Kindleberger argued that during the interwar period, Britain was unable and the United States was unwilling to provide leadership in three major areas.

1. *Maintaining a relatively open market for distress goods.* From the middle of the nineteenth century until 1915, Britain maintained a policy of free trade. In contrast, the United States introduced the Smoot-Hawley tariff (1930) at the first sign of economic trouble. This contributed to the worldwide move to protectionism, which undermined the international monetary system and aggravated the problems of debtor countries.

2. *Providing countercyclical long-term lending.* Before 1913, British foreign lending was negatively correlated with domestic investment. Domestic recessions reduced British imports, but the lack of domestic investment opportunities stimulated lending abroad. A boom in the British economy, on the other hand, reduced foreign lending by creating more opportunities for domestic investment, but higher incomes increased imports into Britain. From the point of view of Britain's economic partners, when British lending to support investment in their economies decreased, this was offset by an increase in their exports. Similarly, an increase in British lending was offset by a decrease in exports to Britain. The lending pattern was thus countercyclical. For the United States, in contrast, foreign lending in the 1920s was positively correlated

66   Chapter 4

with domestic investment and therefore procyclical in that U.S. imports and foreign lending rose and fell simultaneously, reinforcing the business cycle, not dampening it down. Kindleberger suggests that the difference between the American and British lending patterns may have been a result of American inexperience in foreign lending. For a country that has a long experience in international investment, savings are likely to be allocated between domestic and foreign uses, depending upon relative demand, so that domestic lending and foreign lending are inversely related. When a country first begins lending, however, it finds itself faced with numerous new opportunities so that as domestic savings increase they are invested at home and abroad simultaneously. As a result, domestic and foreign lending are directly related.

3. *Discounting in a crisis.* The United States did not provide countries that were experiencing balance of payments problems with sufficient short-term lending.

It is worth noting that the failure of U.S. leadership was not entirely a failure of government leadership. The U.S. federal government certainly had responsibility for trade policy and the U.S. Federal Reserve could have used monetary levers to undertake discounting, but foreign lending was made by private investors through the market. Although governments could prohibit foreign lending, they could not force private investors to increase foreign lending. Kindleberger also points out that until 1931 it was not clear that Britain could no longer provide the leadership the country had provided before 1913. During the 1920s, there were British-led League of Nations programs for the stabilization of the currencies of Austria and Hungary, while the Dawes and Young plans to settle German reparations, though they had American frontmen, were dominated by British experts. Only in 1931, with British abandonment of the gold standard, was it clear that Britain could no longer provide the necessary leadership.

Finally, the United States was not the only country at fault during the 1920s. As Kindleberger points out, France in this period played a negative role, too. Although it was not big enough to stabilize the world financial system, it was big enough to destabilize it. France's conversion of its sterling holdings into gold after 1928 put severe pressure on the pound, while the conversion of French holdings of dollars into gold in 1931–1932 forced the U.S. Federal Reserve into implementing deflationary policies. In both cases France pursued what it saw as its national interests without adequately taking into account the repercussions on world economic stability.

The Gold Standard

Other economists have placed greater emphasis on the failure of the gold standard. Certainly the collapse of the gold standard in 1931 imposed a severe shock on the international economy and converted a severe slump into a great international depression. However, in the longer run, the abandonment of gold-enabled countries to pursue expansionary monetary policies began the process of recovery.

The European Financial Crisis of 1931

Until the spring of 1931, there was some hope that the slump, though severe, would be short lived, but all optimism ended with the financial crisis in Europe. This began in Austria when the country's largest bank, the Credit-Anstalt, was revealed to be insolvent. Panic spread to Germany, whose banks had close commercial ties to Austria, and then to Britain, whose banks had advanced to both Austria and Germany short-term credit, which was now frozen. The resulting drain of gold from London was made worse by two unfortunately timed official reports: that of the Macmillan Committee, which revealed that short-term claims by London banks on foreigners were greatly exceeded by the short claims by foreigners on London; and the report of the May Committee, which projected a deficit in the government's budget, a serious violation of the economic orthodoxy of the era. In normal times such reports might have had only a minor impact but in the circumstances of 1931, they created panic in already nervous markets. Following massive gold outflows, Britain suspended the convertibility of externally held pounds into gold in September 1931. The pound immediately fell relative to currencies still on the gold standard. To maintain their competitiveness many other countries soon followed Britain off gold so that by the end of 1932, thirty-two countries had suspended gold payments. The death of the gold standard also saw the birth of the Sterling Area, which was to last until after British entry into the European Community in 1972. After their departure from the gold standard, many countries chose to link their currencies to the pound sterling. There were three major reasons for this.

1. The pound was widely used and had prestige for historical reasons.

2. Britain was a major export market for many countries.

3. Britain was still a major creditor for many countries, which wished to ensure that their debt service payments would be unaffected by currency fluctuations.

"Fetters of Gold and Paper"

Eichengreen and Temin, in *Fetters of Gold and Paper* (2010), explain the international transmission of the Depression from the United States to other countries by the deflationary impact of the gold standard and see lessons for the present in the experience of the 1930s. They argue that the admittedly severe economic downturn of 1929 was converted into the Great Depression by the actions of central banks and governments, especially during the currency crisis of 1931. Their policies were perverse in that they sought to preserve the gold standard rather than stabilize output and employment. At the time central bankers believed that the maintenance of the gold standard would restore employment, while attempts to increase employment directly would fail and they clung stubbornly to this view in the face of all the evidence. The gold standard was supposed to prevent the collapse of output and employment, but when this occurred, rather than revising their worldview, the defenders of the gold standard became more and more strident. The authorities were accused of not being rigorous enough in sticking to the gold standard rules.

68   Chapter 4

Under the gold standard, the supply of money and credit depended on the quantity of gold and the quantity of foreign exchange convertible into gold held by central banks. As uncertainty grew about the stability of the key currencies, central banks liquidated their foreign balances and tried to replace them with gold. This meant that they increased interest rates competitively in their efforts to obtain more of the very limited world stocks of gold reserves. If they had recognized their interdependence they could have simultaneously cut interest rates to counter deflation without individually running the risk of losing gold, but this kind of co-operation was not part of the gold standard mandate. The fundamental weakness of the gold standard, as with other fixed exchange rate systems, was a lack of symmetry. While it is important in fixed exchange rate systems for deficit countries to live within their means, it is also important for surplus countries to increase their spending. Their refusal to do so forces deficit countries to deflate more severely than would otherwise be necessary.

During the interwar period the gold standard acted as a mechanism for transmitting internationally the effects of mistaken U.S. policies. Restrictive policies in the United States induced restrictive monetary policies in other countries because of their need to limit the loss of gold reserves, a problem made worse by the fact that tighter U.S. policies occurred at a time when gold was already moving to the United States. In addition, the tighter U.S. policy coincided with recessionary tendencies in capital-importing countries such as Germany and Canada, which were adversely affected by the reduction in American capital outflows which had been occurring even before the onset of the U.S. slump as a result of the speculative boom on the stock market.

The International Economy, 1933–1940

The end of the gold standard and the long, slow recovery from the Depression that began in 1933 saw a number of developments that were to continue in importance after the Second World War.

International Monetary Arrangements

After Britain's withdrawal from gold the panic in world financial markets became focused on the United States. The U.S. Federal Reserve found itself forced to adopt deflationary policies to stop the outflow of gold. Such policies in the midst of a severe depression were obviously undesirable, and it was to escape this situation that the United States suspended gold payments in 1933. This meant the virtual end of the gold standard, though a small number of countries remained on gold for a few more years. There now emerged five regional currency systems (or "blocs").

1. *The Sterling Area,* which centered on Britain consisted primarily of the British Empire and several Western European countries. Its members held their reserves primarily in the form of British pounds.

2. *The Dollar Area,* which centered on the United States consisted of countries in North and South America. Its members adopted the U.S. dollar as their reserve currency.

3. *The Exchange Control Area,* which was dominated by Germany, consisted mainly of countries in Central and Eastern Europe. The Exchange Control Area was characterized by a complex system of exchange controls and bilateral agreements, as discussed below.

4. *The Yen Area* consisted of East Asian countries. For these countries the Japanese yen served as the principal reserve currency.

5. *The Gold Bloc,* which consisted of countries still on gold, the major ones being France, Italy, and Belgium. Those countries still on gold now found their currencies overvalued compared to those of countries that had left gold and depreciated their currencies. As a result of the speculative flight of capital from its member countries the Gold Bloc had effectively disintegrated by the end of 1936.

Exchange Controls

The interwar period saw a growth in the use of exchange controls to restrict payments between countries and import controls to restrict movements of commodities between countries. Exchange controls involved requiring exporters to deposit moneys received from sales abroad with either the central bank or a government agency, while importers had to buy foreign exchange from those same agencies. Official rates of exchange for both buying and selling were fixed arbitrarily by the government. Exchange controls were initially introduced to prevent capital flight in times of crisis but sometimes came to be used as a means of allowing the introduction of expansionary domestic policies without the danger of causing a currency collapse. They were also used to prevent currency depreciation which might lead to inflation or an increase in debt-servicing costs.

Bilateral Trading Agreements

Exchange controls were often associated with bilateral agreements, which took three major forms.

1. *Compensation agreements (between governments) and private compensation agreements (between firms).* These were essentially a modern form of barter and, like traditional barter, they were difficult to operate because they required a coincidence of wants.

2. *Clearing agreements.* These provided a procedure for offsetting financial claims. For example, a clearing agreement between two countries, say Germany and Hungary, would require German importers of Hungarian goods to pay marks into a Hungarian account at the German central bank (at that time the Reichsbank). These marks would be "blocked" in the sense that the Hungarian exporters could only use them to buy German goods, not the goods of a third country. A similar account would exist in Hungary to receive payments of Hungarian peng⊠, used to pay for imported German goods.[7] Germany played the leading role in developing such clearing arrangements

---

[7] The peng⊠ was replaced by the *forint* in 1946 after an episode of hyperinflation.

70   Chapter 4

and in the 1930s negotiated agreements with most European countries and several Latin American countries. In this way the Exchange Control Area was established.

3. *Payments agreements.* Unlike clearing agreements, which were negotiated only between countries using exchange controls, payments agreements were often negotiated between an exchange control country and a free exchange country. The best-known example was the Anglo-German Agreement of 1934, under which Germany's imports from Britain in any month were limited to 55 percent of the value of its exports to Britain during the last month but one. The resulting 45 percent surplus was used partly to service Germany's debts to Great Britain, with the balance being available to the Reichsbank.

Exchange controls distorted trade from its normal channels and therefore imposed a welfare cost relative to the situation of free trade. It should be remembered, however, that a liberalized payment system was not considered to be an option in the conditions of the 1930s and bilateral trading agreements made possible some trade that would not otherwise have occurred.

Tariffs and Quotas

Tariffs remained a more widely used obstacle to trade than exchange controls during the 1930s. With respect to such trade restrictions, there were two notable features of the period. The first was the conversion of Britain from free trade to protectionism, a conversion marked by the Import Duties Act of 1932, which imposed duties of 10 percent ad valorem on most imports. The second was the growth in the use of import quotas. These are even more damaging to international trade than tariffs, since they operate independently of the price mechanism. In the Depression period, however, they were often the only way of protecting vulnerable domestic industries from sales of imported goods at distress prices.

International Financial Cooperation

The Bank for International Settlements (BIS) was set up in Basle, Switzerland, in 1930 to manage German reparations payments. It also had a secondary function of promoting cooperation between central banks and it continued to fulfill this secondary function after the reparations moratorium of July 1931 brought an end to its primary function. At this time the BIS was of minor importance, but it has been of greater significance since the Second World War.

Also of greater significance in the future than at the time was another attempt at international cooperation. The Tripartite Monetary Agreement between Britain, France, and the United States in 1936 recognized the need for international cooperation in a system of managed exchange rates and has been seen as a precursor of the IMF. At the time, however, it had only a very limited impact, coming as it did on the eve of a new world war.

Regional Economic Cooperation

In the 1930s there were several attempts at regional trade agreements but only one was to be of lasting importance. This was the system of British Commonwealth Preferences[8] established

---

[8] Then known as "Imperial Preferences."

as a result of the Ottawa Agreement of 1932. The British Commonwealth countries agreed to impose lower tariffs on each other's goods than those on the goods of other countries. In practice this was achieved less by a reduction of tariffs within the Commonwealth than by increases in the tariffs imposed on countries outside the Commonwealth.

International Commodity Control Schemes

Several multilateral agreements to control the prices of rubber, tea, and other primary products were set up in the 1920s, but these had mostly collapsed by the end of the decade. After 1931, a number of commodity agreements were established. But, unlike the agreements of the 1920s which applied mainly to primary products, they had a major impact on manufacturing industries. These agreements tended to divide world markets into spheres of commercial influence. For example, agreements between British and American firms would assign the North American market to U.S. firms and British Empire markets to British firms.

Fiscal Expansion in Germany and Sweden

An active fiscal policy played no part in the economic recovery of the United States, although a fiscal contraction contributed to the recession of 1937. There were, however, fiscal expansions in Germany and Sweden and the question naturally arises as to whether or not fiscal policy played a major role in the economic recovery of those countries. Construction of the autobahns under the Nazi regime is often assigned a major part in the German recovery from the Depression. The importance of public expenditures in Germany in bringing about recovery has, however, been exaggerated. It is certainly true that there was a rapid growth in government expenditure after the Nazis came to power in 1933, but it was only in 1936 that public investment in highways became significant, and by that time the German economy was approaching full employment. Public spending before 1936 was driven by rearmament. This could, of course, have caused economic expansion but the expansionary effects of increased military spending were greatly reduced by maintaining taxation at high levels. Public-sector deficits as a proportion of GDP did not show a growing trend until after 1937, so while fiscal expansion may have prevented Germany from slipping into recession after 1936, it played only a minor role in the recovery between 1933 and 1936. The persistence of low-wage rates, a restructuring of the banking system, and a general world recovery have all been suggested as alternative explanations for the German recovery.

In the case of Sweden, the Social Democratic government explicitly adopted expansionary fiscal policies in 1933. The fiscal expansion was, however, very modest, amounting to about 0.5 percent of GDP. Most economist and economic historians believe that it had only a minor effect on Sweden's economic recovery in the 1930s. The undervaluation of Sweden's currency (the kronor) after the country went off the gold standard in 1931 likely played a much bigger role.

Monetary Expansion in Britain

The decline in income during the Great Depression in the United Kingdom was much less severe than that in the United States or Germany. Industrial production fell by 11 percent for

72   Chapter 4

Britain between 1929 and 1932, compared with falls of 45 percent in the United States and 41 percent for Germany (see Table 4.1). Nevertheless, the effect of the Depression on employment was severe. Unemployment rose from 1.5 million in 1929 to 3.4 million in 1932 and was still 1.8 million in 1937. The partial recovery of Britain after 1932 was driven by a policy of "cheap money," which was adopted after Britain's withdrawal from the gold standard in September 1931.[9] Prior to that date monetary policy was generally tighter than was justified by domestic economic conditions because of the constraints imposed by the gold standard. Subsequently, with the bank rate kept at 2 percent through most of the 1930s, cheap credit fueled a housing boom.

It is notable that a Keynesian solution of expansionary fiscal policy was not attempted at that time. The public-sector deficit was actually reduced by £50 million between 1929 and 1933, and it was not until the beginning of rearmament in 1937 that the United Kingdom experienced a fiscal stimulus. In Britain, as in the United States, fiscal policy was not used to counter the effects of the Depression but, instead, an expansionary monetary policy was implemented.

The Great Depression and the Great Recession

The economic crisis of 2008–2009, sometimes referred to as the "Great Recession," has been compared to the Great Depression of the 1930s, which gives rise to the question of whether the earlier crisis has lessons for policy makers attempting to cope with the first major economic crisis of the twenty-first century. There are some obvious similarities between the 1920s and the three decades prior to 2008, though the comparisons are not exact. Two obvious similarities are an increase in inequality of wealth and income in the industrial countries and an increasing reliance on credit to maintain consumption. It has long been established that credit-fueled booms eventually lead to busts, although this seems to be a lesson that has to be constantly relearned. Every credit-fueled boom is said to be different from all previous ones until the inevitable bust occurs. Whether increasing income inequality necessarily leads to a greater reliance on credit to maintain consumption is less clear, but this seems to have been the case in both the 1920s and the roughly thirty-year period prior to 2008.

Another notable feature of the decade before the Great Depression was the widespread acceptance of a rigid fixed exchange rate system, the gold standard, and a tendency for countries to look narrowly to what they perceived as their own national interests. Although the gold standard is long gone and many countries have floating exchange rates, less universal systems of fixed exchange rates now exist. Eichengreen and Temin (2010) have pointed to similarities between the gold standard and modern examples of fixed exchange rates such as European Monetary Union. Adopting the euro is an absolute commitment, at least as binding as adopting the gold standard but, as with the countries on the gold standard, there has been a lack of coordination between countries adopting the common currency. Various mechanisms for European cooperation exist, such as the Stability and Growth Pact (1997), the Excessive Deficit Procedure (1992), and the Broad Economic Policy Guidelines, but these have often been ignored. In southern Europe deficit spending and government debts have been allowed to get

---

[9] Though not immediately afterwards. Lower interest rates were not introduced until some months later.

The Great Depression **73**

out of control, while in Central Europe there is a chronic deflationary bias. The fundamental weakness of the gold standard and other fixed exchange rate systems, such as the European common currency, is a lack of symmetry. While it is true that deficit countries have lived beyond their means and need to exercise restraint, it is also important for surplus countries, such as Germany, to increase their spending. Their refusal to do so forces deficit countries to deflate much more severely than would otherwise be necessary.

If governments and their economic advisers failed to prevent an economic crisis in 2008, however, their response in dealing with it has been much more enlightened than the reactions of the authorities during the onset of the Great Depression. In terms of monetary policy, interest rates have been kept at low levels and the authorities have moved quickly to prevent the widespread bank failures characteristic of the 1930s. It is recognized that widespread bank failures can result in the drying up of credit, especially for small businesses.

An even more striking difference between the reaction to the Great Depression of the 1930s and the response to the Great Recession is in terms of fiscal policy. During the Great Depression there was little use of fiscal policy. Governments felt unable to break with the orthodoxy of the time, which placed a great emphasis on balanced budgets. The response to the economic downturn of 2008–2009 was very different. In December 2008 the member countries of the European Union agreed to stimulus measures amounting to 1.5 percent of GDP, while in the following February the U.S. Congress approved a stimulus package of $787 billion in tax cuts and spending increases. In April 2009 the leaders of the G20 countries announced in London a concerted fiscal expansion. The difference in response between the 1930s and 2008–2009 was partly due to advances in economic theory, particularly the theories inspired by John Maynard Keynes in the "General Theory" (1936).

Are there any other lessons from the Depression years for those living in the aftermath of the Great Recession? The experience of the recession of 1937–1938 shows that it is dangerous to abandon an economic stimulus before the economy is again approaching full employment. To switch prematurely to austerity can set back recovery from an economic crisis. Perhaps an even more important lesson is that a willingness to adjust one's worldview in the face of experience is essential. After 1931, supporters of the gold standard refused to abandon their view that maintenance of the gold standard would restore employment, in spite of all the evidence to the contrary. Far from revising their worldview they became increasingly strident in insisting that the problem was that the authorities were not sticking closely enough to the gold standard rules.

References

Books

Bernanke, Ben S. (2004). *Essays on the great depression.* Princeton: Princeton University Press.

Friedman, Milton, and Schwartz, Anna J. (1963). *A monetary history of the United States.* Princeton: Princeton University Press.

Galbraith, John Kenneth. (1961). *The great crash.* Cambridge, MA: Riverside Press.

Kenwood, A. G., and Lougheed, A. L. (1999). *The growth of the international economy 1820–1990* (4th edition). London: Routledge.

74   Chapter 4

Kindleberger, Charles P. (1973). *The world in depression*. London: Penguin.
Parker, Randall (2002). *Reflections on the Great Depression*. Northampton, MA: Edward Elgar
  Publishing.
Smiley, Gene. (2002). *Rethinking the great depression*. Chicago: Ivan R. Dee.
Temin, Peter. (1976). *Did monetary factors cause the great depression?* New York: W. W. Norton.

Articles

Benjamin, D. K., and Kochin, I. A. (1979). Searching for an explanation of unemployment in interwar
  Britain. *Journal of Political Economy, 87.*
Bernanke, Ben S. (1983). Nonmonetary effects of the financial crisis in the propagation of the great
  depression. *American Economic Review, 73*(3).
Brown, E. Cary. (1956). Fiscal policy in the thirties: An appraisal. *American Economic Review, 46.*
Eichengreen, Barry. (1992). The origins and nature of the great slump revisited. *Economic History
  Review, XLV.*
Eichengreen, Barry, and Temin, Peter. (2010). Fetters of gold and paper. *NBER Working Paper 16202.*
Fisher, Irving. (1933). The debt–deflation theory of great depressions. *Econometrica, 1*(4).
Middleton, Roger. (2010). British monetary and fiscal policy in the 1930s. *Oxford Review of Eco-
  nomic Policy, 26*(3).
Ritschl, Albrecht. (2000). Deficit spending in the Nazi recovery, 1933–1938: A critical reassessment.
  University of Zurich: I.E.W.-Working Papers 1442-0459.
Romer, Christina D. (1993). The nation in depression. *Journal of Economic Perspectives, 7*(2).
Roose, Kenneth D. (1948). The recession of 1937–38. *Journal of Political Economy, 56*(3).
Temin, Peter. (1994). The great depression. *NBER Working Paper h0062.*

Online Article

Parker, Randall E. (2004). An overview of the great depression. *Economic History Network On-Line
  Encyclopedia,* http://eh.net/encyclopedia

Chapter 5

Bretton Woods and the International Institutions

The First World War had cast its shadow over the entire interwar period (1919–1939). A major feature of that period was a failure to cope with the changes on the global economy as a result of the war. The period had also been notable for a tendency for countries to "go it alone." There were some attempts at international cooperation but they were strikingly inadequate. Much of the responsibility for this state of affairs rests with the United States, which was both unable and unwilling to play a leadership role in either political or economic affairs. The political aspect of its attempt to withdraw from world affairs was shown by the refusal of the U.S. Senate to approve the membership of the United States in the League of Nations. The failure to provide economic leadership was shown by the American refusal to countenance the cancellation of war debts.

The situation after the Second World War was very different. Although this war was even more destructive than the First World War and more genuinely global in scope, full recovery occurred remarkably quickly and the three decades following the war saw the highest overall growth rates of the world economy yet recorded. This was due, in large part, to a general recognition of the fact that countries were inextricably linked economically and to a willingness by the United States to provide leadership in dealing with international problems. It was now accepted that the lack of coordination in the international economy, so characteristic of the period between the two wars, had played an important role in causing the Great Depression. Since it was also believed that the Nazis would not have come to power in Germany had it not been for the Depression, it followed that the Second World War would probably not have occurred if economic affairs had been better managed.

In contrast to the situation after the previous war, the years immediately following the Second World War saw a rapid rebuilding of war-damaged economies, with the assistance of the Marshall Plan, and the establishment of the international institutions that still play a leading role in international economic affairs. Two of these institutions, the International Monetary Fund (IMF) and the World Bank, were set up as a result of the Bretton Woods Conference which met in New Hampshire in 1944. The other institution, the World Trade Organization (WTO), officially came into existence only in 1995, but its precursor, the General Agreement on Tariffs and Trade (GATT) was signed in 1947.

Chapter 5
The Legacy of the Second World War

The Second World War was by far the most destructive war in history. Total military deaths were between 22 and 24 million, while civilian deaths were between 40 and 50 million, including victims of the Nazi Holocaust. The physical destruction associated with the Second World War was also much greater than that associated with the First. Not only were many countries subject to ruthless and destructive foreign occupation but many belligerent countries, whether occupied or not, experienced aerial bombardment, while submarine attacks on merchant shipping were even more devastating than they had been in the earlier conflict. The result was that in many countries the transportation infrastructure was scarcely functionable. The railway networks in France and Germany were largely destroyed and many ports in Western Europe were unusable. On the other side of the world, Japan had lost 90 percent of its merchant marine. There was also widespread destruction of housing and other buildings.

Germany lost 40 percent of its housing during the course of the war, while Britain lost 30 percent, France lost 20 percent, and Japan lost 25 percent.[1] The war saw the destruction of capital stock but also, however, a more intensive use of economic resources. While GNP for West Germany in 1948, three years after the end of the war, was still only 45 percent of its 1938 level, the GNP of the United States was 65 percent higher.

Germany, Japan, and the Soviet Union suffered the most destruction. The Soviet Union at least acquired increased territory in 1945, but Germany and Japan not only

Fire fighting during the London blitz.

lost considerable territory as a result of their defeats in the war but were threatened by famine in the immediate postwar years and had to rely on food relief from the United States. Inflation, as after the First World War, was a serious problem for most of the formerly belligerent countries. Although Germany did not again experience the inflation of the early 1920s, hyperinflations occurred in Hungary (1945–1946), Greece (1944), and the Republic of China (1948–1949). The Hungarian hyperinflation of 1945–1946 was even more severe than the German hyperinflation of 1921–1923. At its peak, prices were doubling every 15 hours. Other countries, while avoiding this kind of situation, nevertheless had to cope with serious postwar inflation fueled by the deficit spending and money creation adopted to finance the war and the postwar reconstruction. Even the United States experienced an inflation of 17 percent per annum between June 1946 and February 1948.

Some countries came out of the war stronger than they had previously been. This is particularly true of the two superpowers of the coming Cold War era. The Soviet Union suffered as much as 20 million deaths during the war but, by annexing the Baltic States and part of

---

[1] Herman Van Der Wee. (1986). *Prosperity and Upheaval: The World Economy 1945–1980.* Los Angeles, CA: University of California Press, p. 26.

Poland, it acquired increased territory. It also benefitted from the fact that during the war it had developed previously backward areas east of the Urals. Finally, it was able to dominate the new Communist regimes set up in Eastern Europe. The United States, though suffering greater human losses than during the First World War, had suffered little physical destruction and had greatly expanded its employment level and its capital stock. Even before joining the war in 1941 the United States had benefitted economically from its role as the "arsenal of democracy" for the previous two years. Some smaller countries also prospered. Neutral countries, such as Sweden and Switzerland, were able to sell goods and services to both sides, while those less-developed countries that were not actually theaters of war benefitted from the high price of foodstuffs.

The most important positive effect of the war, from the point of view of the global economy, was that the United States was converted to a much more enlightened view of its international responsibilities. It now recognized its interdependence with the rest of the world. There was to be no repetition of the isolationism that followed the First World War. The United States now stood ready to provide international leadership and to assist countries in dire straits.

The Marshall Plan and the European Payments Union

There were widespread food shortages in the immediate aftermath of the war, with some countries on the verge of famine. The immediate crisis was dealt with through emergency supplies of food, clothing, and medical supplies distributed by the United Nations Relief and Rehabilitation Administration (UNRRA), which was primarily financed by the United States. Once the emergency was over it was hoped that American loans would be sufficient to bring about economic recovery in the European countries. By 1947, however, it was obvious that recovery was occurring very slowly.

Parade in Greece honoring the Marshall Plan.

The major reason for this was that the European countries lacked the dollars needed to buy from the United States the capital goods necessary for rebuilding their economies and, until their economies were rebuilt, they were unable to acquire dollars through exporting goods and services. This made for a vicious circle. Additional circumstances that made economic recovery even more difficult in 1947 were postwar inflation in the United States, which was raising the cost of imports, and the exceptionally severe European winter of 1947, which caused widespread harvest failures.

The Truman administration was aware that recovery would only be possible with substantial American help. Fortunately, there was strong domestic support within the United States for a program of assistance. American exporters were aware that aid to Europe would enable

78   Chapter 5

TABLE 5.1. Index of Gross Domestic Product at Constant Prices Before and After the Second World War (1937 = 100)

	1937	1950
France	100	117
West Germany	100	99
Italy	100	115
United Kingdom	100	118
Soviet Union	100	128
Europe	100	117
United States	100	175
Japan	100	98

Source: Calculated from data in Angus Maddison. (2001). *The World Economy: A Milennial Perspective.* OECD Development Centre; and Broadberry, S., and Klein, A. (2012). Aggregate and Per Capita GDP in Europe, 1870–2000: Continental, Regional and National Data with Changing Boundaries. *Scandinavian Economic History Review, 60*(1).

the Europeans to import American goods. At the same time the Cold War with the Soviet Union was underway. The effective occupation of Eastern Europe by Stalin and the strength of Communist parties in a number of Western European countries, notably France and Italy, caused considerable alarm, and the Truman administration was able to build support for its policies within the Congress by pointing out that deprivation in European countries would serve to fuel Communism.

In June 1947, General George Marshall, the American secretary of state, announced a far-reaching plan of assistance for the European economies. Officially named the European Economic Recovery Plan, it is more commonly known as the Marshall Plan. Under the plan the United States provided Europe with $13 billion between 1948 and 1952, partly in loans but mostly as direct grants. At the same time, the United States and Canada granted access to their markets for European products, while permitting the European countries to temporarily limit access of North American goods to their own markets in order to conserve scarce American dollars. North American exporters accepted these temporary restrictions because, in the long run, they stood to gain from the expansion of European markets as a result of economic recovery.

The plan was a remarkable success. As shown in Table 5.1, France, Italy, and the United Kingdom had exceeded their 1938 production levels by 1950, although West Germany still lagged due to the fact that the Allies had adopted a policy of reducing German industrial capacity at the end of the war. This policy included a ban on the production of strategic products, such as aluminum and synthetic rubber, and the restriction of steel capacity to 50 percent of its

1929 level. After 1948, however, these restrictions were lifted in the three zones occupied by the western Allies (United States, Britain, and France) as West Germany came to be seen as a partner in the conflict with the Soviet Union. After that, West Germany made a rapid recovery and German economic expansion was underway. In 1951 industrial production was more than twice its 1948 level and 36 percent higher than its level in 1936.

In the broader European context, the Marshall Plan made possible a renewal of transportation systems, the modernization of industrial and agricultural equipment, and a revival of international trade, both within Europe and across the Atlantic. The evident success of the Marshall Plan in reviving economic activity in such a short period of time has since been cited from time to time by supporters of foreign aid. After all, if a massive aid plan was so successful in Europe would not a modern Marshall Plan for less developed countries have a similarly dramatic effect in promoting economic growth in the less developed countries? Such arguments fail to take account of a very important difference between the Western European countries in 1948 and less developed countries in other parts of the world. While it is true that the countries of Western Europe had been devastated physically by the war and in terms of infrastructure were actually in a worse state in 1945 than most less developed countries today, it is also true that they had the experience of having been industrialized. They may have lacked physical capital but they had ample supplies of human capital in the form of educated, well-trained labor and skilled, experienced managers. It is this training and experience that is most difficult to acquire.

In the longer term, the Marshall Plan contributed to the revival of London as an international financial center and gave some impetus toward closer economic cooperation between the countries of Western Europe. Cooperation between countries was promoted by the fact that the United States gave aid to Europe as a whole. The aid was then allocated to individual countries by a European organization set up specifically for that purpose—the Organization for European Economic Cooperation (OEEC), to which belonged all the major countries of Western Europe. Even after the Marshall Plan had expired the OEEC continued to exist. Subsequently, non-European industrialized countries were allowed to join and the OEEC was renamed the Organization for Economic Cooperation and Development (OECD) in 1961, with the stated purpose of promoting economic progress and world trade.

Once the immediate problems of postwar reconstruction were resolved, the next step was to move toward the multilateral payments system envisaged in the Bretton Woods Agreement (described below). This required the removal of restrictions on payments for trade in goods and services, though not for capital flows. A severe shortage of international reserves put this outside of the immediate reach of most European countries so as a first step toward liberalization, the European Payments Union (EPU) was established in 1950. The Union was a means by which the countries of Western Europe were able to economize on scarce foreign exchange while reducing restrictions on trade between each other. Every month each member country's payments or surpluses with respect to other members were totaled and the balances were settled by EPU credits granted by the other member countries. In this way the states of Western Europe were able to expand their trade with each other without needing to fear the loss of scarce reserves of gold or dollars. At the same time the OEEC worked to promote trade liberalization among its member countries. By 1958, when the EPU was effectively dissolved, there were very few

80   Chapter 5

restrictions on payments within Europe and the European economies had recovered to the point where they were able to acquire sufficient reserves of dollars by exporting. At the end of the 1950s most European currencies became freely convertible into U.S. dollars and a multilateral payments system came fully into operation. This payments system was developed as a result of negotiations at the Bretton Woods Conference, to which we now turn.

The Bretton Woods System

Even before the end of the war, delegates from forty-four nations gathered at the Mount Washington Hotel in Bretton Woods, New Hampshire, in July 1944 for the United Nations Monetary and Financial Conference, generally referred to as the Bretton Woods Conference. In the discussions the delegates were very much aware of the need to avoid the failures of the interwar period, which had led to the economic collapse of 1929. Though they had disagreements about the details of the international economic machinery needed to avoid those failures, there was a good deal of consensus about the main problems of the 1920s and 1930s. It was believed that the Depression resulted from a combination of four major economic failures.

1. *A collapse in aggregate demand.* To prevent such collapses in the future, it would be important for governments to be able to spend freely to maintain aggregate demand. Given the degree of war devastation experienced by many countries, the immediate need was to create a mechanism by which they could receive funds to rebuild their economies. In the longer term there was a danger that governments pursuing expansionary fiscal policies would be faced with capital flight, as had frequently occurred in the past. In order to prevent this, governments were not only allowed but actively encouraged to establish controls over international capital flows.

2. *A collapse in the international monetary system.* There was a need for a single multilateral system of payments to replace the currency blocs of the 1930s with their associated competitive devaluations. It was also felt, however, that the gold standard had broken down because of its excessive rigidity. It was therefore necessary to design a system that would be more flexible than the gold standard of the 1920s but more stable than the currency blocs of the 1930s. The solution adopted at the conference was to establish an international organization to keep exchange rates stable and to provide short-term credit to countries experiencing balance of payments difficulties. The International Monetary Fund (IMF) was set up for this purpose.

3. *A collapse of international trade.* Between the two world wars, international trade had declined as a proportion of world production and this was believed to have been responsible for low or even negative growth in world output between the wars. The decline in trade was seen as being in large part due to protectionism. The Bretton Woods Conference itself did not resolve the issue of protectionism but negotiations between individual countries in the immediate postwar years led to the reduction of trade barriers and the establishment of the General Agreement on Tariffs and Trade (GATT), the ancestor of the World Trade Organization.

4. *A collapse in international lending.* There would need to be some mechanism to restore international lending, without which the global economy could not function. At the end of the Second World War and for some years afterward it seemed unlikely that the private sector alone would provide the necessary credit. This would have to be done by governments and the international institutions set up by them. The World Bank was established to provide long-term credit to help war-devastated countries to rebuild themselves.

The negotiations at the conference centered on alternative plans produced by John Maynard Keynes, the head of the British delegation, and Harry Dexter White, the leading member of the U.S. delegation. Keynes proposed the establishment of an international clearing union which would be responsible for controlling a new international currency he called "bancor." This would become the new international reserve currency and would be used in settling accounts between central banks. The Keynes plan also envisaged a system of automatic credit facilities for countries with deficits on their balance of payments and a mechanism by which members of the clearing union would be permitted to discriminate against countries running persistent balance of payments surpluses. This would remove the need for countries running deficits to restore equilibrium by adopting deflationary policies. This, of course, had been a problem with the gold standard as it had operated in the 1920s.

The plan proposed by White on behalf of the United States was more conservative. The White plan was that reserves should be kept in the form of national currencies linked to gold. Credit would be made available to members of an international monetary institution but this would come from contributions by countries in the form of national currencies and gold. While Keynes envisaged the clearing union as a sort of international central bank that could resolve payment imbalances through a whole range of measures directed at both deficit and surplus countries, the White plan envisaged that fundamental balance of payments disequilibria could be resolved only by exchange rate adjustments, and these would require the permission of a majority of the member states. In practice this came to mean that adjustments almost always had to be made by deficit countries, which would usually have to adopt deflationary policies, while there would be no pressure on surplus countries. The White plan thereby failed to correct one of the greatest flaws of the prewar gold standard.

Given the greater power of the United States at the end of the war, the American plan largely prevailed over the British one though, as a concession to the British point of view, a means of potentially bringing pressure on surplus countries was included in the final agreement. This was the "scarce currency clause," included in Article VII of the IMF charter. Under this provision, if a member state had too large a balance of payments surplus, to the extent that the IMF was faced with larger demands for its currency than could be met out of its normal resources, the Fund could "invoke the scarce currency clause." This would allow the member states of the IMF to restrict imports from the surplus country through protectionist measures. It was a recognition of the fact that countries which run persistent surpluses force other countries to run persistent deficits, and adjustments should be made by both surplus and deficit countries, not just the latter. The scarce currency clause, however, was never used. It was disliked by the United States, which believed it was the intended target of the clause in the circumstances of the 1940s, when there was a great deal of concern about a "dollar shortage." Consequently, it enforced such a narrow interpretation on the clause that it became virtually unusable.

The international organization established to oversee the international payments system, the International Monetary Fund, usually referred to more succinctly as the IMF or "the Fund," was much more limited in scope than the clearing union envisaged by Keynes. When established, the Fund had two major roles: to administer a system of fixed exchange rates and to lend foreign currencies to its members when they experienced balance of payments difficulties. At the start of its operations in 1945 the IMF had 29 member countries and in 2011, 187 members.

Under what came to be known as the "Bretton Woods System," there were to be two "key currencies" linked to gold. These were the U.S. dollar and the pound sterling, of which the dollar was much the more important. For this reason the system is sometimes referred to as the "Gold Dollar Standard." The dollar was to have a fixed exchange rate with respect to gold at a rate of $35 to the ounce. Since most member countries of the system linked their currencies to the dollar, the system was an indirect gold standard with the dollar having a fixed exchange rate relative to gold and other countries having fixed exchange rates relative to the dollar.[2] Most international reserves would be in the form of U.S. dollars, though some reserves were held in the form of gold or of the other key currency, the pound. Under this system, "convertibility" meant that most currencies were convertible into dollars, while the dollar itself was convertible into gold.

An important respect in which the Bretton Woods System differed from the gold standard was that exchange rates were "fixed but adjustable." Under the gold standard exchange rates were meant to be permanently fixed, but under the Bretton Woods System it was envisaged that adjustments in exchange rates would take place from time to time provided that the IMF, which was to act as referee in the system, could be convinced that a country had a "fundamental disequilibrium" in its balance of payments. Unfortunately, it was usually difficult to prove one way or the other whether or not a "fundamental disequilibrium" existed since the term was never precisely defined. In the years immediately following the Second World War the IMF adopted a permissive approach and adjustments in exchange rates were relatively frequent, as had originally been intended. In the 1950s, however, a more conservative approach came into vogue and exchange rate adjustments were frowned upon. This meant that in practice adjustments were made through changes in domestic prices and incomes, as had been the case with the gold standard. Also as with the gold standard in its interwar incarnation, this meant that deficit countries were forced to pursue deflationary policies, while there was no real pressure on surplus countries to pursue expansionary policies, so that the system acquired

---

[2] To be more precise, the actual exchange rate had to remain within a band between 1 percent above and 1 percent below the official rate. If it fell outside of this range the central bank would have to intervene by buying or selling foreign exchange.

a deflationary bias. Nevertheless, the new system did have advantages over the interwar gold standard. A fundamental advantage was the way in which it economized on gold. Because of this the gold shortage of the 1920s was less of a problem. A second major advantage was that the system was not expected to be automatic as the gold standard was believed to have been. Central banks regularly intervened in currency markets to maintain the official parity between the dollar and their national currencies. They also regularly consulted with each other and cooperated in dealing with currency issues in a way that had not been so evident in the 1920s.

There was also another feature of the Bretton Woods System, which was a system of credit to assist countries that were experiencing short-term balance of payment difficulties, as opposed to a long-term disequilibrium. Countries in this situation would be able to borrow reserves of gold and international currencies from the IMF. This feature of the Bretton Woods System still exists, having survived the end of the fixed exchange rate regime in 1971. The IMF acquires reserves through quotas, which are compulsory contributions made by member states. Each member country is assigned a quota based on the size of its economy and its share of world trade. This means that the richest countries have the largest quotas and, since votes at the IMF are allocated according to the size of quotas, they also have the most power. Since major decisions require a "supermajority" of 85 percent, the United States effectively has a veto power, as does the European Union. One-quarter of the quota originally had to be paid in gold or a convertible reserve currency and the rest was paid in national currency. Since 1978, gold deposits have no longer been required and it is now expected that a member pay a quarter of its quota in the form of foreign currencies or special drawing rights.[3]

When a country has a balance of payments deficit and needs a loan from the IMF it can buy foreign currency with its own currency, which acts as a kind of "deposit" and which eventually has to be bought back with foreign currency. Withdrawals are made through a series of "tranches." The "gold tranche," known since 1978 as the "reserve tranche," is equal to 25 percent of the country's quota. Requests to draw on the reserve tranche are granted automatically. The deficit country can then apply to borrow successively four "credit tranches," each consisting of 25 percent of its quota. The IMF will usually grant these requests but impose increasingly severe conditions on successive borrowings of reserves. A country can therefore borrow up to 125 percent of its quota, but after the first 25 percent the loans will normally be contingent on the adoption of domestic policies to counter its balance of payments deficit. The funds available to the IMF, however, were never adequate to meet the credit needs of member countries facing balance of payment difficulties and at the same time it came to regard exchange rate adjustments with extreme disfavor. The result was that member countries were forced to adjust domestic policies to eliminate balance of payments deficits, something which the Bretton Woods Conference had intended to prevent.

Not all credit needs were, however, driven by short-term balance of payments needs. At the end of the war many countries were faced with large expenditures needed to rebuild their industries after the destruction caused by the war. The IMF was not designed to provide the

---

[3] There was an agreement in 1969 to allow the IMF to create "Special Drawing Rights" (SDRs) as a supplement to the major foreign exchange assets, namely gold and U.S. dollars. The value of SDRs are expressed in terms of a weighted average of major currencies and may be allocated or loaned to countries by the IMF.

84   Chapter 5

kind of long-term credit needed for such reconstruction. Instead this was to be provided by a parallel institution, the World Bank. When it began its operations in 1945 it was officially named the International Bank for Reconstruction and Development (IBRD). Subsequently four other institutions were created which now, along with the IBRD, form the World Bank Group. From the beginning, however, the IBRD was more commonly referred to as the World Bank. As its name indicated, the original primary purpose of the International Bank for Reconstruction and Development was to provide assistance to the war-torn countries of Europe and Asia as they engaged in reconstructing their economies. As it turned out, recovery from the Second World War occurred much more quickly than had been the case for the First World War. For Europe, this was in part due to the Marshall Plan, managed by the U.S. government, though some assistance did come through the World Bank. By the start of the 1950s the Bank had found itself a new niche by concentrating on the second part of its mandate, which was to provide development assistance for less-developed countries.

Like the IMF, the World Bank originally consisted of a small number of countries, but it has since expanded to include most of the countries in the world and, as of 2011, it has 192 members. As with the IMF, the World Bank gets most of its resources from quotas imposed on its members. These quotas determine voting rights within the organization and since major decisions require a "supermajority" of 85 percent, the United States, which has 16.4 percent of the total votes, can exercise a veto power, as can the European Union, with 32 percent of the votes. It has become a convention that the president of the World Bank will come from the United States and the managing director of the IMF will be a European, though in recent years this division of authority has come under challenge from the emerging economic powers of Asia and Latin America.

The IMF and the World Bank survive to this day, but the Bretton Woods System of fixed exchange rates eventually collapsed for two reasons. First, as seen above, the interpretation of "fundamental disequilibrium" became less flexible over time, which created serious difficulties for countries experiencing balance of payments deficits, without exerting pressure for adjustment on countries with persistent balance of payments surpluses. Second, there was a decline in confidence in the U.S. dollar, which was, after all, the keystone of the whole system. This dependence on the American dollar was a fundamental weakness of the Bretton Woods System, a problem that was pointed out by the Belgian-American economist Robert Triffin as early as the late 1950s.

The Triffin Dilemma

Triffin pointed out that there was a fundamental contradiction in a system that depended on a national currency as the principal source of international reserves. On the one hand, in a growing international economy there was a need for a corresponding growth in international liquidity. Otherwise there would be a worldwide deflationary trend that would choke off growth. Under the Bretton Woods System, also known as the gold dollar standard, reserves were composed of gold and the two key currencies, the pound sterling and the U.S. dollar. Growth in liquidity depended on the growth of gold supplies and the willingness of the United Kingdom and the United States to provide the world with the key currencies by

Bretton Woods and the International Institutions   85

TABLE 5.2. Gold Reserves of Selected Countries as a Proportion of Total World Gold Reserves, 1950–1971 (%)

	1950	*1955*	*1960*	*1965*	*1970*	*1971*
United States	65.2%	58.3%	44.1%	32.6%	26.9%	24.%
United Kingdom	8.2	5.4	6.9	5.2	3.3	1.9
Japan	0.0	0.1	0.6	0.8	1.3	1.7
France	1.9	2.5	4.1	10.9	8.6	8.6
Germany	0.0	2.5	7.4	10.2	9.7	9.9

running balance of payments deficits. Since the price of gold was fixed at the low price of $35 per ounce there was no incentive to increase the gold supply. Britain was weak economically, had very limited gold reserves and could not afford to flood the world with pounds with insufficient gold cover. That left only the U.S. dollar as a growing source of international reserves. As a result, international prosperity depended, first, on the United States to provide the world with ample supplies of U.S. dollars through running balance of payments deficits and, second, on the continued willingness of other countries to accept those U.S. dollars.

Until the mid-1960s the system functioned well enough. International liquidity, created mostly through U.S. balance of payments deficits, grew at a rate sufficient to maintain a high rate of growth in world output without generating inflation. The gold dollar system also suited the United States, which was able to pay for its balance of payments deficits with its own currency. Other countries felt no need to convert their dollar holdings into gold since they were confident that the United States, which held two-thirds of the world's total gold reserves at the end of World War II could, if necessary, easily convert all foreign holdings of its dollars into gold. For a considerable period this was a reasonable assumption, but it became less plausible over time as U.S. gold reserves shrank.

There was thus a contradiction in the gold dollar standard. Growth in international trade required a steady growth in foreign holdings of U.S. dollars as reserves. As foreign holdings of dollars increased, however, U.S. gold reserves gradually shrank as a result of some of these dollars being converted by other countries into gold. The shift in gold reserves from the United States (and the United Kingdom) to the other major industrial countries which occurred between 1950 and 1971 is shown in Table 5.2. Confidence in the dollar was bound to decrease as it became increasingly obvious that the United States no longer had sufficient gold reserves to convert all foreign holdings of its dollars into gold. Eventually loss of confidence in the dollar would bring down the whole system as countries refused to accept dollars. This would be a serious obstacle to multilateral flows of international trade and investment.

In the 1940s and most of the 1950s this possibility seemed remote. At the time there was a seemingly unquenchable thirst for dollars and concerns were expressed about the "dollar shortage." A decade and a half of U.S. balance of payments deficits changed the situation. In the 1960s the concern was increasingly about the "dollar glut" or "dollar overhang" as countries found themselves holding larger and larger reserves of dollars which they were no longer convinced could be converted into gold. The dilemma was that the system could only be preserved if there was a reduction in the quantity of U.S. dollars abroad in the world. This could be accomplished by drastic deflation in the United States, but that would not only create economic problems in the United States but also lead to a world recession by depriving the global economy of the reserves needed to fuel trade and investment. The cure might, therefore, be as bad as the disease. Triffin's solution was similar to the plan proposed by Keynes at the Bretton Woods Conference. He proposed the creation of an international central bank at which all national central banks would deposit their reserves. The international central bank would issue an international currency which would function as the official reserve currency for the whole world. At the time this proposal was too radical to be accepted, particularly by the United States, which still wished to preserve its power as the head of the international financial system. Nevertheless, there was an agreement in 1969 to allow the IMF to create Special Drawing Rights (SDRs) as a supplement to the major foreign exchange assets, namely gold and U.S. dollars. SDRs, the value of which are expressed in terms of a weighted average of major currencies, are allocated by the IMF to its member countries based on their quotas, and can be exchanged for the major currencies. Since the number of SDRs created has been very low, however, they have not become a major component of international reserves.

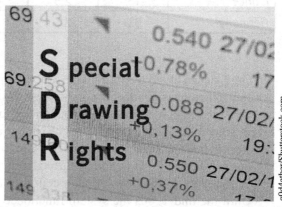

With the collapse of the Bretton Woods System in 1971 the issues raised by Triffin appeared less relevant. Recently, however, there has been a revival of interest in the proposals of Triffin and of Keynes before him. Following upon the financial crisis of 2007–2008, China has expressed concerns about the stability of a world economy in which the U.S. dollar is the reserve currency. In 2009 Zhou Xiaochuan, governor of the People's Bank of China, referred to the proposals of both Triffin and Keynes for an international currency. China recommended that the role of the U.S. dollar as the global reserve currency be gradually diminished and greater use made of SDRs. Similar concerns were raised about the international role of the U.S. dollar in July 2011 when China's official Xinhua News Agency questioned whether or not the dollar should continue to serve as the world's reserve currency. This was a result of the brinksmanship in the U.S. Congress over raising the debt ceiling. The consequent downgrading of U.S. government debt from AAA to AA+ by the Standard and Poor credit rating agency served to strengthen such concerns.

The General Agreement on Tariffs and Trade

At the end of the war it had been anticipated that there would be an international organization to mediate trade relationships, just as the IMF was to manage exchange rates and provide countries with short-term credit and the World Bank was to provide long-term credit. In

1947 the United Nations Economic and Social Council organized a conference to establish an International Trade Organization (ITO). At that time, however, there was too wide a divergence of views between countries for such an ambitious undertaking to be successful. On the one hand, the United States wanted institutional arrangements that would move quickly toward multilateral free trade, while, on the other hand, the European countries believed they needed to be able to protect their still fragile economies from foreign competition. In 1948, a compromise of sorts was reached with the Havana Charter, but it deviated so far from the American point of view that the Congress refused to ratify it and the ITO was stillborn. Not until 1995 was something very close to it to come into existence in the form of the World Trade Organization.

In the meantime, however, a much less ambitious series of trade negotiations were underway. In 1946–1947, twenty-three countries engaged in a series of talks related to tariff reductions for specific products. The tariff reductions agreed to (which at the time covered about one-fifth of world trade) were summarized in a document called the General Agreement on Tariffs and Trade (GATT), which also set out rules for future trade negotiations, established a code of behavior, and instituted a secretariat. It was expected that GATT would come under the authority of the ITO, once it was established, but since the ITO was never created the GATT began an independent existence.

It proceeded to organize a series of "trade rounds." Between 1947 and 1960 there were five such rounds of talks, each lasting a few months. They were very successful at eliminating quotas and reducing tariffs on manufactured products, but they avoided the more difficult issues such as agricultural protectionism, dumping, and nontariff barriers. Progress became more difficult once later rounds of GATT talks began addressing these issues, and this is reflected in the lengths of these rounds. The Kennedy Round, which included antidumping provisions, lasted three years (1964–1967), while the Tokyo Round, which attempted to establish rules related to nontariff barriers, lasted six years (1973–1979). The eighth and final round of GATT negotiations was the Uruguay Round (1986–1994), which aimed to reduce agricultural protectionism, establish rules related to foreign investment, and liberalize trade in services such as banking and insurance. It had some limited success in these areas but its most important achievement was the establishment of the WTO, which began its operations in 1995.

In addition to acting as enabler for trade discussions the GATT, as indicated, included an elementary code of behavior for its member countries. The most important provision of this code was the principle of nondiscrimination. Under the GATT's "Most Favoured Nation Clause" any concessions made by one member country to another would have to be extended to all other GATT members. There was an important exception to this rule with respect to free trade agreements such as NAFTA or the European Union, but the rule nevertheless meant that tariff concessions tended to escalate as trade deals between pairs of individual countries came to be enjoyed by all members. There was also a principle that countries, on becoming signatories to the GATT, should make concessions to the other members in order to avoid free riding. The success of the GATT is shown by the expansion in its membership, which increased from twenty-three countries in 1947 to seventh-five by the time the World Trade Organization was established in 1995.

The World Trade Organization

The World Trade Organization (WTO), which began its operations on January 1, 1995, now has 153 members. Its principal functions are overseeing the operation of the WTO agreements, providing a forum for negotiations, and providing a dispute settlement mechanism. The GATT is still the treaty governing trade in goods but the WTO is also responsible for administering other agreements covering a variety of issues, including trade in services and intellectual property rights. WTO negotiations
occur through Ministerial Conferences, which meet every two years, and through rounds of trade negotiations. The first such round to take place under the auspices of the WTO is the Doha Round, which was launched in 2001 and has the dual objectives of furthering trade liberalization and providing assistance to less-developed countries. The dispute settlement mechanism is the responsibility of the Dispute Settlement Body (DSB), which includes representatives of the WTO member governments and generally acts on the recommendation of a Dispute Panel. If a member country successfully demonstrates that another member has violated WTO agreements, the DSB can direct the offending member to change its laws or policies so that they conform with those agreements. If it fails to do so within a reasonable period of time the DSB may authorize the complainant to take retaliatory measures.

Unlike the IMF or the World Bank the World Trade Organization has, in principle, a one-country one-vote system, but in practice, decisions are made by consensus and the countries with the largest economies tend to carry the most weight.

The Rise and Fall of the Bretton Woods System, 1947–1973

It was not until the late 1950s that the Bretton Woods System was firmly established. Although the IMF began its operations in 1947 its role in practice was very limited for the first ten years of its existence, despite its imposing role on paper as the official provider of short-term credit for countries in difficulty and as overseer of the multilateral payments system. There were three major reasons for this.

1. The IMF had very limited resources, so that for at least a decade after the end of the war countries in difficulty preferred to deal directly with the U.S. government. In any case, the IMF was generally viewed at this time as an arm of that government.

2. Exchange controls, a legacy of the war and the Depression, were still widely in force. Very few currencies were convertible before 1952, so that there was not yet an effective multilateral payments system for the IMF to police.

3. Throughout most of the 1950s many countries preferred to adopt regional payments agreements, of which the most important were the Sterling Area and the European Payments Union (EPU) (to both of which the United Kingdom belonged).

The Sterling Area and the EPU were clearing arrangements. The members of the Sterling Area, which consisted of most of the British Commonwealth plus a few small countries in Europe and the Middle East, used British pounds as their official reserves and settled payments with each other through the Exchange Equalization Account held in London. This permitted the free movement of currencies within the Sterling Area but exchange controls governed transactions between members of the Sterling Area and countries outside it. The EPU was a similar arrangement between Western European countries. As indicated, every month each member country's payments or surpluses with respect to other members were totaled and the balances were settled with EPU credits.

During the 1950s the payments situation improved, especially for those countries most devastated by the war. As they rebuilt their agricultural and manufacturing industries their export industries recovered. After 1958 the United States almost always had balance of payments deficits, fueling an outflow of gold and dollars to build up the reserves of countries in the rest of the world. In the 1960s an increasing number of countries adopted current account convertibility, meaning that expenditures related to the current account were convertible into dollars, although capital account expenditures, relating to foreign investment, were still subject to exchange controls. As a truly multilateral system of international exchange developed, the IMF began to assume a more prominent role in international lending. This was helped by a substantial revision in IMF quotas in 1958, increasing the Fund's resources from $5.1 billion to $14.5 billion. There were further increases in quotas in 1965 and 1970 and the General Arrangements to Borrow (GAB) (1962) allowed the IMF to borrow, if necessary, the currencies of the ten major trading countries (then known as the Group of Ten).

By the mid-1960s the flaws described by Triffin were becoming more evident. Gold supplies were only growing slowly, so that the global economy was dependent on a growing supply of U.S. dollars and, to a lesser extent, pounds sterling. Dollars and pounds were being supplied through American and British balance of payments deficits, but these deficits increased the danger of a loss of confidence in the key currencies. For a time the dollar remained strong despite growing U.S. balance of payments deficits, driven by American foreign military commitments and especially by the Vietnam War. There was, however, increasing speculation against the pound since Britain's gold reserves were clearly inadequate. Finally, in 1967, the pound was devalued. This not only undermined the prestige of the pound but also represented a serious blow to confidence in the dollar. After all, if one key currency could be

90   Chapter 5

devalued, why not the other? The First Amendment of the Articles of Agreement of the IMF (1969), which created the Special Drawing Right (SDR) as a supplement to gold and U.S. dollars, was an attempt to deal with the danger of a potential loss of confidence in the dollar as the principal reserve currency. While potentially very important, however, the actual role of SDRs has so far been small since, as noted earlier, they have not been created in sufficient amounts to resolve the problem for which they were designed. In addition, the timing of their introduction was unfortunate since the 1970s were to witness increasing concerns about inflation, so that the problem facing the global economy came to be seen as one of too much liquidity rather than too little.

The liquidity problem was not the only one that was to undermine the Bretton Woods System. As with the prewar gold standard, exchange rates became misaligned and too rigid. As we have seen the Bretton Woods Conference of 1944 had intended that the exchange rate regime would be one of "fixed but adjustable" rates. It had been envisaged that while exchange rates would normally fluctuate within a very narrow band, they would be adjusted from time to time to prevent the external values of currencies from getting too much out of line with their equilibrium values. This represented a recognition that one of the major weaknesses of the gold standard had been excessive rigidity with respect to exchange rates. During the first few years of the gold dollar standard several currency devaluations did in fact occur. In the 1950s, however, and even more in the 1960s the view developed that a devaluation represented a severe blow to national prestige for countries with overvalued exchange rates, while the system put no pressure on countries with undervalued currencies to revalue. The Scarce Currency Clause, which had been introduced into the Bretton Woods Agreement at British insistence, was intended to pressure surplus countries, but it effectively remained a dead letter. The result was that, as under the prewar gold standard, only countries with overvalued exchange rates were under pressure to adjust and, to all intents and purposes, they could adjust only through implementing deflationary domestic policies.

After the devaluation of the pound in 1967 the attention of financial markets was drawn to the U.S. dollar which, after years of balance of payments deficits, was clearly overvalued. The problem was that if it had become difficult for any country to devalue, it was especially difficult for the United States because of the central role of the U.S. dollar in the world payments system. The gold dollar standard depended on the U.S. dollar maintaining a fixed price of gold. A solution to this quandary would have been the revaluation of the currencies of surplus countries, such as West Germany and Japan, but these countries were reluctant to take this step, which would have raised the price of their goods in foreign markets and hurt their export industries.

Consequently, the last years of the Bretton Woods regime saw a series of unsuccessful attempts at propping up the U.S. dollar and some half-hearted attempts at more serious reform, never followed through, such as the introduction of SDRs in 1969. Finally, in August 1971, after $22 billion in reserve assets had fled the United States over a six-month period, President Nixon unilaterally suspended convertibility of the dollar into gold. This was intended to merely put pressure on surplus countries to revalue their currencies, but it marked the beginning of the end for the Bretton Woods System. The Smithsonian Agreement (December 1971) was an attempt to patch up the system through a realignment of currencies and the introduction of a band of fluctuation of 2.25 percent (as opposed to 1 percent), but after a further devaluation of the U.S. dollar in February 1973, there was a general floating of currencies.

Post-Bretton Woods

After the so-called Nixon Shock of August 1971 the IMF Board of Trustees began considering reforms to the international monetary system. Their recommendations were accepted in the Jamaica Agreement of 1976 and incorporated into the Second Amendment of the Fund Agreement.[4] The Jamaica Agreement demonetized gold by breaking its link with the U.S. dollar and legitimized the concept of the managed float. Henceforth governments were free to intervene in currency markets to adjust the values of their currencies, a process known as "managed floating." It might be expected that after the end of fixed exchange rates the power and prestige of the IMF would have been reduced but in fact the reverse has been the case. Since 1976 the prominence of the IMF has grown. There are a number of reasons for this. First, the international economy has been subjected to more frequent and more severe crises since 1971 than before, and the IMF has been called upon to help resolve these crises. Second, not all currencies have floated but some have instead been tied to one or other major currency. The countries concerned need access to IMF assistance when faced with balance of payments difficulties. Third, IMF resources have increased substantially in the last forty years, as a result of increases in quotas, gold sales, and the creation of new loan facilities. Quotas were doubled in 2010 and had been increased five times since 1976. On a number of occasions, most recently in 2009, the Fund has added to its resources by selling part of its gold holdings, generally at a substantial profit. Finally, new types of loans have been created. These include the Structural Adjustment Facility (SAF), which gives the Fund leverage to insist on structural reforms in low-income countries, and the Supplemental Reserve Facility (SRF), which allows the provision of financial assistance to countries facing difficulties because of sudden withdrawals of foreign capital. South Korea was the first country to get assistance under the SRF.

Labour and Environmental Issues and the International Institutions

Since the Second World War international trade has become more liberalized than in any previous period in history. Quantitative restrictions on trade survive in only a few industries and tariffs have been substantially reduced. The major obstacle to further growth in trade is the existence of different regulations between countries in a whole range of areas, such as product and workplace safety. The harmonization of such regulations is known as "deep integration," in contrast to the removal of formal barriers to trade, known as "shallow integration." Increasingly international economic negotiations are focusing on labor and environmental standards. These are areas that encroach on very sensitive issues of national sovereignty, and there is a great deal of disagreement about whether or not they are legitimate topics for international agreements or whether they should be left to national governments. There are also differing views as to whether or not the international organizations should be involved in enforcing international labor and environmental standards.

---

[4] The First Amendment had created SDRs in 1969.

With respect to international standards for both labor and the environment, three alternative approaches can be identified. The first approach is to harmonize standards. The problem then becomes which standards to adopt and how often should the standards be revised. If the highest standards are adopted some countries may already be very close to achieving those standards and require little adjustment, while other countries might have to incur considerable expense in changing their practices. If low or medium standards are adopted some countries may be faced with lowering their standards. There is also the danger of "freezing" inadequate standards if they cannot easily be changed without international agreement. The second approach is "mutual recognition" by which countries have different but "comparable" standards. The problem here is defining how "comparable" is to be distinguished from "different." The third approach is to give up the fight and agree to have "separate standards." From the point of view of maintaining national sovereignty this may be the most convenient approach but it gives rise to the possibility of a "race to the bottom" in which some countries, by adopting low standards, force other countries to similarly lower their standards or put themselves at a serious cost disadvantage in international markets.

Attempts to harmonize standards, however, are difficult. Even countries at similar levels of economic development have differing preferences about appropriate labor or environmental standards, but the problems of reaching agreement are all the greater when countries have large differences in income levels. With respect to labor standards, for example, it is clearly unrealistic to advocate an international minimum wage since any such wage would either be unaffordable to poorer countries or so low as to be meaningless in richer countries. A more fruitful approach to labor standards could be to emphasize the process by which labor relations are conducted rather than the results in terms of wage rates. The International Labour Organization (ILO), a UN-affiliated organization based in Geneva, has proposed five basic rights of labor: prohibition of forced labor, freedom of association, the right to collective bargaining, no exploitation of child labor, and nondiscrimination in employment. It might seem that there would be universal agreement on these basic rights but even they are controversial. A prohibition on the use of child labor, for example, may be uncontroversial in rich industrialized countries but in less-developed countries children are often major breadwinners and the alternatives for them are not work or school but work or starvation. Also countries with corrupt or inefficient administrative systems and large "underground economies" may not be able to enforce prohibitions on child labor even if they wish to. Finally, the poorer countries fear, perhaps with some justice, that concerns about labor conditions may sometimes be a pretext for protectionism in rich countries.

Just as there are concerns that some countries may seek a trade advantage by allowing very low standards to prevail with respect to wage rates and working

Child worker in Mali.

conditions (a process known as "social dumping"), there are also concerns that countries may act as "pollution havens" by allowing corporations to gain a cost advantage through needing to meet only low environmental standards. With respect to the environment, however, there is an added complication. Environmental standards have "transboundary" as well as "non-transboundary" effects. Non-transboundary effects are those that arise from a country acting as a pollution haven with the aim of attracting investment from foreign corporations or giving local firms a cost advantage over firms operating in countries with higher or more rigorously enforced standards. The danger here, as with low labor standards, is a "race to the bottom." With respect to the environment, however, there may also be transboundary effects, which are spillovers that occur between neighboring countries. If, for example, firms in Hungary dump waste into the Danube this will have a direct impact on other countries through which the Danube flows, such as Austria. Similarly, pollution in Tijuana, Mexico, affects San Diego, California. Pollution is no respecter of national boundaries. For this reason the need for international cooperation with respect to the environment is more widely accepted than the need for coordination in labor standards.

"Man, I'm feeling good. We saved eighty bucks in taxes by defeating that environmental initiative."

More contentious is the role of international institutions in enforcing cooperation with respect to labor or environmental standards. Nevertheless, Bagwell and Staiger (2001) have suggested a way in which trade negotiations under the auspices of the World Trade Organization could play a role in the improvement of labor standards. When countries agree to reduce formal barriers to trade, such as tariffs and quotas, they may resort to other means of giving domestic industries cost advantages, such as lowering labor standards. If they negotiate tariff reductions through the WTO, however, they are implicitly making a commitment to permit greater market access to their trading partners. Bagwell and Staiger argue that if a country subsequently reduces market access by reducing its labor standards a case could be brought to the WTO by the other member countries seeking redress. This could mean raising tariffs against the offending country.

Sylvia Ostry, in discussing the role played by environmental nongovernmental organizations (ENGOs) in the World Bank, has described how the maintenance or improvement of environmental standards can be promoted in the international arena. She starts by making a distinction between "mobilization networks" and "technical/legal networks." Mobilization networks aim to increase public awareness of issues such as environmental problems and tend to be critical of the role played by international organizations. These networks certainly attract great publicity through such means as public protests and demonstrations, but it is doubtful if they exert much influence on the decisions made by the international organizations. Technical/

94   Chapter 5

legal networks, on the other hand, seek to operate within rather than outside of institutions such as the World Bank and are arguably more successful in promoting their viewpoint. The IMF is relatively impervious to influence from pressure groups since it has a small staff with a well-defined worldview, but the World Bank is more open to outside influence, partly because it has a much larger, more diverse staff than the IMF and partly because it deals with a greater variety of issues and needs outside technical advice. The ENGOs are well placed to provide this advice with respect to environmental issues because they generally have more technical knowledge in this area than most governments or corporations. Therefore, they can influence the World Bank from within. They also seek to influence decisions of the World Trade Organization by demanding the right to present amicus curiae briefs under the WTO's Disputes Settlement mechanism.[5] Many low-income countries are opposed to this tendency, however, since it opens the way for not only environmental NGOs but also lawyers acting for Western corporations and labor unions to influence WTO decisions. The low-income countries fear that they would find themselves legally "outgunned" in such an environment.

References

Books

Cameron, Rondo. (1989). *A concise economic history of the world.* New York: Oxford University Press.

Lairson, Thomas D., and Skidmore, David. (2003). *International political economy: The struggle for power and wealth.* Belmont, CA: Thomson Wadsworth.

Maddison, Angus. (2001). *The world economy: A milennial perspective.* OECD Development Centre.

Rider, Christine. (1995). *An introduction to economic history.* Cincinnati, OH: South-Western College Publishing.

Van Der Wee, Herman. (1986). *Prosperity and upheaval: The world economy 1945–1980.* Los Angeles, CA: University of California Press.

Articles

Bagwell, K., and Staiger, R. W. (2001). The WTO as a mechanism for securing market access property rights: Implications for global labor and environmental issues. *Journal of Economic Perspectives, 15*(3).

Broadberry, S., and Klein, A. (2012). Aggregate and per capita GDP in Europe, 1870–2000: Continental, regional and national data with changing boundaries. *Scandinavian Economic History Review, 60*(1).

Brown, Drusilla K. (2001). Labor standards: Where do they belong on the international trade agenda? *Journal of Economic Perspectives, 15*(3).

Eichengreen, Barry. (2010). Out-of-the box thoughts about the international financial architecture. *Journal of International Commerce, Economics and Policy, 1*(1).

Green, Timothy. (1999). Central bank gold reserves: An historical perspective since 1845. *Centre for Policy Studies, World Gold Council,* London.

Ostry, Sylvia. (2001). Dissent.com: How NGOs are re-making the WTO. *Policy Options.*

---

[5] An "amicus curiae" is an individual or organization which, while not a direct party to a case, offers information to a court to help it reach a decision.

Chapter 6

International Institutions and International Financial Crises

International financial crises, though not new, have become more frequent and generally more severe during the last forty years. This is partly due to the fact that greater international economic integration has made it easier for crises to spread from country to country so that economic difficulties that would have been localized in the past now affect the world economy.

The interesting questions relate to what causes crises in the first place and what can be done by individual countries and international institutions to alleviate them in their country of origin and prevent them from spreading to other countries. It is useful to place financial crises into three major categories: those that arise out of domestic macroeconomic imbalances, those that arise from structural problems in the financial sector, and those that are a result of contagion, though these are not mutually exclusive—international financial crises may be a result of macroeconomic imbalances in some countries, which have contagion effects that affect other countries. In the last two decades, crises have increasingly come to be associated with weaknesses in the regulation of financial markets. In this chapter we will, first, consider each of these types of crisis. Second, we will describe the phenomenon of financial globalization and analyze its role in increasing the frequency of international crises. Third, we will discuss crisis avoidance, Fourth, we will analyze the role of international institutions, particularly the International Monetary Fund (IMF), in resolving or worsening these crises. Finally, we will describe some of the major international financial crises of the last forty years.

Macroeconomic Imbalances

Some crises are the result of fiscal or monetary imbalances in one economy or several economies simultaneously. Examples are the Debt Crisis of the 1980s and the Mexican Peso Crisis of 1994–1995. The immediate triggers of the Debt Crisis were a fall in oil prices and a decline in international lending, but the deeper cause was the failure of the strategy of import substitution industrialization that had been implemented for several decades by a number of less industrialized countries,

"Those were years of such ambitious plans ... before the money ran out."

95

particularly in Latin America. This strategy, which will be discussed more fully later in this book, required high levels of government spending. Since low-income countries generally had inefficient taxation systems and poorly developed domestic capital markets, governments raised the necessary revenues to finance this spending by a combination of foreign borrowing and domestic money creation. The result was large budget deficits, high levels of foreign debt, and high rates of price inflation. Import substitution usually also involved maintaining low and stable nominal exchange rates so that favored domestic industries could import equipment and raw materials cheaply. As a result, a situation developed in which countries with high levels of foreign debt had increasingly overvalued exchange rates. In situations such as this, markets become increasingly doubtful about whether the exchange rate can be supported and capital flight begins as investors seek to convert their money into a strong currency. An exchange rate crisis then develops, as happened in the case of the debt crisis and the peso crisis, followed by a collapse in the exchange rate. In principle this situation might be avoided by an orderly devaluation, but in practice that is very difficult to achieve.

Contagion

Financial crises have also been attributed to contagion. This type of crisis spreads from country to country through trade and investment ties and can affect even countries that have sound macroeconomic fundamentals. Contagion may be made worse as a result of increased volatility in flows of financial capital, which cause a domino effect as capital flees from one country after another. In recent decades the increased importance of short-term capital flows relative to long-

term flows and the development of communications technology increasing the speed with which money can be transferred from country to country have worsened the "contagion effect" that has always existed to some degree. Financial flows are now extremely sensitive to interest rate differentials and since there is very little time in which to undertake analysis, a "herd effect" develops, in which investors copy the actions of each other. The problem is worse for countries in which the banking sector borrows internationally long term and lends domestically short term, counting on the possibility of rolling over the debt. Even countries for which this is not the case, however, may suffer contagion to some degree.

The East Asian Crisis of 1997, discussed later in this chapter, is often cited as an example of a crisis that spread through contagion, though structural weaknesses in the banking sectors of the affected countries also played a major role. By 1997 it was apparent that some East Asian countries (such as Thailand and South Korea) had developed macroeconomic imbalances, while others (such as Taiwan and Hong Kong) had sound macroeconomic fundamentals in that they had high levels of foreign exchange reserves relative to their foreign debt, low rates of inflation, and balanced or nearly balanced budgets. The Asian crisis was partly

International Institutions and International Financial Crises   **97**

due to capital that flowed into Asian countries in the 1980s and early 1990s without due care being taken as to whether the recipient economies were really stable. When panic set in, the countries with weak macroeconomic positions certainly suffered more than those with strong macroeconomic fundamentals, but even countries such as Taiwan experienced some difficulties. Being in the same geographical region as more troubled economies meant that they experienced contagion and suffered downward pressure on their exchange rates or foreign exchange reserves.

Padma Desai (2003), in describing contagion, distinguishes between "first generation transmission," in which a crisis is the result of trade flows, and "second generation transmission," in which the problem is the result of loss of confidence by a creditor or creditors. In first-generation contagion a country is faced with an economic downturn that reduces its ability to import goods from its trading partners. If this results in a currency depreciation for the afflicted country it has the effect of reducing the exports of other countries by giving the first country a competitive advantage in third-country markets. In this way the problems of the first country spread to other countries by reducing their exports. Second-generation transmission occurs as the result of actions by creditors. If a country or a group of countries has a high level of foreign debt, then they obviously become vulnerable to reductions in lending by foreign creditors. This could be exacerbated by reliance on a single large creditor country. By 1997, a number of East Asian countries had borrowed heavily from Japan and were seriously affected when Japanese banks, becoming nervous because of their heavy exposure in an increasingly troubled Thailand, began recalling loans not just from Thailand but also from neighboring countries. A similar kind of contagion can also occur if creditors in several countries become nervous about the economic viability of a region and a herd effect develops. This situation applied in the Latin American Debt Crisis of the 1980s, when banks from the industrialized countries in general became alarmed about the financial situation in Latin America and cut back on lending to all countries in the region.

Globalization and Capital Mobility

We have already seen how financial crises may pass from country to country. Globalization and, in particular, the growth in international financial flows have caused an increase in the frequency and severity of financial crises over the last forty years. The term "globalization" refers to an increase in the interdependence of countries and since the Second World War, particularly since the collapse of the Bretton Woods System in 1973, it has been associated with an increase in the power of financial capital relative to that of governments.

98   Chapter 6

More formal definitions of globalization include five major elements: (1) a rapid growth in international financial transactions, such as international lending; (2) a rapid growth in direct foreign investment, often, though not necessarily, by multinational corporations; (3) a rapid growth in international trade; (4) the convergence of prices between countries as a result of increased trade; and (5) a faster diffusion of technology across national borders as a result of improved transportation and communications systems.

Of the above factors, the growth in international financial transactions has been particularly associated with an increase in economic instability. At the end of the Second World War governments dominated international financial transfers, but the private sector rapidly grew in importance during the 1950s. This was evident with the growth of the Eurodollar (later called the Eurocurrency) market. As soon as the European economies began recovering from the destruction of the war, American manufacturing firms began investing in Europe, partly to take advantage of the lower costs (especially wage costs) in the region in comparison to the United States and partly to be better able to compete with local European producers without having to cover the cost of transporting goods across the Atlantic. Despite this, there was at first a dollar shortage in Europe. From 1958 onward, however, the United States was almost permanently running balance of payments deficits so that large balances of American dollars began accumulating in European banks, particularly London banks. Those banks were able to lend these dollars at lower rates of interest than American banks since they escaped the banking regulations of the United States, which had been relatively strict since the Great Depression. In this way the "Eurodollar Market" was born. It expanded still further as American banks set up branches abroad to escape U.S. banking controls and soon developed into a "Eurocurrency Market" as other strong currencies, in addition to the U.S. dollar, came to be traded in this largely unregulated financial system. This international private-sector financial market soon outstripped the government sector. By 1973, the value of currencies in the Eurocurrency market was already at least nine times the value of the international reserves of the U.S. government.

The growth of the international financial market accelerated in the 1970s as a result of the energy crises. During the first crisis of 1973–1974 the posted price of oil quadrupled and during the second crisis of 1979–1980 it almost tripled. This led to a huge increase in the holdings of foreign currencies, mostly U.S. dollars, by the oil exporting countries. These dollars, which came to be known as "petrodollars," were deposited in banks in the major money centers and subsequently lent out by these banks to their foreign customers. The resulting growth in international financial markets occurred at a time when financial regulations were being relaxed. When a slowdown in world economic growth occurred in the 1970s, conservative governments began implementing tax cuts and deregulation, including financial deregulation, in the belief that this would increase savings and investment and thereby bring about higher rates of economic growth. Deregulation proceeded still further in the 1980s, which saw a reduction in the restrictions on capital flows which had been a key feature of the Bretton Woods System. The removal of controls over short-term capital flows by the United States after 1974 and the United Kingdom after 1979 forced other countries to follow suit so as to prevent capital from migrating to New York or London.

One indicator of the extent to which financial markets have become globalized over the last forty years is the growth of trade in foreign exchange. The Bank for International Settlements estimated that daily average foreign exchange market turnover in April 2010 was $4 trillion.[1] This compares with $1.9 trillion in April 2004. A second indicator of globalization in financial markets is the growth in foreign exchange trading relative to the reserves of foreign exchange held by governments. By the mid-1990s daily trading in foreign exchange far exceeded the total foreign exchange reserves held by all governments.

This growth in the size of foreign exchange markets has been associated with increasing trade in financial assets for their own sake. The buying and selling of foreign exchange was historically associated with the needs of international trade in goods and services but this connection is now much weaker than before. By 2009, annual trade in foreign exchange was over 300 times the value of world exports. Along with this increase in currency trading came a vast increase in international borrowing and trading in equities. The volume of international lending more than doubled between 1990 and 1994 and has continued to increase since then.

As noted, this vast growth in the scale of international financial markets is partly owing to a reduction in government controls over international capital flows, but it is also partly a result of changes in technology. Developments in computer technology and a greater variety of financial instruments since the 1980s have undoubtedly made it more difficult for governments to enforce controls. The shift in ideology toward the deregulation of financial markets, however, began in the 1970s, predating the explosion in communications technology, though it was in the 1980s that deregulation really got underway.

More recently a number of economists have argued that free capital mobility, especially mobility of short-term capital, has few if any benefits, and is very destabilizing. Jagdish Bhagwati (1998) argues that while free trade in goods may increase economic efficiency, this is not necessarily true of free mobility of capital because of the potential for destabilizing speculation. Supporters of free capital mobility argue that it results in a more efficient allocation of capital worldwide and enables emerging economies to grow more quickly by giving them greater access to capital which would otherwise be in scarce supply domestically. But critics of this view point out that there is little empirical evidence to support these claims. China and Japan, the two countries that have had the most impressive records of growth since the Second World War, both achieved these growth rates at times when they had strict controls over capital inflows. Bhagwati and others argue that the best that can be said is that the benefits of free capital mobility are possible but unproven, while the experience of the last three decades shows that capital mobility has been associated with severe economic crises, beginning with the debt crisis of the 1980s. They argue that countries which currently have restrictions on capital mobility and are contemplating liberalizing should be careful to take account of the potential downside of liberalization.

On a more general level, there have been proposals for measures that might slow down short-term capital movements. One such proposal, which has attracted some attention, though so far only limited support, is the Tobin tax. The Tobin tax, first described by James Tobin in 1972, would be a small tax on foreign exchange transactions which would be insufficient

---

[1] *BIS Quarterly Review,* December 2010.

100   Chapter 6

to discourage long-term investments but would deter speculators, who move money from country to country at short intervals and would have to pay the tax each time they did so. In 2001 Tobin suggested 0.5 percent as a possible tax rate. There is controversy as to whether or not it is technically feasible to collect such a tax, given the difficulty of measuring financial transactions, and even if it is technically feasible it would be necessary to get international cooperation to introduce the tax since any country that implemented it alone would be faced with capital flight. At present there seems to be little prospect of a Tobin tax being adopted.

An alternative approach is to introduce restrictions on capital inflows rather than capital outflows. Chile adopted a policy of penalizing capital inflows between 1978 and 1982 and again between 1991 and 1998. During these two periods foreign investors were required to deposit a proportion of their investment with the central bank of Chile in a noninterest earning account. This had the same effect as a tax on foreign investment and, while it had only a minor effect on long-term lending, it had a significant effect on short-term lending. Supporters of the policy argue that it lengthened the average maturity of Chile's foreign debt and helped to protect the country from the effects of the Mexican peso crisis of 1994. Others, however, doubt that the capital controls significantly lengthened the maturity of Chilean debt and maintain that, even if temporarily effective, such controls lose their impact over time as financial institutions find ways of getting around the controls.

Crisis Avoidance

Two issues are generally raised in discussions of how to reduce the probability of an international financial crisis: moral hazard and exchange rate policy. We will discuss each of these in turn.

Moral Hazard and the Basel Accords

"Moral hazard" refers to the removal of the costs of failure from the financial sector and the danger that this may encourage inappropriate behavior on the part of financial institutions. If financial institutions and international investors know that they will be protected by taxpayers and international institutions when market conditions become unfavorable, they may be encouraged to engage in high-risk activity. In the normal course of events, risky investments and loans to high-risk borrowers command a "risk premium" to compensate for the high probability of the investment making a loss or the borrower defaulting. In the case of moral hazard, investors have an incentive to engage in high-risk activity since there is a high return if the investment pays off, but if it fails the cost is borne not by the investor or lender but by governments or international institutions. There is thus a gap between the expected private return on investments and their true or social rate of return. The gap between private and social rates of return may be even further widened when governments influence the credit system to favor certain industries or firms, a practice sometimes referred to as "crony capitalism." Ideally, investors and lenders should have to bear the costs of failure so that they will more carefully weigh the true risk of their actions.

Attempts have been made to minimize the effects of moral hazard through the Basel Accords. In 1975 the Basel Committee on Banking Supervision, named after its base in Basel,

Switzerland, was set up by a group of ten countries for the purpose of improving banking supervision. In 1988 the committee published a series of guidelines setting capital requirements for banks. Initially known as *the* Basel Accord, Basel I classified bank assets according to credit risk and applied to these assets weights ranging from zero for assets considered to be absolutely safe (home country sovereign debt) to 100 for high-risk assets (corporate debt). Banks engaged in international lending were required to hold capital equal to 8 percent of their risk-weighted assets. Basel I was superceded by Basel II (originally known as the New Basel Capital Accord) in 2004. In addition to refining and expanding upon capital requirements, Basel II proposed new tools for financial regulators and developed a set of disclosure requirements designed to help markets measure the adequacy of an institution's capital. In 2010 the Basel Committee agreed on Basel III, which is designed to deal with the inadequacies of financial regulation as revealed by the financial crisis of 2008–2009. It increases bank capital requirements and regulatory requirements on bank liquidity and leverage. In summary, the Basel Accords are intended to decrease the dangers of moral hazard with respect to banks by requiring them to meet a minimum capital requirement. The problem with the accords is that the Basel Committee has no power to enforce its recommendations and though some countries have adopted these recommendations there may be delays in implementing them.

Exchange Rate Policy

In addition to moral hazard, exchange rate policy has been an important issue with respect to recent international crises. Less-developed countries frequently seek to maintain exchange rate stability as a tool for fighting inflation. This policy, known as a "nominal anchor" approach, requires "pegging" the country's currency to that of a country with low inflation, frequently the United States. The objective is to force the domestic rate of inflation down to that of the United States since local firms trying to raise prices at a rate significantly higher than the U.S. rate of inflation would not be able to compete with foreign imports. The issue then becomes whether a "crawling peg" or a "hard peg" should be adopted. A "crawling peg" occurs when the peg is supposed to be periodically revised whenever the country finds itself experiencing balance of payments difficulties. The problem with a crawling peg is that as soon as signs emerge that a country's currency is overvalued, the markets anticipate a devaluation and the country is faced with capital flight. This erodes its foreign exchange reserves and may force a larger than desirable currency depreciation. In other words, there is a problem of credibility. The alternative is a "hard peg." In this case the country undertakes never to revise its exchange rate, which is supposed to provide greater credibility and prevent capital flight. The problem, of course, is that such a policy, if not accompanied by appropriate domestic fiscal and monetary policies, generally means that the exchange rate becomes more and more overvalued. Even with appropriate policies it is almost certain that the exchange rate will become temporarily overvalued because there is a momentum to inflation and it is unlikely to fall immediately upon adoption of the fixed exchange rate. Eventually it becomes obvious that the peg with the dollar cannot be maintained. At this point there is massive capital flight and a massive currency collapse.

The experience of Argentina in 2001 is a good example of the problem of maintaining a hard peg without appropriate fiscal and monetary policies. In 1991 Argentina adopted a hard peg to the U.S. dollar as a counter-inflationary measure. The policy was, indeed, successful in bringing down the rate of inflation, which decreased from an annual rate of 1,344 percent in 1990 to 7.4 percent in 1993. There were, however, persistent fiscal deficits, a rising foreign debt, and growing trade deficits as Argentinian goods became less competitive in foreign markets relative to those of other South American countries whose currencies were not pegged to the dollar. Eventually, in 2001, faced with massive capital outflows, a severe recession, and a banking crisis the exchange rate regime was abandoned. The lesson was that a hard peg could not be maintained in the face of persistent fiscal and current account deficits.

The international institutions and most economists now believe that there should be some flexibility in exchange rates. There are still, however, disagreements among policy makers and economists as to what constitutes the best exchange rate regime. One view is that a nominal anchor approach is still useful in countering inflation in the early stages of stabilization but a fixed exchange rate, whether it be a crawling peg or a hard peg, should be adopted only on a temporary basis and subsequently replaced with a flexible rate. The obvious problem is that it is difficult to make a transition from a fixed to a flexible exchange rate without generating a massive capital outflow and a foreign exchange crisis. On this basis some economists argue that it is better for less-developed countries to adopt floating exchange rates and rely on monetary and fiscal policies to counter inflation.

Role of the IMF and the World Bank

The IMF was established to assist countries experiencing short-term balance of payments difficulties and consequently has played a major role in the management of international financial crises when they occur. The three major functions of the Fund are (1) to provide surveillance of the balance of payments situations of member countries, (2) to provide loans of hard currencies to member countries when needed, and (3) to provide technical assistance in helping poor countries to improve their access to financial markets. The second of these functions implies acting as the lender of last resort to countries in difficulty. Increasingly, in recent years, the Fund has acted in concert with the World Bank. When they were established at the time of the Bretton Woods Conference in 1944, it was envisaged that the IMF and the World Bank would have separate areas of responsibility. The Fund was to have responsibility for macroeconomic and financial sector issues, while the Bank was to focus on providing assistance to countries in the areas of infrastructure and financial reform. In recent years, however, the activities of the two institutions have increasingly overlapped. The World Bank, like the IMF, plays a role in providing emergency assistance through structural adjustment loans (SALs), in which balance of payments financing is linked to reforms in broad sectors of the economy. In providing such assistance the IMF and the World Bank are careful to coordinate their activities. Such cooperation is made easier by the fact that both institutions are based in Washington, DC, and have interlocking boards of directors.

The IMF exercises its surveillance functions through Article IV Consultations, which provide for regular consultations between the Fund and member countries with an emphasis on the prevention of financial crises. Originally the IMF emphasized the adequacy of international reserves in its lending decisions and policy recommendations, but other factors have been given increasing emphasis, notably the ability of governments to finance budget deficits, financial regulation, and overall economic policy, including fiscal and monetary policy and structural policies. When providing loans to countries in need, the Fund usually provides less than what is needed, but it is hoped that when a country receives IMF assistance this will act as a signal to official and private-sector lenders that it is creditworthy.

IMF loans usually have to be repaid in one to three years. Four major categories of loans are available.

1. Stand-by Arrangements (SBAs) and the Supplemental Reserve Facility (SRF), which may be made available to any member country of the International Monetary Fund. Most lending through the IMF is through SBAs, which are usually disbursed between one to two years and repaid within three to five years. The SRF was introduced in 1997 to provide very short-term financing on a large scale. It is designed to deal with a sudden and disruptive loss of market confidence and allows a country access to funds in excess of the normal borrowing limits based on that country's quota. Loans under the SRF command a higher interest rate than other IMF loans and have to be repaid within twelve to eighteen months of disbursement.

2. The Extended Fund Facility, established in 1974, which helps countries deal with medium-term balance of payments problems related to structural programs. This overlaps considerably with the World Bank SALs.

3. Loans through the Poverty Reduction and Growth Facility, established in 1999, under which loans with interest rates of 0.5 percent and maturities of up to ten years are provided to the IMF's poorest member countries.

4. The Exogenous Shocks Facility, established in 2005, which is designed to assist low-income countries faced with problems arising from sudden exogenous shocks.

Invariably conditions are attached to these loans and recipients normally have to agree to adopt a stabilization program drawn up by the Fund. The stabilization programs are intended to correct current account deficits and increasingly also to reassure financial markets of the creditworthiness of the recipient country. The elimination of current account deficits entails adopting policies to reduce domestic consumption and hence reduce the demand for imports. Such policies are invariably unpopular since they include reductions in public spending and increases in taxation, but even more controversial are economic liberalization policies often demanded, such as deregulation and privatization of state-owned assets.

104   Chapter 6

The IMF and its partner, the World Bank, have come under considerable criticism for their handling of crises in recent decades but from quite different directions. Some critics question whether it is desirable to have a lender of last resort at all in the international economy. Proponents of this view generally believe that the availability of emergency credit creates a moral hazard problem, encouraging governments to adopt lax fiscal and monetary policies in the belief that if worst comes to worst the IMF and its partner, the World Bank, will bail them out. A milder variant of this view accepts the need for a lender of last resort but believes that the IMF has been overly generous in providing financial support to countries pursuing unsound economic policies.

A more common criticism of the Fund and the Bank takes the opposite point of view, chastising them for imposing overly severe and ideologically motivated conditions on the loans they provide. The IMF, in particular, has also been criticized for "mission creep." When first established the Fund saw its role as providing financial assistance and guidance to countries in dealing with the immediate consequences of a crisis. Since the 1970s, however, it has seen its role as one of pressuring countries to adopt what it feels are appropriate policies for the overall economy. This has been justified on the grounds that if governments implement "unsound" economic policies, balance of payments problems will recur in the future.

Joseph Stiglitz, a former chief economist at the World Bank, is a strong critic of both the IMF and the World Bank with respect to what he sees as their emphasis on free markets. He points out that in the 1990s the number of people living in poverty worldwide increased by almost 100 million. At the same time there has been an increase in economic instability as a result of financial contagion. In his view the international institutions, which were originally established to offset flaws in financial markets, have now become advocates of free markets. The Bretton Woods Agreement of 1944 envisaged the role of the IMF as providing loans to countries facing economic downturns and, by means of the Scarce Currency Clause, putting pressure on member countries to maintain global aggregate demand. These functions reflected the view that markets were flawed and sometimes required corrective action from international institutions. In Stiglitz's view, by the 1980s, at the latest, the IMF had adopted a very different position. It had become a missionary for the free market system and, far from pressuring countries to maintain aggregate demand, was pressuring them to pursue deflationary policies. The World Bank moved in the same direction after 1981 with a new emphasis on free markets as the solution to the problems faced by less-developed countries The World Bank's SALs, introduced in the 1980s, were tied to the same conditions as those imposed by the IMF. As a result, the two institutions were marching in lockstep, imposing the pro-market conditions envisaged in what has been described as the "Washington Consensus," so-called because it was supported by three major institutions based in Washington, namely the IMF, the World Bank, and the U.S. Treasury.

In Stiglitz's opinion the 1980s not only saw a greater faith in free markets on the part of the Fund but also a phenomenon he describes as "IMF imperialism." When it was founded in the aftermath of the Second World War the International Monetary Fund was expected to limit its attention to macroeconomic and financial issues but in recent decades the Fund's view of its role has expanded enormously on the grounds that almost any structural issue can be seen as affecting the balance of payments or the government's budget. The Latin American Debt

Crisis of the 1980s, in particular, played a large role in encouraging the IMF and the World Bank to get more involved in what used to be regarded as strictly political issues. Since the debt crisis was in large part a result of out-of-control budgets and lax monetary policies, the Fund and its backers had a valid case in emphasizing the need for cutting budget deficits and implementing tighter monetary policies.

More controversial, however, was the IMF emphasis on capital market liberalization, a policy that was strongly promoted when the Fund was called upon to assist in dealing with later crises, notably the Asian Crisis of 1997. The controversy is not so much about lifting controls on long-term investment as about liberalizing controls on short-term financial flows. As is evident from the section of this chapter on globalization and capital mobility, Stiglitz is not alone in arguing against the removal of controls over short-term capital flows. Even some economists who maintain that capital market liberalization is desirable in principle believe that caution should be exercised when introducing it. Kenneth Rogoff, a former chief economist of the IMF, now accepts that liberalization was pursued too hastily. In some cases and in particular in the leadup to the Asian crisis in the 1990s, the IMF had insisted on rapid capital market liberalization. Since the countries of the region lacked sound banking structures or adequate standards of financial regulation, the result was excessive inflows of financial capital, frequently to engage in speculative activities. Rogoff argues that the *sequencing* of reforms is important. In other words, it was unwise to insist on capital market liberalization before the establishment of strong financial institutions.

The IMF and the Washington Consensus do, however, have their defenders. Anne Krueger, a former chief economist of the World Bank and senior official at the IMF, argues that a greater emphasis on liberalization is appropriate in dealing with balance of payments crises because the nature of those crises has changed in recent decades. Until the 1970s, balance of payments crises were usually the result of problems with the current account, but since then, and particularly since the 1990s, they have more often been caused by problems on the capital account. Capital account crises differ from current account crises in two major ways: First, they require a much more rapid response since flows of financial capital can change direction much more rapidly than flows of goods and services. Second, they occur when investors lose confidence in the ability of a country to service its debt. This can occur even when a country has sound macroeconomic fundamentals, such as low budget deficits and low inflation. The important thing is to reassure markets by giving them what they like. Markets will be reassured by pro-market structural policies, such as deregulation and privatization, and an emphasis on transparency of policy.

Even if this view is accepted, however, the need to reassure markets does not justify introducing financial liberalization where it does not already exist. It may also be noted that the structural reforms urged by the IMF and the World Bank have not always been successful in reversing capital outflows.

Major International Economic Crises Since 1980

There have been numerous international economic crises over the last 30 years. Three of the most important will be discussed in this section.

The Debt Crisis of the 1980s

The origins of the debt crisis lie in the 1970s, when the less-developed countries (LDCs) began to rely increasingly on commercial bank credit to finance their development strategies. During the 1950s and 1960s they had relied primarily on foreign direct investment to supplement domestic savings in financing capital formation but, given the dominance of transnational corporations, this created concerns about threats to national sovereignty. Domestic firms,
sometimes state owned, were promoted to counter this perceived threat. In the 1970s, however, low interest loans were readily available from the Western banks as a result of the oil shocks of that decade. Sharp increases in oil prices in 1973–1974 and again in 1978–1979 by the members of the Organization of Petroleum Exporting Countries (OPEC) dramatically increased the holdings of U.S. dollars by the oil-exporting countries. Unable to fully absorb these "petrodollars" the oil exporters deposited large amounts of them with the commercial banks in the major money centers, such as London and New York. Flooded with loanable funds, the banks offered large sums at low nominal interest rates. Once inflation took hold after 1973 (another consequence of the increase in oil prices) nominal interest rates lagged behind inflation and real interest rates fell rapidly. On occasions nominal rates actually fell below the rate of inflation and real interest rates became negative. Not surprisingly, this led to an increase in borrowing by governments and institutions supported by government guarantees.

There were, however, risks that were not sufficiently taken account of by either the borrowers or the lenders. The banks lent very large sums to countries whose creditworthiness was dubious. The eagerness of banks to engage in this high-risk behavior was a result of various factors, including the following:

1. *Lack of historical memory,* which seems to be a recurring feature of financial markets. There had been many Latin American debt crises in the past, the most recent in the 1930s, but this was apparently forgotten.

2. *Deficiencies of regulation.* The rapid growth of the Eurocurrency market had outstripped the ability of the regulators to supervise the actions of banks and financial institutions.

3. *Recession.* The oil shocks not only stimulated inflation worldwide but they also plunged the industrialized countries into recession in the mid-1970s. This was the era of "stagflation" (simultaneous high inflation and economic stagnation). Lacking demand for loans in the recession-hit industrialized countries, banks became more interested in low-income countries, which seemed to have an unquenchable thirst for funds.

The eagerness of low-income countries, especially those in Latin America, to borrow was the result both of developments specific to the 1970s and of more long-standing factors.

1. Several countries had long been pursuing strategies of import substitution industrialization. These strategies required large levels of government spending and, because they necessitated imports of capital goods, tended to increase current account deficits. Given the difficulties typically faced by LDC governments in collecting taxes, it was tempting to cover budgetary and current account deficits by borrowing.

2. Borrowing from foreign commercial banks seemed like a bargain given low nominal interest rates and high rates of price inflation. Unfortunately for the borrowers, as it turned out, most of the lending was at floating interest rates, which could be adjusted upwards if credit tightened. In the 1970s this did not seem to be a problem since it was expected that interest rates would fall rather than rise. The situation became, however, very different at the end of the decade when monetary policy was tightened in the industrialized countries and interest rates began to rise sharply.

3. As indicated, there was at this time a distrust of direct foreign investment by transnational corporations. This distrust was well founded in some cases. There were examples of Western governments undermining governments in less developed countries when they threatened the interests of transnational corporations. Notable examples were in Iran in 1953, when the CIA engineered a coup against the government of Mohammad Mossadegh, who threatened the interests of Western oil companies, and in Guatemala in 1954, where the government of President Arbenz was overthrown in an American-backed coup when he threatened the interests of the United Fruit Company.

The lenders were happy to satisfy the thirst for loans on the part of low-income countries in the mistaken belief that loans to sovereign borrowers were always low risk. As indicated, this reflected historical amnesia and the performance of the debtor countries should have raised some concerns long before the crisis eventually occurred. A further problem arose from the fact that many Latin American countries had adopted overvalued exchange rates in order to curb inflation and to enable favored import competing firms to buy foreign-produced capital goods cheaply. These caused large current account deficits, which were then covered by further external borrowing. Once it became clear that the overvalued exchange rates could not be maintained indefinitely, capital flight began to occur as the wealthy converted their financial assets into U.S. dollars and other hard currencies. For a time this was covered by even more borrowing.

The problems inherent in this situation came to light in the early 1980s as a result of the second oil price hike engineered by OPEC in 1979. Import prices for those debtor countries that relied on imported oil were increased and, more importantly, by igniting the fear of further inflation on the part of central banks in industrialized countries, it led to the introduction of very tight monetary policies in those countries. This had the effect of causing a severe recession in the industrialized countries, a sharp rise in U.S. interest rates, and a consequent appreciation in the external value of the U.S. dollar. Most LDC loans were denominated in U.S. dollars and, as noted, much of the LDC debt was at floating interest rates. This caused a sudden and large increase in the debt burden. By 1982 debt payments were consuming 70 percent of the export revenues of the largest non-oil-exporting debtor countries. In 1973 the proportion had been only 36 percent.

108   Chapter 6

Everything came to a head in August 1982. With foreign banks refusing to provide new funding to finance the large payments falling due on its old debts Mexico, the second largest debtor country, announced that it could no longer cover its scheduled loan payments, thereby raising the spectre of defaults not just by Mexico but by other debtor countries as well. The stability of the international banking system seemed in doubt. The IMF, the U.S. government, and the commercial banks provided emergency finance to Mexico but the crisis continued to grow.

After Mexico, numerous countries in Latin America and elsewhere sought (mainly in vain) to secure new loans and renegotiate the terms of the old loans. The IMF responded by providing some assistance but only on condition that stringent adjustment packages were adopted. The emphasis was on improving trade balances by reducing imports, which meant tight fiscal policies and currency devaluations. Undoubtedly there was a need to bring government budget and current account deficits under control, but the combination of fiscal tightening and currency devaluations resulted in a decade of economic stagnation and inflation for the debtor countries. For a remarkably long time the IMF and its backers, the Western governments, persisted in believing there was a simple problem of short-term liquidity. When the banks were reassured that sound policies were being implemented they would resume lending. Not until 1987 was it accepted by the IMF and its backers that it would be necessary to reduce the debt obligations of the debtor countries.

Meanwhile the debtor countries and the banks experimented with a variety of measures. By 1987 the creditor banks were seeking to protect themselves by making additions to their loan loss reserves and diversifying their loan portfolios. A secondary market for LDC debt developed, in which debts would be bought and sold for a discount. In some cases debtors took advantage of this market by buying back their own debt at discounted prices in a procedure known as "cash buy-backs." Other methods of reducing debt were "debt-for-equity swaps" and "debt-for-debt swaps." In the former case, foreign corporations would buy LDC debts at a discount from banks and then sell the debt to the debtor country's central bank in exchange for local currency, which would then be used to finance investments in the local economy. In this way the debtor country would erase some of its debt without using scarce foreign exchange. The end result, of course, would be more foreign ownership of the country's economy. With "debt-for-debt swaps" old unguaranteed loans would be exchanged, at a discount, for new loans, which were guaranteed either by the LDC government or a foreign government. Mexico was able to exchange part of its old debt at a discount for new debt backed by U.S. government–guaranteed securities. Between 1985 and 1988, about 2 percent of LDC debt was eliminated by these three methods.

That still left nearly $1.3 trillion of debt. By now it was generally accepted that there would need to be some debt forgiveness if the Latin American countries were to get back on their feet. In 1989 Nicholas Brady, then the U.S. secretary of the Treasury, proposed a program to forgive $70 billion over several years for a group of fifteen countries, amounting to a 20 percent reduction in the outstanding debt of those countries. Under the Brady plan the banks would be invited to exchange existing loans for new bonds with lower principal or interest rates. The incentive for doing this was that the new bonds would be guaranteed by special funds financed through loans issued by the IMF, the World Bank, and the governments of the industrialized countries. The plan was criticized as being too generous to the banks and not sufficiently generous to the debtor countries. It has been argued that a moral hazard problem

International Institutions and International Financial Crises   109

was created since taxpayers in industrialized countries were assuming part of the cost of the misjudgements of commercial banks. On the other hand, it was true that the banks still had to absorb part of the cost of their mistakes.

Others criticized the Brady plan for providing too little debt reduction and for imposing on the debtor countries policy changes against their will, for relief was contingent on the borrowers showing a willingness to adopt economic reforms. These reforms reflected the view already referred to as "the Washington Consensus." The term "Washington Consensus" was originally coined in 1989 by the economist John Williamson to describe ten specific policy prescriptions, but it came to refer more loosely to a neoliberal or free market approach to economic policy. As indicated earlier, its name derives from the views of three major organizations based in Washington, D.C., namely the IMF, the World Bank, and the U.S. Treasury. The most widely held interpretation of the Washington Consensus is that its policy prescriptions fall under three broad headings. First, the adoption of macroeconomic policies to minimize inflation and balance government budgets or at least reduce the size of budget deficits. Second, the privatization of state-owned assets and deregulation of the economy. Third, the opening of economies to trade and to foreign investment.

The adoption of macroeconomic stabilization policies was clearly necessary. Inflation, which had always been a problem for the debtor countries, became worse in the early 1980s, in large part as a consequence of government attempts to deal with the worldwide recession of the time by increased spending. Given the difficulties governments of low-income countries usually have in collecting taxes and the impossibility of financing spending through international borrowing, because of the debt crisis, the increased spending was financed through money creation. This inevitably led to severe inflation and in some cases hyperinflation. Bolivia, the worst affected country, experienced inflation of over 8,000 percent in 1985. The only way to end this was through cutting budget deficits and reducing the rate of money creation.

The second and third themes of the Washington Consensus involve structural reforms. Privatization and deregulation accord with the belief of the IMF and its Western backers that such reforms will bring about greater efficiency through freeing the market and undoubtedly reflect a pro-market ideology that is not universally shared. These were the most controversial of the reforms imposed on the debtor countries. Another aspect of the structural reforms involved the opening of the economies of the debtor countries to international trade and investment. This, it was believed, would bring about greater competition and efficiency. In the late 1980s and 1990s there were significant reductions in tariffs and nontariff barriers and a greater openness to foreign direct investment on the part of almost all Latin American countries.

How successful were the reforms? The answer to that question depends on the time frame adopted for analysis. Undoubtedly most debtor countries, especially those in Latin America, performed much better in the 1990s than in the 1980s. A comparison of the 1990s with the 1960s and 1970s is not so favorable, however, as can be seen from Table 6.1, which compares annual growth rates in real GDP per capita for the four largest Latin American countries between 1960 and 1999. For three of the four countries shown, annual growth rates were significantly lower between 1990 and 1999 than between 1960 and 1980. At the same time there was undoubtedly a worsening of inequality in the distribution of income and wealth in countries where inequality was already very severe.

110   Chapter 6

TABLE 6.1. Annual Growth in Real GDP Per Capita for the Four Largest Latin American Countries (%)

Country	1960–80	1980–90	1990–99
Argentina	1.9%	−2.2%	3.6%
Brazil	4.5	+0.7	1.5
Colombia	2.8	+1.5	1.2
Mexico	3.9	−1.0	0.9

The Asian Crisis

The Asian Crisis of 1997 differed from the debt crisis of the 1980s in a number of significant ways. While the structural and fiscal problems of the Latin American countries had been clearly apparent in the years before the debt crisis, the Asian countries in the years before 1997 were generally believed to have sound "fundamentals." For two decades they had experienced high rates of economic growth, along with high savings rates, low inflation, full employment, and an outward orientation, in contrast to the inward, import substitution stances of the Latin American countries in the 1970s. Government budgets were balanced, in surplus, or exhibited only very small deficits. The Asian Crisis was not in fact due to failures of fiscal policy but to excesses in the financial markets and to the impact on the Asian economies of external shocks. Once the failures of the financial sector became apparent, however, they imposed a heavy burden on the fiscal balances of the affected countries. There are obvious parallels between the situation facing the Asian countries in 1997 and the burdens imposed on the budgets of the developed countries as a result of measures to support the financial sector during the aftermath of the crisis of 2008–2009.

The Asian crisis began with the collapse of the Thai baht in July 1997. The collapse was attributable to a number of immediate causes. One cause was a recent decline in Thailand's exports as a result of a fall in the prices of computer chips. Another contributing factor was a rising vacancy rate in Thailand, which alarmed foreign lenders whose money had been funneled into real estate speculation. There followed panic withdrawals of funds from Thailand. The situation was made worse by the fact that over half of the country's foreign borrowing came from a single creditor country, Japan, making it vulnerable to nervousness on the part of Japanese banks.

The panic spread to other countries and Thailand's crisis rapidly became an "Asian Crisis." The Thai devaluation made exports from neighboring countries less competitive, but there was also undoubtedly a herd effect in financial markets, with panicked withdrawals of funds from all countries of the region. The worst affected countries were Thailand, Indonesia, the Philippines, Malaysia, and South Korea, but even Taiwan and Singapore, which had large foreign exchange reserves, came under speculative attack, though they were able to ride it out. During the twelve-month period after July 1997, almost all East Asian countries experienced falls in the external values of their currencies with the devaluations for the worst-hit countries ranging from 34 percent (the South Korean won) to over 83 percent (the Indonesian rupiah). Many businesses in the affected countries were forced into bankruptcy as creditors recalled loans and interest rates rose sharply. This led to sharp rises in unemployment in a region where social services were generally inadequate and the worst affected countries all experienced sharp reductions in real GDP in 1997–1998. For most of them, however, recovery followed soon afterwards. The economies of South Korea and Malaysia resumed growth again 1999, while Thailand had recovered by 2001. The economy of Indonesia, on the other hand, had still not fully recovered from the crisis by 2005.

While the crisis was made worse by herd effects in the financial sector, there are differing views as to the fundamental cause of the problems of the East Asian economies. One view holds that the crisis was the result of moral hazard. A tradition of public guarantees for financial institutions and nonbank corporations encouraged risky behavior. It was possible for banks to borrow internationally and lend locally to finance speculative ventures because financial institutions and corporations were believed by investors to have implicit government guarantees.

Abandoned building in Bangkok.

An alternative interpretation of the crisis is that it was primarily the result of structural problems in the financial sectors of the Asian economies, specifically weak prudential regulation and low required capital adequacy ratios. One indicator of financial weakness was a serious mismatch between the foreign liabilities and the foreign assets of Asian banks and nonbank firms since domestic banks borrowed from foreign banks but lent mostly to domestic firms. The rapid financial liberalization of the 1990s magnified these problems.

Apart from the moral hazard and structural problems in the financial sector, numerous other factors influenced the timing and severity of the crisis. The most important were as follows:

1. The appreciation of the U.S. dollar relative to the Japanese yen and the European currencies in 1995. Many Asian currencies were pegged to the U.S. dollar and, as the dollar rose in value, these currencies became overvalued. Pegging was intended to provide a nominal anchor to combat inflation but inertia inflation persisted and, in combination with fixed *nominal* exchange rates, caused a rise in *real* exchange rates. It took time for inflationary expectations to be dissipated and, in the meantime, wage demands persisted. It is worth noting, however, that despite the fact that the Korean won was not pegged to the dollar, South Korea was one of the most hard-hit countries in the crisis.

2. A drop in real estate and stock market prices in 1997, which caused large losses and defaults in the corporate and financial sectors.

112   Chapter 6

TABLE 6.2. Proportion of Foreign Borrowing from Japanese Banks (December 1996) (%)

Thailand	54.5%
Indonesia	39.7
Malaysia	36.9
South Korea	24.0

3. Current account deficits. Some of the most hard-hit countries had substantial current account deficits on the eve of the crisis though, again, South Korea was an exception.

4. High growth rates in the East Asian economies which, perversely, contributed to their problems by creating an overly optimistic belief that expansion would persist indefinitely. This belief encouraged rapid capital inflows, which were even more rapidly reversed when the Asian economies appeared to weaken.

5. The openness of the East Asian economies which, though it was a major factor in the development of the Asian economic "miracle," made these economies vulnerable to trade shocks. The appreciation in real exchange rates as a result of pegging to the U.S. dollar therefore hit these economies very hard.

6. The continuing stagnation of the Japanese economy, which reduced the demand for exports from Japan's neighbors.

7. The increasing competition of manufacturing exports from China.

8. A fall in demand for semiconductors in 1996. Semiconductors were a major export for some East Asian countries.

9. Dependence on a single creditor. As mentioned, a number of Asian countries were heavily dependent on a single creditor, namely Japan, and were therefore vulnerable to shifts in the attitude of Japanese banks. As can be seen from Table 6.2, the most seriously affected of the Asian countries had received a large proportion of their foreign loans from Japan and were therefore vulnerable to a withdrawal of credit from this one lender. Thailand's economy was severely hit when Japanese banks began recalling loans in 1997.

Role of the IMF

Few observers, including the International Monetary Fund, anticipated a crisis as severe as that of 1997, though some concerns had been expressed about potential weaknesses in the economies of some Asian countries, especially Thailand. The traditional measures of vulnerability to a crisis, such as government budget deficits, failed to signal the dangers facing the East Asian economies because the cost of bailing out the banks was not taken into account until after the event. Once the crisis was underway the IMF stepped in quickly, but its measures

International Institutions and International Financial Crises 113

to resolve the crisis were controversial at the time and have remained so. Emergency loans were provided to the most hard-hit countries, with $35 billion of IMF support being provided to Indonesia, South Korea, and Thailand. In addition, $85 billion was committed from other sources, though not all of it was actually taken up. Strict conditions were attached to these loans, including sharp rises in interest rates, currency devaluations, cuts in government spending, deregulation, and privatization of state-owned enterprises. Though some of these measures did not appear to be directly related to the crisis they were defended on the grounds that they were needed to reassure markets.

Critics of the IMF argued at the time and have argued since that it had helped to create the crisis in the first place through its promotion of free capital markets and subsequently made the crisis more severe through the adjustment packages imposed upon the afflicted countries. During the 1990s the Fund had pressured the East Asian countries to dismantle controls over capital markets. Its critics believe that this was because of an ideological commitment to capital mobility, but even those who generally support the IMF now concede that capital liberalization was premature, given the inadequacy of the systems of financial regulation in the East Asian countries. It is now widely accepted that capital liberalization should be undertaken, if at all, only after an efficient system of prudential regulation is in place. In terms of the IMF response to the crisis after it occurred, the Fund's critics believe that (1) the rescue packages were inadequate; (2) the adjustment packages were draconian and impracticable; and (3) a timely debt restructuring would have been better for the affected countries than the austerity packages that were actually imposed.

The Subprime Mortgage Crisis of 2007 and the Great Recession

The world is still feeling the effects of the financial crisis that began in the United States in 2007. Financial innovation, integration of global financial markets, financial deregulation, and global savings imbalances all played a part in causing this crisis.

The international collapse began as the subprime mortgage crisis in the U.S. housing sector. Easy initial loan terms had encouraged low-income borrowers with low credit ratings to take out mortgages ("subprime mortgages") in the hope that they would be able to service them through rising incomes or from the sale of houses with rising prices. In the run up to the 2007 crisis over a trillion dollars was channeled into the subprime mortgage market. When housing prices began falling many of the borrowers either chose to default or were forced into default.

The U.S. subprime mortgage crisis became a financial global crisis because of a number of developments that had taken place in the 1990s and the early years of the twenty-first century, including financial innovation and the globalization of financial markets. Prior to the 1990s banks took deposits and lent them as mortgages to home buyers. Their profits came directly from the interest charged on the mortgages. In the 1990, however, banks and other financial institutions began bundling large numbers of loans together and selling shares in the resulting packages in a process known as "securitization." Purchasers of shares in these packages would receive a return based on the interest paid by the home buyers. This procedure was supposed to increase efficiency by spreading risk, but the ultimate owners of the securities generally knew very little about the loans contained in the package. Since financial markets had become globalized, these products were sold not only in the United States but also internationally, which meant that the problems of the U.S. housing market and, by extension, the U.S. banking system, infected world financial markets.

Deregulation of financial markets also contributed to the crisis. Not only were new types of financial assets being marketed but at the same time there was a greater use of computers and complex mathematical models. As a result there appeared a range of financial products which hardly anyone could understand, including the regulators and corporate heads. At the time, however, inability to understand the new financial products seems to have been of little concern to those responsible for regulation since the prevailing opinion was that financial markets should be allowed to self-regulate. This view was strongly supported by Alan Greenspan, chairman of the U.S. Federal Reserve Board between 1987 and 2006. In his testimony before Congress in October 2008 Greenspan confessed that he had always believed that the self-interest of lending institutions would protect shareholders' equity and he was "in a state of shocked disbelief" to find that this was not so.

The final factor contributing to the crisis was a global imbalance in savings. A number of countries, notably China, Germany, and Japan, have consistently run large current account surpluses, which has meant that other countries, such as the United States, Spain, and the United Kingdom, have consistently run deficits financed with capital inflows from the surplus countries. Without access to the high savings of countries like China, borrowers in the United States would have found borrowing more expensive and the housing bubble would not have grown to such an extreme degree.

Alan Greenspan.

So where do we go from here? Reinhart and Rogoff (2008) conducted a series of historical studies of international banking crises and have drawn some sobering conclusions from them. They found that financial crises invariably result in collapses in asset markets which are deep and prolonged, typically lasting over three years. The aftermath of the crises is associated with severe declines in output and employment, with unemployment, on average, rising for almost five years. Finally, the real value of government debt increases dramatically, primarily as a result of collapsing tax revenues due to contractions in output and, in some cases, increased spending for countercyclical fiscal policies. The actual cost of bank bailouts tends to be only a minor contributor to the debt. As of this writing (2016) the debt problems of governments have become very obvious. On the basis of past experience, such high levels of government debt usually lead to sovereign default and high inflation. Technical defaults have become rare since the 1980s because of intervention by the IMF and the World Bank, but debt reschedulings, which effectively are partial defaults, have occurred from time to time. Reschedulings give debtors a longer period in which to repay their loans, thereby reducing their annual debt repayments and causing a real loss to the creditors. Such reschedulings may be adopted as a face-saving form of default. Reinhart and Rogoff also observed that inflation and default tend to go together since governments can reduce the real burden of the public debt at the expense of long-term bondholders through inflation. This displeases the markets, but governments desperate enough to default will hardly be too concerned about that.

The Asian countries were, of course, able to recover from the crisis of 1997 relatively quickly. The current situation facing the industrialized countries, however, seems much less promising. Given the global nature of the crisis, the option of growing their way out of recession through increased exports will not be as available to the industrialized countries as it was for the Asian countries. In addition, growing out of the recession will not be made any easier when several of the affected countries seem to be set on pursuing deflationary policies in an effort to reduce government debt. As in the 1930s, unemployment may end up being passed from country to country via a shrinking demand for exports.

References

Books

Desai, Padma. (2003). *Financial crisis, contagion, and containment: From Asia to Argentina*. Princeton: Princeton University Press.

Gerber, James. (2011). *International economics*. Boston: Addison-Wesley.

Lairson, Thomas D., and Skidmore, David. (2003). *International political economy: The struggle for power and wealth*. Belmont, CA: Thomson Wadsworth.

Articles

Bagwell, K., and Staiger, R. W. (2001). The WTO as a mechanism for securing market access property rights: Implications for global labor and environmental issues. *Journal of Economic Perspectives, 15*(3).

Bhagwati, Jagdish. (1998). Why free mobility may be hazardous to your health: Lessons from the latest financial crisis. Prepared for the NBER Conference on Capital Controls in Cambridge, MA.

Brown, Drusilla K. (2001). Labor standards: Where do they belong on the international trade agenda? *Journal of Economic Perspectives, 15*(3).

Calcagno, A., Manuelito, S., and Titelman, D. (2003). From hard peg to hard landing? Recent experiences of Argentina and Ecuador. *Financiemento del desarrollo, 125*.

Corsetti, G., Presenti, P., and Roubini, N. (1998). What caused the Asian currency and financial crisis? Part I: A macroeconomic overview. *NBER Working Paper 6833*.

Edwards, Sebastian. (1999). The mirage of capital controls. *Foreign Affairs*.

Frankel, Jeffrey. (1998). The Asian model, the miracle, the crisis and the fund. Delivered at the U.S. International Trade Commission.

Ostry, Sylvia. (2001). Dissent.com: How NGOs are re-making the WTO. *Policy Options*.

Reinhart, C. M., and Rogoff, K. (2008). This time is different: A panoramic view of eight centuries of financial crises. *NBER Working Paper 13882*.

Reinhart, C. M., and Rogoff, K. (2009). The aftermath of financial crises. *American Economic Review, 99*(2).

Stiglitz, Joseph E. (2004). Capital-market liberalization, globalization, and the IMF. *Oxford Review of Economic Policy, 20*(1).

Chapter 7

Regional Trade Agreements

There have been a number of attempts to form regional trade agreements (RTAs) since the Second World War. The majority of these regional associations are a product of bilateral agreements between pairs of countries or agreements, which relate to a limited number of industries or sectors. Associations with larger membership or wider coverage have been fewer in number and are generally short lived. There are, however, three such associations that have been more far reaching and longer lived than the others. The North American Free Trade Agreement (NAFTA), an agreement between the United States, Canada, and Mexico, has been in existence since 1994. The European Union (EU) has been in existence even longer and has expanded considerably both in membership and scope since its first incarnation as the European Economic Community (EEC) in 1958. Finally, Mercosur (Mercado Común del Sur) is an association of South American countries formed in 1991.

Regional associations are often categorized into a hierarchy of four types, increasing in terms of degree of integration. A "free trade area" is an association of countries in which goods and services are traded across borders without being subject to obvious trade restrictions such as tariffs or quotas. There is, however, no common external tariff for the association as a whole. This means that the agreement covering the free trade area will invariably include some provision specifying that only goods with a certain minimum proportion of value added by the member countries will be free of tariffs. This is necessary in order to prevent one of the members from imposing lower tariffs than the others and then re-exporting imported goods to fellow members of the free trade area, which have higher external tariffs. Each member of the free trade area maintains its own regulations with respect to product standards and working conditions. NAFTA is an example of such a free trade area.

Next in the hierarchy of regional associations is a "customs union," in which the member countries not only trade goods and services free of tariffs between each other but also have a common external tariff. The member countries agree that they will all impose the same tariffs on countries outside the customs union. Mercosur is an example of a customs union. Next comes a "common market," which is a customs union with the additional feature of members allowing the free mobility of capital and labor between each other. The European Economic Community (EEC), before it became an economic union (the European Union) in 1993, was a common market. The most complete level of economic integration occurs with an "economic union." This is a common market in which there is a great deal of economic harmonization, such as common regulations, with respect to product standards, tax structures, and social policies. There may also be a common currency. As already indicated, the European Union is an economic union.

116

Regional Trade Agreements   117

All regional trade agreements are discriminatory and might therefore be thought to violate the rules of the World Trade Organization (WTO) and its predecessor, the General Agreement on Tariffs and Trade (GATT). The rules of these institutions, in general, mandate nondiscrimination between member countries. But there is a provision in the GATT (Article XXIV) that allows the formation of customs unions or free trade agreements between *some* GATT members without their having to extend equal trade advantages to *all* GATT members, provided that parties to the regional trade agreement do not impose tariffs or trade restrictions on nonparties that are more restrictive than those that existed prior to the agreement. Free trade agreements have been permitted as a result of this loophole.

Trade Creation and Trade Diversion

Regional trade agreements may either increase or reduce welfare. Their welfare effects are often analyzed using the concepts of trade creation and trade diversion first suggested by Jacob Viner in 1953. Trade creation occurs when relatively high-cost domestic production is replaced by imports from a lower cost producer. This increases welfare because it brings about a more efficient allocation of resources. An example would be if Peru had originally imposed a duty of 50 percent on wine imports from all countries so that domestic consumers purchased only Peruvian wine, even though wine from Chile would be the cheaper option in the absence of the tariff. If Peru then enters into a free trade agreement with Chile and starts to import wine from Chile, there is an improvement in efficiency as Chile increases wine production and the less efficient wine producer, Peru, shifts out of wine production and into other industries.

Trade diversion occurs when the free trade agreement causes a switch in imports from a low-cost supplier to a higher cost supplier. Suppose that Peru had originally imposed a 25 percent duty on all imports of wine, and let us further suppose that Argentinian wine is 10 percent cheaper than Chilean wine and 27 percent cheaper than Peruvian wine (before imposition of the duty). With the duty of 25 percent, Peru imports wine from Argentina, but after the signing of the free trade agreement Chile pays zero duty, while Argentina still pays a 25 percent tariff. Now Peru imports wine from Chile because the tariff on Argentinian wine makes it more expensive to Peruvian consumers than the tariff-free wine from Chile. This reduces welfare and efficiency because it diverts production away from the most efficient producer, Argentina, toward a less efficient producer, Chile. As a result, there is a less efficient allocation of resources from a worldwide perspective, although consumers in Peru will gain access to cheaper wine than they had before the introduction of the free trade agreement. There is also, however, a loss of revenue to the government of Peru as a result of the lower tax on imports. If this revenue loss is sufficiently large there might be a decrease in the economic welfare for Peruvians, as well as for the world at large.

A question that can be asked with respect to a particular regional trade agreement is whether it is likely to create trade, on balance, or divert trade. In the former case the agreement would lead to an increase in economic efficiency. In the latter case it would lead to a decrease in efficiency. Two general indicators of the likely effect of a regional trade agreement are the share of trade of the member countries with each other and the level of tariffs before the signing of the agreement. If a group of countries traded mostly with each other before they entered a trade agreement, it is generally presumed that the RTA is beneficial because the scope for trade diversion is small. Similarly, if the members of the RTA had previously imposed very high tariffs on other countries it may be supposed that the agreement is likely to be trade creating since foreign trade for these countries would originally have been very small, so that there is little scope for trade diversion. In a study of the effects of regional trade agreements Anne Krueger (1999) found that the European Union had the effect of liberalizing trade, but Mercosur may have been much more trade diverting, with a negative effect on the welfare of its members. It might also be expected that NAFTA has had an overall positive effect since trade between the three NAFTA countries was already very large, giving little scope for trade diversion. A fuller account of these three regional economic associations follows.

The North American Free Trade Agreement (NAFTA)

NAFTA, an agreement between the three North American countries (the United States, Canada, and Mexico) came into existence on January 1, 1994. It was built, however, upon an earlier agreement between the United States and Canada, the Canada–U.S. Free Trade Agreement (CUSTA), which came into existence five years earlier, on January 1, 1989.

NAFTA and CUSTA both contained three major provisions:

1. Most trade barriers were removed.
   The barriers to trade between Canada and the United States had been generally low before 1989, though significant in some sectors. The United States also imposed relatively low tariffs on Mexican goods. Mexico, however, had a protectionist regime before 1994, so most of the change in trade restrictions occurred on the part of Mexico.

2. North American content rules were included in the agreements, as was to be expected for a free trade area. At least 50 percent of the value added to a good must be North American if it is to qualify for reduced tariffs. Clearly such a provision increases the possibility of trade diversion, but there is no doubt that in the absence of a common external tariff no agreement would have been politically possible without it.

3. A system of disputes resolution was established. In case of a dispute between a pair of NAFTA countries a binational panel would be established and would issue a ruling.

CUSTA had been controversial in Canada but was relatively uncontroversial in the United States. NAFTA, however, which brought Mexico under the free trade umbrella, aroused considerable opposition within the United States, though much less concern in Canada. American interest groups, in general, had few concerns about free trade with Canada because, first, Canada and the United States are both wealthy, industrialized countries and, second, in 1989, there were already very few restrictions on trade between the two countries. Mexico, however, was a very different case. Unlike Canada it is a low-income country, which raised concerns about competition between American workers and their lower paid Mexican counterparts. In addition, prior to NAFTA there were considerable restrictions on trade between the United States and Mexico, though admittedly these were mostly on the Mexican side. For Canada, admitting Mexico into the fold was less of a concern because trade between the two countries was relatively small and likely to remain so.

Table 7.1 shows the diversity in income levels of the three members of NAFTA and the size of the combined market of the three countries. The table shows GDP on a purchasing power parity (PPP) basis, which adjusts income for differences in prices. It can be seen that the United States is overwhelmingly dominant, both in terms of population and GDP. In this respect NAFTA is very different from the European Union (EU), for which the largest country (Germany) accounts for less than 17 percent of the total population and less than 20 percent of total GDP. In contrast, the United States accounts over 68 percent of the population and 83 percent of the GDP of the three NAFTA members. In this respect NAFTA bears a closer resemblance to Mercosur, in which Brazil greatly outweighs all the other member countries in both population and GDP.

The dominance of the United States within NAFTA is still clearer when trade figures are considered. Even before the signing of the agreement trading ties between the three NAFTA members were already very close. Canada was the largest trading partner of the United States, while Mexico was the third largest trading partner, after Canada and Japan. On the other hand, there was relatively little trade between Canada and Mexico. Since 1994 Mexico has overtaken Japan, but China has overtaken both Canada and Mexico in terms of exports to the United States, though not in terms of total trade (exports plus imports). From Table 7.2 it can be seen that while Canada and Mexico are both important trading partners of the United States, they are far from being its only important trading partners. Table 7.3, on the other hand, shows that the United States dominates the trade of both Canada and Mexico to an extraordinary degree.

The dominance of the United States within NAFTA is very clear. It is much more important to Canada and Mexico than either of them are to it. Furthermore, both of the two smaller countries are much more dependent on international trade than their larger partner,

TABLE 7.1. Population and GDP for NAFTA Countries, 2010

Country	Population (in millions)	GDP (US$ billions, PPP) (2010)	GDP per Capita (US$)
Canada	34.6	1,327	38,353
United States	312.5	14,582	46,662
Mexico	112.3	1,652	14,711
Total	459.4	17,561	38,239

Source: GDP: World Bank.

120   Chapter 7

TABLE 7.2. Principal U.S. Trading Partners, 2010

Country	Exports (US$ billions)	Imports (US$ billions)	Proportion of US Exports (%)	Proportion of US Imports (%)
Canada	248.8	276.5	13.5	11.8
Mexico	163.3	229.7	8.9	9.8
China	91.6	364.9	5.0	15.6
Japan	60.5	120.3	3.3	5.1

Source: U.S. Census Bureau.

TABLE 7.3. U.S. Share of Total Exports and Imports of Canada and Mexico, 2010

Country	U.S. Share of Total Exports (%)	U.S. Share of Total Imports (%)
Canada	74.9	50.4
Mexico	73.5	60.6

Source: CIA World Factbook.

TABLE 7.4. Openness Ratios of the NAFTA Members, 2010 (%)

United States	21.9
Canada	59.7
Mexico	38.6

Source: CIA World Factbook.

as is clear when we compare the openness ratios of the three economies as shown in Table 7.4. This statistic is simply the ratio of the sum of exports and imports to GDP and is a rough indicator of a country's dependence on international trade. It is much higher for Canada and Mexico than it is for the United States, which is hardly surprising since large economies are more likely to be self-sufficient than small or midsize economies It does indicate, however, that the United States is even less dependent on its NAFTA partners than the simple trade figures would suggest.

Clearly there is a great disparity in economic power between the three member countries of NAFTA. Also striking is the diversity in average incomes of its three member countries. The average Canadian income is about 82 percent of the average American income, but the average Mexican receives about 32 percent of the average American income and 38 percent of the average Canadian income.

Canada and the United States

Trade between Canada and the United States was influenced by two major trading agreements before NAFTA. One of these agreements, the Auto Pact, was based on a single industry, while the other, the Canada–U.S. Free Trade Agreement (CUSTA) was the direct precursor of NAFTA.

The single largest component of Canadian–U.S. trade was and is in automobile products. Prior to 1965 the three major car producers, General Motors, Ford, and Chrysler, were the same in both countries, but Canadian content rules stipulated that, to be free of tariffs, cars sold in Canada had to be assembled there with mostly domestically produced components. Since the Canadian home market was relatively small, few economies of scale were available and productivity in the Canadian automobile industry was about 30 percent lower than that of the U.S. industry. In 1965, in order to avoid a trade war with American manufacturers, the Canadian government signed with the U.S. government the "Agreement Concerning Automotive Products," more commonly known as the Auto Pact. This agreement brought in free trade in cars and car parts with a proviso that the value added on vehicles produced in Canada had to be at least as high as that of 1964. It could be argued that the agreement represented a violation of the nondiscrimination rule of GATT, and it was in fact declared illegal by the World Trade Organization in 2001. By that time, however, it had been effectively superceded by NAFTA. While it was in operation the Auto Pact was a resounding success from Canada's point of view and was often cited during the Canadian debate in the 1980s between supporters and opponents of a more comprehensive trade agreement with the United States. Between 1963 and 1969 Canadian exports to the United States increased by 169 percent, most of this being in automotive products. At the same time the productivity gap in the industry between the two countries disappeared. This was the result of the fact that car manufacturers now produced for a North American market; some vehicle types were produced in American plants for the joint Canada–U.S. market, whereas others were produced in Canadian plants. Canadian supporters of a more general free trade agreement in the 1980s later pointed to the productivity increases associated with the Auto Pact, while opponents stressed that, unlike the Canadian–U.S. Free Trade Agreement, the Auto Pact contained a provision guaranteeing that Canadian manufacturing operations would not all be transferred south of the border.

In 1989 Canada and the United States entered the Free Trade Agreement, which was later widened into NAFTA when Mexico joined the other two North American countries. The agreement with Canada gave rise to relatively little opposition in the United States, certainly less than did the later agreement with Mexico, but aroused considerable controversy in Canada. The Canadian federal election of 1988 was fought primarily on this issue. The government of Brian Mulroney advocated a Free Trade Agreement with the United States on two major grounds. First, it was argued that there was a growing climate of protectionism within the United States, which could create serious problems for Canada, given the country's heavy dependence on the American market. The government believed that a trade treaty would provide some defense against American protectionism. Second, the government of Canada believed that opening up the Canadian market to more competition from American firms would force Canadian firms to be more competitive. This would increase Canadian productivity, especially in manufacturing, which had been lagging behind that of its neighbor.

122   Chapter 7

The opponents of the free trade agreement put forward the following arguments. First, Canadian firms would be unable to compete with American firms, which had access to greater economies of scale because of the larger U.S. market. Second, the free trade agreement would force Canada to reduce its social programs, especially its public health system, to the levels prevailing in the United States. This would be necessary so that Canadian business taxes could be lowered to make Canadian firms competitive with their U.S. counterparts. Third, Canadian cultural industries, such as publishing, which are important to Canadian national identity, would be forced out of business through American competition. Fourth, part of the price paid by Canada for American acceptance of a free trade agreement was the dismantling of restrictions on foreign investment.

There is still some debate about whether the free trade agreement benefited or harmed Canada. The third and fourth concerns raised by the opponents of the agreement are seldom discussed. The agreement specifically included protections for Canadian cultural industries and, since the 1980s, the trend has been for restrictions on foreign investment to be reduced not only by Canada but by other countries as well. There is still, however, some disagreement about the first two concerns raised by the opponents of CUSTA. As far as output and employment are concerned, much depends on the time scale analyzed. In the short run, some regions of Canada undoubtedly saw decreases in employment and income as a result of CUSTA, while others clearly benefited. The principal manufacturing region of Canada, Ontario, experienced rising unemployment, while other regions, such as Alberta and British Columbia, thrived as a result of gaining better access to the American market for the natural resources, such as oil and lumber, that they exported. In the long run the effects on Canadian manufacturing were probably beneficial. Daniel Trefler (2001) estimates that in the short run the agreement resulted in a 15 percent decrease in employment and a 10 percent fall in income for those manufacturing industries most affected by the tariff cuts, but, in the long run, productivity increased by 17 percent, or 1 percent a year.

The other major fear on the Canadian side about the agreement related to its effects on social programs, and there were undoubtedly major cuts in social programs in Canada during the years following the signing of CUSTA. These, however, were mainly a result of the severe deflationary policies introduced by the Canadian federal government during the 1990s and had more to do with high Canadian interest rates and fear over the size of the government debt. They had little to do with the free trade agreement.

Mexico and the United States

When Mexico sought to join a free trade association with its two northern neighbors, its motivations were very different from those of Canada in advocating CUSTA. To understand Mexico's position, it is necessary to briefly review its economic policies and experience in the forty years prior to the implementation of NAFTA.

The economic strategy adopted by Mexico in the 1950s, along with several other Latin American countries, was one of import substitution industrialization (ISI), meaning the promotion of industrialization through protectionist policies. It was hoped that domestic manufacturing would flourish by producing for a home market from which imports were excluded. This policy seemed to work well until the 1970s, but it involved high levels of government spending to subsidize high-cost manufacturing industries and penalized exports through an overvalued exchange rate. Eventually ISI resulted in both high budget deficits and high current account deficits.

Already in the 1970s, the Mexican government had found itself in trouble as a result of borrowing heavily on the global financial market and had accepted an International Monetary Fund (IMF)  stabilization program in 1976. Shortly afterward, however, things seemed to pick up as Mexican exports benefited from rising oil prices. Encouraged by the prospect of increased export returns, the government of José Lopez Portillo borrowed heavily on international financial markets and poured money into social programs and economic development. Mexico's credit rating remained solid because of its known oil reserves.

Two developments of the early 1980s ended this rosy scenario. First, world oil prices started falling. Second, the U.S. Federal Reserve and other Western central banks tightened their monetary policies to combat inflation. As a result, Mexico faced falling oil revenues and rising interest rates on its debt. The resulting debt crisis led to the "lost decade" of the 1980s, during which the country's growth in GDP was almost zero. With little foreign capital flowing into Mexico and interest on existing debt flowing out, there was a sharp fall in investment. A deal worked out between the Mexican government on the one hand and the IMF, the U.S. government, and a cartel of foreign banks on the other, simply made things worse. Clearly the Mexican economy had serious weaknesses but the prescribed policies of severe budget cuts and a large peso devaluation simply resulted in a rise in inflation and a dramatic fall in real income, which fell by more than 15 percent between 1982 and 1986.

It was clear, however, that there was no going back to the policies of the 1970s. It was neither possible nor desirable to continue with the macroeconomic policies of the past. Budget deficits would have to be eliminated or at least reduced to low levels. Since this could only be achieved by constraining public expenditures, the country was deprived of the option of promoting growth through government spending. The funds to finance recovery would have to come from another source. Consequently, it was accepted that Mexico would have to change its development strategy from one of state intervention to one that placed a greater emphasis on markets as a way to attract foreign capital for investment.

The process of reducing the economic role of the state began during the presidency of Miguel de la Madrid (1982–1988), who reduced trade barriers and managed to bring down the size of the budget deficit, but it was the next president, Carlos Salinas (1988–1994), who went furthest in promoting the new strategy. Salinas accelerated the privatization of state enterprises and continued the reduction in tariff levels, with the aim of attracting foreign investment. There was still a problem, however, in that the markets would need reassurance that the policy changes were to be permanent. There were good reasons for the markets to be doubtful about

124   Chapter 7

the ability of Mexican governments to persist with their economic policies. Between 1929 and 1997 the presidency of Mexico and both houses of Congress were always controlled by a single political party, the *Partido Revolucionario Institucional* (Institutional Revolutionary Party) (PRI).[1] Consequently the president of Mexico had enormous power during his term of office. The president was, however, limited by the Constitution to one term of six years, a period known as a *Sexenio*. As a result of this limitation, there was always the potential for major changes in government policies every six years, when a new president assumed office. This invariably triggered fears in the markets and, as a result, there occurred at regular intervals a "sexenio crisis." Such events would usually be associated with large outflows of financial capital, a loss of official reserve assets as the Mexican authorities fought to stabilize the exchange rate, and a large increase in short-term foreign debt as the government borrowed to offset its loss of reserves. If Salinas was to succeed in his objective of attracting more foreign investment he would need to reassure the markets that his successor would not change his policies to any significant degree. By constraining the actions of future Mexican leaders, a free trade agreement would lend credibility to the economic reforms. Access of Mexican exports to the American market was not as much of an issue for Mexico as it had been for Canada since American tariffs on Mexican goods were already low, considerably lower than Mexican tariffs on American goods, so that Mexico would be giving up more than the United States in terms of tariff reductions. The primary objective was to reassure markets and thereby attract foreign investment.

The Maquiladora

From Mexico's point of view NAFTA appeared to serve its purpose. Between 1990 and 1993 foreign capital poured in. The capital inflow has not, however, been an unmixed blessing. It has been claimed that capital inflows were responsible for the peso crisis (discussed below), and questions have also been raised as to whether the majority of Mexicans have received long-term benefits from foreign investment. One of the consequences of the reforms of Salinas and his predecessor was a rapid growth in the output of firms operating in export processing zones along the Mexican–U.S. border. These export processing zones had originally been established as a result of Mexico's Border Industrialization Program (BIP), which had set up an export processing zone in 1965 to provide employment for Mexican workers at a time when government policy in Mexico was still very protectionist. Under the BIP foreign firms could set up assembly operations in the export processing zone and be exempted from Mexican tariffs on the parts and materials that they imported, provided they exported the goods that they assembled. The firms that located in Mexico to take advantage of this program were known as *maquila,* and the export processing industries as a whole came to be referred to as the *maquiladora*.[2] The BIP program has since been phased out as a result of NAFTA, but the maquiladora continue to flourish just south of the U.S. border with Mexico. Foreign firms can minimize transportation costs by locating their assembly operations close to the United States, their principal market, and take advantage of wage rates much lower than American rates.

[1] The party lost control of Congress for the first time in 1997 and the presidency in 2000.

[2] A *maquila*, in Spanish, means a "miller's portion," the charge millers traditionally imposed for processing other people's grain.

The maquiladora grew rapidly in the 1980s as a result of devaluations of the peso and the removal of controls over foreign investment. By 1998 the maquila were employing nearly 1 million workers and producing about one-third of Mexico's manufacturing output. On one level the maquiladora are clearly a success story but there is also another side to them. It has been pointed out that they are insulated from the rest of the Mexican economy, importing most of their inputs and skilled labor. They have provided jobs for unskilled workers but otherwise have had little impact on Mexican economic development.

The Peso Crisis

In 1994 and 1995 Mexico experienced the peso crisis. Partly as a result of its impending association with Canada and the United States in NAFTA, Mexico attracted financial inflows of $91 billion between 1990 and 1993. These inflows were accompanied by inflation and by large current account deficits as Mexico imported capital equipment for investment. As a result of the combined effects of inflation and the current account deficits the peso was becoming dangerously overvalued by 1994. The resulting nervousness of financial markets was worsened by the Chiapas Rebellion, an uprising by peasant farmers in southern Mexico. When the government of Mexico tried to pacify the markets by announcing a devaluation of 15 percent in December 1994 the nervousness turned into panic and the peso collapsed in value. By June 1995 it had fallen by 78 percent since December of the previous year.

Mexico recovered from the peso crisis relatively quickly and for this NAFTA deserves some of the credit. Though the trade agreement may have helped to prompt the inflow of foreign capital, which contributed to the crisis in the first place, there is no doubt that Mexico received more assistance in dealing with the crisis than would have been the case if it had not been associated with Canada and the United States in NAFTA. Eager to reassure the markets and preserve NAFTA, the U.S. government, under President Bill Clinton, arranged a massive financial assistance package for Mexico worth about $50 billion. The United States itself organized currency swaps and loan guarantees worth $20 billion, the IMF and the Bank for International Settlements (BIS) provided stand-by credit worth a total of almost $28 billion, and the Bank of Canada offered assistance worth $1 billion.[3] As a result the peso stabilized and by 1996 recovery was well underway.

The Side Agreement on Labour

While there have been doubts about the extent to which NAFTA benefited Mexico, there have also been reservations about NAFTA within the United States. Concerns about the establishment of closer economic ties with Mexico focused particularly on issues of labor and the environment. Some of the concerns with respect to labor were invalid. The frequently raised apocalyptic "pauper labour argument" implied that because average wage rates in Mexico are substantially lower than those in the United States there would be a mass exodus of firms south of the border. This argument confuses wage rates with labor costs, which actually

---

[3] A currency swap is an exchange of specific amounts of different currencies. At an agreed-upon maturity date the principal amounts are swapped back. There will also be arrangements for payments of interest during the intervening period. In the case of the rescue package for Mexico, dollars were swapped for pesos.

depend on productivity as well as wages. Average employment income in the United States is about five times that of a Mexican worker but labor productivity, as measured by GDP per hour worked is also five times as high, so that average wage cost per unit of output is similar for the two countries. This reflects higher average skill levels in the United States, due to better access to education and more technologically advanced methods of production. Even though there is no prospect of firms in all industries migrating to Mexico, however, this may happen in industries that employ low-skilled workers, such as garment workers and unskilled assembly-line workers. For these types of workers, productivity is almost as high in Mexico as in the United States, and wage rates are a lot lower. In response to union concerns raised in low-skill industries in the United States, the "North American Agreement on Labor Cooperation" (more informally known as "the side agreement on labour") was added to NAFTA. The side agreement requires both Mexico and the United States to enforce their own labor laws relating to child labor, minimum wages, and workplace safety. In practice this seems to have had little effect.

The Environmental Side Agreement

Concerns about environmental standards led to the adoption of another side agreement, the North American Agreement on Environmental Cooperation. There were two major concerns related to the environment. The first concern was that American (and Canadian) firms might relocate to Mexico to avoid meeting the costs of stricter environmental standards in the United States. The concern was not that Mexico lacked sound environmental regulations but that enforcement was lax. A second concern related to increases in

pollution as a result of the growth in the maquiladora industries. With the rapid growth in population and manufacturing in Mexican cities along the U.S. border, such as Tijuana and Ciudad Juarez, there was a significant increase in pollution, which inevitably affected neighboring American cities. The side agreement on the environment created a mechanism for investigating environmental disputes and established the North American Development Bank (NADB) to provide financial assistance for cleanup costs.

The Impact of NAFTA

The country most affected by NAFTA has been Mexico. Canada and the United States had low barriers to trade with each other even before the adoption of the Canada–U.S. Free Trade Agreement. The development of CUSTA into NAFTA in 1994 had only limited effects on these two countries since Canada had relatively little trade with Mexico and U.S. tariffs on Mexican goods were already low. Mexico, on the other hand, was required to introduce significant cuts in trade restrictions as a condition of joining NAFTA.

Most studies of the economic effects of NAFTA have found them to be small but positive for Canada and the United States and much more significant for Mexico. In the years immediately following the creation of NAFTA, Mexico experienced a growth in exports and an inflow of foreign investment, though these positive effects were offset by the peso crisis and more recently much of the foreign investment that Mexico had hoped to attract has been flowing to other emerging and faster growing economies such as those of China and India. It is worth noting, however, that not every section of Mexican society has benefited from the agreement. The removal of subsidies for small farmers has dislocated many people, especially in the poorer southern regions.

The European Union (EU)

The European Union (EU) is potentially the largest integrated market in the world. Already larger in terms of population than NAFTA, it is still expanding. In 2010 it had twenty-seven member countries, a total population of 502 million, and a total GDP of $15.9 trillion (measured in terms of purchasing power parity). This compares with the three NAFTA countries which, in 2010, had a population of 459 million and a total GDP of $17.5 trillion. Additional to the twenty-seven member countries are some countries, such as Norway, which are not members of the EU but are included in its common market area, meaning that their citizens can move freely, invest, and trade throughout the European Union.

The European Union, previously known as the European Economic Community (EEC), was originally established by the Treaty of Rome of 1957 but was built upon an earlier association, the European Coal and Steel Community, which had been established in 1951 by the six countries which were to become the founding members of the EEC. The original six countries were also influenced by the successful example of the Benelux Customs Union between Belgium, the Netherlands, and Luxembourg, which had been in operation since 1948.

The European Coal and Steel Community (ECSC) was established in 1951 as the result of a proposal by the French Foreign Minister, Robert Schuman, to pool the European coal and steel industries. After the Second World War the Allied Powers had occupied the Ruhr Valley, Germany's most heavily industrialized region and source of much of the European continent's coal reserves. The Ruhr remained under foreign occupation even after West Germany had been restored to independence because other European countries, still in the process of rebuilding their war-damaged economies, did not wish to be cut off from access to the Ruhr's coal reserves. There was also still some residual fear of possible German aggression if Germany had unrestricted access to the Ruhr's resources. Naturally this did not sit well with the German government. Schuman's plan got around the problem by returning the Ruhr Valley to German sovereignty while at the same time preserving the access of other countries to its coal reserves and steel industry.

The ECSC consisted of France, West Germany, Italy, Belgium, the Netherlands, and Luxembourg. The United Kingdom had also taken part in the negotiations to form the ECSC but had decided to stay out, displaying even at this early stage an ambivalence toward the European project, which has been apparent ever since. Within the ECSC, the High Authority had regulatory powers over the coal and steel industries of the member countries. It has been

128   Chapter 7

said that as a result of its policies there was overproduction of steel during the 1950s but as an example of cooperation the ECSC was very successful.[4] Six countries which had very recently been engaged in a bitter war with each other had been able to harmonize their policies toward two major industries. It became clear, however, that it was impracticable to regulate the iron and steel industries in isolation from the rest of the economy. Therefore, it was proposed to form a wider economic association. The result was the Treaty of Rome, agreed to by the six member countries of the Coal and Steel Community in 1957. The European Economic Community formally came into existence on January 1, 1958.

Institutions of the European Economic Community and the European Union

The European Economic Community (EEC) and its successor, the European Union, have four governing bodies.

1. *The European Commission.* The Commission is in many ways the central institution of the EU. It administers and enforces the Treaty of Rome and the treaties since passed to amend or expand upon the founding treaty. In this capacity it manages the EU budget and rules on disputes over treaty articles and, like the national governments, it can submit proposals for new EU laws. The Commission now consists of twenty-seven members, one from each member country, who are expected to adopt a European-wide perspective rather than simply reflect the interests of their countries of origin. They elect a president and each member is assigned specific responsibilities, so that there is, for example, a commissioner for agriculture and a commissioner for finance.

2. *The European Council and the Council of Ministers.* The European Council, principal policy-making body of the EU, consists of the heads of government of member countries meeting to discuss fundamental issues, such as the budget or major legislative changes proposed by the commission or a member government. The presidency of the European Council used to rotate from country to country on a six-month basis, but it is now chaired by a permanent president, whose position was created by the Treaty of Lisbon, which came into force in 2009. The Council is also attended by the High Representative for Foreign Affairs and Security Policy (described below) and the president of the European Commission. As well as chairing the Council, organizing its agenda, and representing the Council before the European Parliament, the president of the European Council is intended to represent the EU internationally. However, because the president of the Commission and the High Representative also claim to do this, there is considerable overlap in their areas of responsibility. It has been suggested that the president of the European Council is responsible for broad strategy, the president of the European Commission is responsible for implementing policy, and the High Representative is akin to a foreign minister. Nevertheless, there have been conflicts of jurisdiction between the two presidents, which have led some to suggest that their positions should be merged. When discussing issues related to some particular policy area, decisions are taken by the Council of Ministers, which is attended by departmental ministers rather than the heads of government.

---

[4] See Van Der Wee (1986).

For example, the ministers of agriculture will meet to discuss issues related to the common agricultural policy. The presidency of the Council of Ministers, unlike the presidency of the European Council, continues to rotate among member countries every six months except when the Council consists of the foreign ministers, when the chair is taken by the High Representative for Foreign Affairs and Security Policy. This position was created in the Lisbon Treaty and, like the president of the European Council, the High Representative is appointed by the European Council. Since the Treaty of Lisbon, most of the voting in the Council is by a "qualified majority" of 255 votes out of a total of 345. The number of votes assigned to each country varies according to their size, with the smallest country (Malta) having three votes and the largest (France, Germany, Italy, and the United Kingdom) having twenty-nine each. A few issues, however, require unanimous approval, the most important being the admission of new members and the changing of EU tax regulations.

3. *The European Parliament.* The parliament is directly elected for five-year terms on a population basis. In the past its main power was the right to question the Council and the Commission. It also had a veto power over the budget in its entirety and could pass a vote of no confidence in the Commission as a whole but could not amend the budget or vote out of office individual commissioners. Since it was long believed that these powers were too extreme to ever be used, there was a sense that the European Parliament had no real power until 1999 when the Parliament actually exercised its powers and passed a vote of no confidence in the Commission, which then had to resign en masse. Since the 1990s there has been some increase in the parliament's powers. It can now amend some EU legislation and, along with the governments of member countries, it has a veto power over the admission of new members to the EU. Nevertheless, there is still a sense that the European Parliament, the only directly elected European institution, has very limited power, and this fact gives rise to complaints about a "democratic deficit" in Europe.

4. *The European Court of Justice.* The Court is effectively the supreme court of the European Union. It interprets the various treaties that govern the EU, and its rulings take precedence over those of national courts. Each member country of the EU appoints a judge to the Court.

Policy Issues

The founders of the EEC and their successors have tended to fall into two camps. One camp envisages a loose federation in which national authorities cooperated with each other to promote trade. The other favors a gradual transfer of sovereignty from nation-states to the European level. Some have even envisaged the eventual creation of a "United States of Europe." Both groups accept a "subsidiarity" principle under which the EEC (and later the EU) has authority over issues that are more effectively handled at the international level, while national governments are responsible for everything else. But this, of course, leaves a lot of room for interpretation. It has come to be generally accepted that the EU should control environmental policy, regional development policy, competition policy, and agriculture. Other areas of

130   Chapter 7

government, such as labor and social policies, are more contentious and, while it is accepted that the EU has a responsibility for agriculture, its specific agricultural policies have generated a great deal of discord between the member countries. Another area of policy that has given EU wide implications, economic and monetary union, is perhaps the most difficult and contentious of all and will be dealt with at some length below. First, however, the difficulties of establishing an efficient agricultural policy for the Community will be described.

The Common Agricultural Policy (CAP)

One of the most controversial aspects of the European Union is its Common Agricultural Policy (CAP). The CAP is a program of agricultural price supports which was established by the original six member countries shortly after the establishment of the EEC, the objective being to replace the various national systems of agricultural supports by a single community-wide system. The ostensible purpose of the CAP is to provide farmers with a reasonable standard of living and consumers with food at a fair price. In practice, however, it has heavily subsidized farmers, imposed high prices on consumers, and resulted in overproduction of agricultural products. To achieve the objectives of the CAP a system of import levies and quotas are imposed to ensure that prices of imported food do not fall below the EU target prices, which are set at levels that are supposed to provide farmers with an acceptable standard of living but which inevitably result in overproduction. There are also internal intervention prices for agricultural products. If prices fall below these, the European Commission buys products in order to raise their prices to the intervention level. The resulting surpluses are stored, which in the past gave rise to costly storage facilities housing "butter mountains" and "milk lakes." Overproduction is made worse by the existence of agricultural subsidies. The CAP is very costly, accounting for about 48 percent of the EU budget, although only 5.4 percent of the EU population works on farms. It already absorbed almost half of the EU budget before the recent expansion in membership, at a time when only about 4 percent of the working population of the member countries were employed in agriculture.

There have been several attempts to reform the CAP by limiting production or reducing the number of small, heavily subsidized farmers but until recently such measures have always met strong resistance from farmers' lobbies and the governments of countries supporting them, notably France. With the expansion of the EU to include countries with large rural populations, however, agricultural reform has gained a new urgency. Since 2003 a number of measures have been proposed and some have even been adopted. A substantial reduction in the guaranteed price of sugar has been agreed upon and there are proposals to reduce direct subsidies to farmers. It remains to be seen how effective the actual and proposed reforms will be in reducing the share of the EU budget which is eaten up by the CAP.

Closer Integration

The Single European Act

Since 1958 the European Community has both "widened" and "deepened." The term *widening* refers to an expansion in membership, while *deepening* means closer economic integration among the existing members. After a period of slow development in the 1980s, when

Regional Trade Agreements   131

there was much talk of "Eurosclerosis," there was a series of moves toward greater integration over the next decade. Much of this dynamism was due to Jacques Delors, then president of the European Commission, who promoted the Single European Act, which came into force in 1987, and in 1988 issued the Delors Report on Economic and Monetary Union.

The Single European Act, adopted in 1987, was the first major revision to the Treaty of Rome since 1957. It included 279 amendments to the Treaty of Rome, most of which came into force by 1992. Since the obvious barriers to trade, such as tariffs, had long since been dealt with, the intention now was to eliminate the more subtle barriers to commerce and investment between the European countries. This would require, first, the harmonization of regulations related to such areas as product standards and safety regulations and, second, the harmonization of fiscal standards, which implied the adoption of common systems of indirect taxation and government procurement. The European Commission estimated that the gains from having a fully integrated European market would be an increase in total GDP of between 4 percent and 6.5 percent. These gains would come from three sources.

1. The reduction in business costs due to the removal of customs and passport checks

2. Economies of scale arising from a single market

3. Increases in efficiency as a result of increased competition between firms in different countries

The actual gains, while substantial, have been less than originally hoped for because of failures to fully implement the terms of the Single European Act and thereby create a unified market across the EU. Difficulties in implementing the act have been significant in the areas of harmonization of product and safety standards and fiscal practices. Harmonization of product standards and safety standards is always difficult to implement because of disagreements over whose standards should be the model. Prior to the adoption of the Single European Act there were many different standards in force across the European Community in such areas as building codes and consumer safety. This gave rise to two potential problems. First, if the common standard adopted was very close to that previously used by one particular country, that country would initially have a competitive advantage over the others since, unlike them, it would not have to introduce costly changes in its practices. Second, a country might have to lower its standards to meet the new common standards and would understandably be reluctant to do so. Because of these potential problems the harmonization of standards has frequently been replaced by the concept of "mutual recognition" of standards, in which countries were allowed to have different standards, provided they were "comparable" or "equal."

The other area of difficulty has been in achieving fiscal harmonization. There are two aspects to fiscal harmonization: taxation and public procurement. With respect to taxation, the EU has a common system of indirect tax, the value added tax (VAT), but VAT rates differ between countries. Evidence from studies of interstate tax differences in the United States shows that if sales taxes differ by more than 5 percent between neighboring tax jurisdictions consumers will cross state borders to avoid higher taxes. Since the different European countries have governments with different political philosophies, they have very different tax rates and reducing the variability in tax rates across the Union has proved to be difficult. It has been agreed that VAT rates should lie between 15 percent and 25 percent, but this makes it possible

132   Chapter 7

for rates to differ by more than 5 percent between jurisdictions. As a result, some controls have been allowed to remain in place to prevent consumers from leaving higher tax jurisdictions in order to buy certain high-cost items, such as cars, in lower tax jurisdictions. With respect to public procurement, the governments of most nations favor nationally owned firms when buying goods and services. The EU has attempted to eliminate this kind of discrimination in public procurement policies but with limited success.

European Monetary Union

The next big step toward integration was the adoption by most members of the European Community of a common currency, the euro. This was the culmination of a process which began in the 1970s but was only brought to fruition in 1999. Before describing the process of adoption of the euro it is worth considering the benefits and costs of adopting a common currency.

Optimal Currency Areas

From a strictly economic point of view the benefits of having a common European currency are uncertain and probably modest, while the costs are certain and substantial. The major economic benefits of the common currency are that it eliminates the costs of currency conversion and reduces the effects of exchange rate uncertainty on international trade and investment. The costs of currency conversion are not insignificant but neither are they massive. They have been estimated at about 0.4 percent of the GDP of the European Union.[5] The other major benefit of having a common currency, eliminating the effects of exchange rate uncertainty on international trade, would once have been a very important consideration. Instability in exchange rates played an important part in reducing international trade during the interwar period. Since then, however, the creation of forward markets through which foreign currencies are bought and sold for delivery at future dates at fixed prices has greatly reduced the risk associated with variable exchange rates.

While the potential economic benefits of monetary union are uncertain, the potential costs are clear. All countries using the common currency are forced to follow the same "one size fits all" monetary policy. This may not be a problem if all the countries concerned have economies that form an optimal (or optimum) currency area. Robert Mundell suggested in 1961 that a geographical region would form an optimal currency area and should have a common currency if the following conditions are met.

1. The countries concerned have closely synchronized business cycles, so that they experience expansions and recessions at the same time. This would mean that the same monetary policy should be appropriate for all.

2. Since perfect synchronicity is unlikely, there should also be mobility of labor and capital across the relevant countries. This enables capital to move to where the best investment opportunities are and labor to move to where the jobs are.

---

[5] Gerber (2011), p. 350.

The European Union falls short of being an optimal currency area on both grounds. Business cycles are far from perfectly synchronized across the EU and while capital is mobile, labor mobility is hindered by language barriers and persistent administrative obstacles. While it is also true that regional economies within countries frequently do not meet the criteria either, this problem is generally dealt with by large fiscal transfers from regions that are prospering to regions that are not. The euro zone shows no signs of being willing to adopt such major transfers between member countries.

The fact that the European Union does not form an optimal currency area, however, was not a deciding factor in the decision to establish a common currency. The motivation behind the decision was political rather than economic. It was hoped that the adoption of a common currency would promote greater economic unity between European countries in the future rather than reflect the existing state of affairs.

The Exchange Rate Mechanism and the Crisis of 1992

The story of European monetary union begins in the 1970s, though the adoption of a common currency was not achieved until 1999. With the final collapse of the Bretton Woods System in 1973, the European countries became concerned about the danger of competitive devaluations, which would increase risk and uncertainty associated with investing and trading across what was then called the European Economic Community (EEC). Since it was now clear that it would not be possible to resurrect a global system of fixed exchange rates the members of the Community sought to develop a local system of fixed exchange rates across the EEC. As a result, the European Monetary System was established in 1979. The ultimate objective was to establish a common currency, but it was recognized that this could not be achieved overnight. In the meantime, an exchange rate mechanism (ERM) was created as a stepping stone to a single currency. Under the ERM, national currencies would be tied to a weighted average of currencies known as the European Currency Unit (ECU). Though not a medium of exchange, the ECU was used as the unit of account for the European Union (until replaced by the euro in 1999) so that contributions to the EU budget were assessed in terms of ECUs while the contributions were actually made in national currencies at the appropriate exchange rate.

As a first step toward fixed exchange rates national currencies were permitted to fluctuate relative to the ECU within a band of fluctuation fixed by the ERM. Initially this was set at ±2.25 percent and it was intended that this would narrow over time until all the national currencies were "locked in" to an exact exchange rate with the ECU. At that point national currencies could be replaced by a common currency. Before monetary union, however, the European Monetary system came under severe stress as a result of the European financial crisis of 1992–1993. By the end of the crisis the United Kingdom and Denmark had dropped out of the ERM completely and have not since adopted the common currency. For those countries that stayed in the ERM the band of fluctuation was widened to ±15 percent.

The crisis was a consequence of the reunification of Germany. In 1990 the Berlin wall came down and the Democratic Republic of Germany (East Germany) was reunited with its western counterpart, the Federal Republic of Germany. The newly united Federal Republic of Germany now faced a major economic challenge. The costs of rebuilding the former Democratic Republic of Germany were enormous. Since the industries of the East were unable to compete with the more efficient industries of the West, unemployment rose among East Germans, who now had access to the generous social programs long enjoyed by their cousins in West Germany. In addition, substantial expenditures were required to improve the infrastructure in the East. Fearful of inflation as a result of large increases in government spending, Germany's central bank, the Bundesbank, sharply raised interest rates. This created a problem for other European countries which in the early 1990s were faced not with inflation but with rising unemployment. Raising interest rates would prevent economic recovery, but failure to raise rates to match those of Germany would exert downward pressure on their exchange rates. The problem came to a head in September 1992 with speculative attacks on a number of European currencies. Some countries, notably France, chose to stay within the ERM, raise interest rates, and suffer a severe recession. Others, such as the United Kingdom and Italy, withdrew from the ERM and allowed their currencies to depreciate. Subsequently Italy rejoined the ERM within a wider band of fluctuation of ±15 percent.

With hindsight this experience should have encouraged greater caution in moving toward a common currency, but the countries that remained within the European Monetary System nevertheless persisted and adopted a common currency, the euro, in 1999. An important factor in achieving monetary union was the apparent success in harmonizing fiscal policies though, again with hindsight, it is clear that the harmonization was less complete than was believed at the time.

The Maastricht Treaty and European Monetary Union

The movement toward monetary union, after the setback of 1992, was renewed with the Maastricht Treaty. The treaty, named after the Dutch city in which it was signed, came into force in 1993, at which point the European Economic Community (EEC) was renamed the European Union (EU). The most important aspect of the Maastricht Treaty from the economic point of view was the mapping of the path to European monetary union. Part of the preparation for monetary union had already been made under the terms of the Single European Act, when controls

European Central Bank, Frankfurt.

over movements of financial capital within the future EU had been lifted. The next step was to establish the European Monetary Institute in Frankfurt in 1994. Once a common currency, the euro was adopted in 1999 by the Monetary Institute, which would become the European Central Bank and control monetary policy for all the countries in the "euro zone." The adoption of a common currency represented a major surrender of national sovereignty since the government of each country adopting the euro lost its power to establish its own monetary policy.

It was for this reason that the United Kingdom and Denmark, while ratifying the Maastricht Treaty, chose to exercise the right to opt out of monetary union. For this reason it is henceforth convenient to distinguish between the European Union (all EU countries) and the euro zone (EU countries which have adopted the euro). Countries that have entered the European Union since the Maastricht Treaty was signed in 1994, however, are obliged to adopt the euro once they have met monetary and budget requirements contained in the treaty.

From the beginning it was clear that there might be difficulties if countries adopted a common monetary policy while having different fiscal policies—a problem that has recently reemerged with a vengeance. For this reason the Maastricht Treaty set out "convergence criteria" which would have to be met by European countries before they adopted the euro. This was intended to force the adoption of similar fiscal policies by countries adopting a common monetary policy. The major criteria were as follows:

1. *Exchange rates.* Countries were required to have joined the exchange rate mechanism for two consecutive years. This meant that their national currencies would have to remain within a band of ±15 percent of the value of the ECU (subsequently of the euro).

2. *Inflation.* Inflation rates had to be no more than 1.5 percentage points higher than the average inflation rate for the three countries with the lowest inflation rates in the euro zone.

3. *Long-term interest rates.* The nominal long-term interest rate could be no more than 2 percentage points higher than the average rate for the three countries with the lowest inflation rates in the euro zone.

4. *Government deficit to GDP ratios.* The ratio of the annual deficit to GDP must not exceed 3 percent, though temporary exceptions might be made in exceptional cases.

5. *Government debt to GDP ratios.* The ratio of gross government debt to GDP must not exceed 60 percent.

To ensure that countries continue to maintain fiscal discipline after adopting the euro, the Stability and Growth Pact was adopted in 1997. Under the pact, euro zone countries are expected to stay within the deficit and debt guidelines included in the convergence criteria for aspiring members. For this reason the pact has been criticized on the grounds that it is too inflexible and prohibits member countries from adopting expansionary fiscal policies in times of recession. In practice, however, the pact has not been rigorously enforced and has been violated by a number of euro zone countries including its strongest advocate, Germany. In the 1990s the adoption of the convergence criteria forced a number of countries to adopt deflationary policies at a time of high unemployment. Even so, it was clear that few, if any, countries would be able to meet all the criteria. Italy and Belgium, for example, both had government debt to GDP ratios of more than 100 percent. The common currency was nevertheless adopted in 1999, as planned, but only as a result of not enforcing conformity with the convergence criteria.

In 1999 eleven of the then fifteen members of the European Union adopted the euro, while Greece adopted it in 2001. Since 2001 five of the newer members of the expanded EU have

136   Chapter 7

joined the euro zone, so that it now includes seventeen of the twenty-seven members of the European Union. In each case there has been a transition period of two years during which the euro and the old national currency coexist. By the end of the two years the national currency will have been phased out. This tends to create a temporary consumer boom, particularly for those countries where tax evasion is a national pastime. All illegal stashes of the old currency have to be spent within two years since converting them into euros would be bound to attract the attention of the authorities.

The ongoing problems that subsequently arose as a result of the failure to enforce fiscal rules will be discussed below under "The European Sovereign Debt Crisis," but it is convenient to first describe the expansion in membership of the EU.

Expansion

Since the establishment of the original European Economic Community (EEC) on January 1, 1958, the membership of the EEC and its successor, the EU, has increased dramatically. With twenty-seven member countries, a total population of 502 million, and a total GDP of almost $16 trillion, it is the largest regional economic association in the world in terms of population and second only to NAFTA in total GDP. It began, however, with six members. Since then it has become not only larger but much more economically diverse, as can be seen from Table 7.5.

TABLE 7.5. Population and GDP for EU Countries (2010)

Country (with date of entry)	Population (millions)	GDP (US$ billions, PPP)	GDP per Capita (US$, PPP)
Original Members			
Belgium (1958)	10.9	407	37,339
France (1958)	65.8	2,194	33,343
Germany (1958)	81.8	3,071	37,543
Italy (1958)	60.6	1,909	31,502
Luxembourg (1958)	0.5	45	112,000
Netherlands (1958)	16.7	706	42,275
Total	236.3	8,332	35,260
Joined 1973			
Denmark (1973)	5.6	219	39,107
Ireland (1973)	4.6	178	38,696
United Kingdom (1973)	62.4	2,231	35,753

(Continued)

TABLE 7.5. Population and GDP for EU Countries (2010) (*Continued*)

Total	72.6	2,628	36,198
Joined 1981–1995			
Austria (1995)	8.4	333	39,643
Finland (1995)	5.4	197	36,481
Greece (1981)	10.8	319	29,537
Portugal (1986)	10.6	272	25,660
Spain (1986)	46.1	1,478	32,061
Sweden (1995)	9.4	365	38,830
Total	90.7	2,964	32,679
Joined 2004–2007			
Bulgaria (2007)	7.4	104	14,054
Cyprus (2004)	0.8	25	31,250
Czech Republic (2004)	10.5	266	25,333
Estonia (2004)	1.3	27	20,769
Hungary (2004)	10.0	203	20,300
Latvia (2004)	2.2	37	16,818
Lithuania (2004)	3.2	60	18,750
Malta (2004)	0.4	10	25,000
Poland (2004)	38.2	754	19,738
Romania (2007)	21.4	306	14,299
Slovakia (2004)	5.4	130	24,074
Slovenia (2004)	2.1	57	27,143
Total	102.9	1,979	19,232
Joined 2013			
Croatia (2013)	(4.3)	(81)	(18,200)
Total for the 28	502.5	15,903	31,648

Source: World Bank (GDP).

138   Chapter 7

Until 1981 the European Union consisted predominantly of high-income, industrialized countries from northern Europe. During the period 1981–1995 it admitted some less-affluent countries from southern Europe (Greece, Portugal, Spain), but they were balanced by the entry of high-income countries (Austria, Finland, Sweden). The major change in the composition of the EU came after 2004, when a large number of poorer, less-industrialized countries entered. Of the twelve countries that joined between 2004 and 2007, eight had a lower per capita income than the poorest of the previous members, and two of the new members had a per capita income of less than half that of the EU members as a whole. Croatia, which is set to become the twenty-eighth member of the EU in July 2013, also has a GDP per capita well below the average of EU members. The admission of these new members places stress on the regional development and agricultural programs of the EU. It also complicates the task of bringing EU members into a closer economic and political union. For this reason members of the EU, such as France, that wish to promote closer integration, a process known as "deepening," have tended to favor a slower expansion in membership. They favor consolidation before expansion. Other countries that support a relatively rapid expansion in membership, a process known as "widening," tend to favor a looser association of countries. The United Kingdom has been the strongest proponent of this view. The collapse of communism in Eastern Europe, however, forced the hand of the European countries. The expansion of 2004–2007 was preferable to the dangers of having economically deprived and potentially politically unstable countries on the borders of the European Union. The last thing the more prosperous European countries wanted was a serious refugee problem.

With the intention of promoting economic and political stability in Southern and Eastern Europe the EU has offered the carrot of membership to European countries that satisfy three major criteria. First, they must be stable democracies with respect for human rights. Second, they must have market-based economies. Third, they must be willing to adopt EU rules, including the eventual implementation of economic and monetary union. A number of countries that hope to eventually enter the European Union have not been admitted on the grounds that they have not yet satisfied these criteria. The most important of these is Turkey, which initially applied for membership in 1987 and has been engaged in negotiations with the EU leadership since 2005. There are, however, substantial political and economic obstacles to its admission into the EU. The economic obstacles are the country's size and relative poverty. In terms of population, Turkey, with a population in 2010 of 73.7 million would, if admitted, be the second largest country in the European Union, but its GDP per capita was $15,142 in PPP terms, which is less than half of the average for the existing member countries. The political obstacles relate to perceived failures by Turkey to preserve freedom of speech, the continuing (though diminishing) danger of a military takeover, and the problem of Cyprus. The northern part of Cyprus, which is ethnically Turkish, has seceded from the rest of the island, which is mainly Greek and is a member of the EU. Turkey is the only country that recognizes the independence of Northern Cyprus and has been reluctant to allow Greek Cypriot ships into its harbors. As a member of the EU, Cyprus has a veto over the admission of new members, which makes the admission of Turkey unlikely until the Cypriot issue has been resolved.

The European Sovereign Debt Crisis

The European sovereign debt crisis is a result of increased borrowing costs and increased government debt due to bank bailouts. Just as the European financial crisis of 1931 was linked to the American Depression of 1929, so the European sovereign debt crisis beginning in 2010 occurred when it did as a result of the global weakening of banks in the aftermath of the American subprime mortgage crisis, which began in 2007. The sovereign debt crisis initially centered on Greece, Ireland, and Portugal, but it now poses a danger to the larger European economies of Italy, Spain, and perhaps, further down the road, to France and the continuation of the single European currency itself. An indication of how the crisis spread occurred in January 2012 when the Standard and Poor's credit rating agency downgraded the credit of France and eight other European countries. Just as the Great Depression revealed the flaws of the gold standard, the current crisis has highlighted weaknesses of the European monetary system, which it had been possible to ignore during the more prosperous years following its introduction in 1999.

The crisis began in 2010 when Portugal, Ireland, and Greece sought assistance from the EU and the International Monetary Fund (IMF). In that year Ireland received a rescue package of €85 billion from the EU and the IMF, while Portugal received €78 billion. Ireland's difficulties were the result of a huge increase in sovereign debt because of government bailouts of banks, which had been fueling a property bubble that had now burst. Portugal's problems stemmed from government fiscal mismanagement. Both countries have since made progress in getting their budgets under control.

Greece offered a much more difficult challenge than the other two countries. Greek governments had a long tradition of running budget deficits even before Greece adopted the euro in 2001, with a ratio of government debt to GDP consistently above 100 percent since 1993. After Greece adopted the euro, however, budget deficits became much worse than before. The government was now able to borrow at lower interest rates because of the belief of financial markets in the stability of the euro (as compared with Greece's former currency, the drachma). The deficit problem remained hidden for a time because the Greek government misrepresented the country's financial position and the other euro area governments chose not to scrutinize Greek finances too closely. In 2009, however, the estimate of the year's budget deficit as a proportion of GDP was revised from 6 percent to over 12 percent, and it has since been revised upward still further. As a result, the Standard and Poor's Credit Rating Agency downgraded Greek government debt in April 2010 and the interest rate on Greek government bonds rose sharply. The Greek government then requested assistance from the EU and the IMF. A loan of €45 billion was provided, and further assistance has since been made available. Assistance was provided to Greece because of fears that it would otherwise be forced to default on its debt, which would have a contagion effect, undermining the confidence of investors in other euro zone countries with high deficits or debt. These include not only Ireland and Portugal but also the much larger countries of Italy and Spain.

There were, however, strings attached to the loans. The government of Greece has been forced to adopt severe austerity measures. Spending cuts and tax increases are estimated (by Citibank) to amount to 12.5 percent of GDP in 2010 and a further 5 percent in 2011. Not surprisingly, this led to widespread protests among the Greek population. The alternative to accepting the package, a unilateral default on its debt, was regarded; however, it was just as disastrous for Greece since it is generally accepted that in this event it would be forced to give up the euro and adopt a national currency, presumably its former currency, the drachma. At least for a time, probably several years, Greece would effectively be frozen out of credit markets and there would be a very real danger of a collapse of the Greek banking system.

Pensioners queuing outside a bank in Thessaloniki.

The abandonment of the euro without defaulting would also create enormous difficulties; however, since a newly revived drachma would rapidly depreciate in value and, since most Greek debt would still be denominated in euros, the drachma value of the debt would soar. Nevertheless, the fiscal austerity being demanded of Greece has become so severe and so unrelenting that some economists now feel that the country might eventually abandon the euro.

"Taking a Haircut"

For over a year the EU leaders refused to acknowledge that Greece and the other indebted countries would never be able to repay all of their debt. The EU leaders persisted in the delusion that Greece and the other heavily indebted euro zone countries faced a liquidity crisis that could be resolved relatively easily through providing reassurance to the markets. The approach was very similar to that taken by the IMF and the creditor banks toward the Latin American Debt Crisis of the 1980s. There was the same slowness in recognizing that there was a solvency crisis that could only be resolved by debt write-downs. This was understandable since it was feared that if debts were restructured to ease the burden of Portugal, Ireland, or Greece the banks might become wary of buying bonds issued by other heavily indebted euro zone countries. Finally, in October 2011, the euro zone leaders accepted the reality which the markets had already taken into account. In July private creditors had to take a 21 percent "haircut" on Greek debt and in October it was agreed that the creditors would "voluntarily" exchange their holdings of Greek bonds for safer debt of half their value. Clearly this was effectively a partial default. To prevent contagion to the rest of the euro zone it was agreed that banks would be forced to increase their capital in order to reduce the danger of collapse as a result of their losses. Contagion did in fact occur, however, as the markets turned their attention to Italy, which has a government debt to GDP ratio of almost 120 percent, though its budget deficit was at a relatively modest level of 4.6 percent of GDP, not much higher than that of Germany (4.3 percent). The financial markets were concerned about the fact that Italy has had a very low rate of economic growth for many years. This raised concerns that its foreign exchange earnings might be insufficient to cover interest payments on its debt if interest rates rose above 7 percent and led investors to see Italian government as a risky asset. In November 2011 the long-term interest rate on Italian bonds did indeed rise above 7 percent. An emergency interim government was formed with the task of introducing austerity measures to reduce the debt and economic reforms to increase productivity. Since then successive Italian governments have struggled to reform the economy. It is still not clear whether whether these reforms will be successful, but the path to prosperity will be difficult to reach in a European environment of fiscal austerity.

The European Financial Stability Facility

The sovereign debt crisis caused the European countries to introduce new mechanisms to assist members of the euro zone, but these have so far proved inadequate. In May 2010 the twenty-seven member states of the European Union, including those that had not yet adopted the euro, agreed to the creation of the European Financial Stability Facility (EFSF). The EFSF, which was guaranteed by the governments of countries in the euro zone, was authorized to sell bonds and use the money raised to make loans to euro zone countries in trouble. Assistance was also available under the European Financial Stabilization Mechanism (EFSM), a funding program relying upon loans guaranteed by the European Commission. The EFSF and EFSM were merged into a single program, the European Stability Mechanism (ESM) in 2013. It was agreed in October 2011 to increase the resources of the EFSF to €1 trillion, but it was not clearly specified how this would be achieved since the euro zone governments were reluctant to devote more taxpayers' money to this purpose. There were suggestions that non-European countries, such as China and Brazil, might be willing to invest in the ESFS but, not surprisingly, they have understandably shown little enthusiasm for doing this. There were also proposals, later discussed at a G20 meeting, to increase the resources of the IMF so that it could provide more assistance to troubled European countries.[6]

The assistance provided through these programs and through the IMF has so far proved insufficient to resolve the crisis, and the stabilization measures associated with them have attracted a number of criticisms. Many economists, such as Joseph Stiglitz, former chief economist of the World Bank, believe that the sums covered by the programs are still inadequate. Though the total sums potentially available now sum close to €1 trillion, this has failed to reassure the markets. Many economists and bankers have also criticized the emphasis on deficit cutting in the conditions attached to the loans. Such large fiscal cutbacks occurring in several countries simultaneously could prevent economic recovery in a still very fragile world economy. Easing the conditions or providing more assistance, however, runs into strong opposition in the more prosperous euro zone countries, particularly in Germany, which would pay the largest share of any increases in bailout funding. Some politicians and bankers in these countries have opposed providing loans to countries in trouble on the grounds

---

[6] The G20 is a group of twenty major economies. It comprises nineteen countries plus the European Union, representatives of which attend G20 meetings even though four member countries of the EU are separate members. The G20 first met in 2008 and collectively accounts for more than 80 percent of world GDP and 85 percent of world trade.

142   Chapter 7

that this violates no bailout provisions in the Maastricht Treaty, by which individual countries are responsible for keeping their fiscal houses in order. There is also the perpetual fear in Germany of supporting any programs that might generate inflation, however remote that possibility may be.

Fiscal Union

Other critics argued that the measures taken so far amounted to merely "kicking the can down the road" and failed to deal with the fundamental problem of European monetary union, which was the inability of a monetary union to cope with an economic crisis in the absence of a fiscal union. A fiscal union would require an institution to oversee the tax and spending policies of member countries of the euro zone. The proposal for a fiscal union was controversial since it would require a massive surrender of sovereignty by the member states.

In the meantime the euro zone countries attempted to coordinate their fiscal policies by reforming the Stability and Growth Pact. In March 2011 reforms were adopted that included an automatic procedure for imposing penalties on countries that breached either the deficit or debt rules of the pact. A more ambitious undertaking occurred a few months later in January 2012 when all the EU leaders except those of the United Kingdom and the Czech Republic agreed to a fiscal pact. The pact was incorporated into a treaty which was signed in March and came into force on January 1, 2013. The pact required that each country that ratified the treaty would implement binding legislation establishing a balanced budget rule by January 1, 2014, though countries would be able to run a structural deficit of up to 0.5 percent of their GDP or up to 1 percent if their government debt/GDP ratio is below 60 percent.[7] The European Commission and the European Council monitor the budgetary plans of countries with excessive deficits and the European Court of Justice can fine countries up to 0.1 percent of their GDP if they fail to observe the rules of the pact. Though it is clear that a monetary union without some kind of fiscal union is unsustainable, critics of the pact argue that it imposes a fiscal straightjacket rather than promotes growth. Unfortunately, the rules imposed through the pact are unlikely to promote either stability or growth in a time of stagnation and potential global recession. It also represents a major transfer of sovereignty from elected governments to unelected institutions. In any case it does not resolve the problem of already existing sovereign debt problem.

The Maastricht Treaty and the European Central Bank

More immediate relief has been provided by the European Central Bank (ECB). The Maastricht Treaty includes a "no bail-out" clause, by which the responsibility of repaying public debt rests with individual member countries. Under the treaty the European Central Bank is required to maintain price stability, defined as an inflation rate of 2 percent, within the euro

---

[7] A "structural" deficit is the excess of government spending over revenues that would occur if the economy were at full employment, given the existing tax structure and spending programs. The actual deficit may be higher than this since in a recession the tax intake is reduced because taxpayers have lower than normal incomes and there will be unusual demands on social services, resulting in higher than normal expenditures.

zone. This means that, unlike central banks in most countries, the ECB is not a lender of last resort and does not have a mandate to pursue policies such as quantitative easing to counter unemployment. Some European leaders, such as the French president, Nicholas Sarkozy, have sought to expand the bank's mandate to focus on employment and growth as well as inflation, but this has been strongly resisted by Germany. The ECB, nevertheless, purchased bonds of some heavily indebted euro zone countries in the summer of 2011, but it did so reluctantly and in the face of allegations that it was exceeding its authority.

It has adopted more aggressive measures, which have given the euro zone some breathing space. In December 2011 the ECB began making low-interest loans to European banks. The loans are not made to governments, but government securities are acceptable as collateral. In December, loans of €498.2 billion were issued and in February 2012 a further €529.5 was made available. The majority of these loans have been taken up by Italian and Spanish banks, which has made it easier for the governments of Italy and Spain to market their bonds. In September 2012 the European Central Bank calmed financial markets when it announced that it would provide unlimited support for all euro zone countries involved in a bailout program from the European Stability Mechanism. Successful debt issues by euro zone countries, including Ireland, Spain, and Portugal, were a sign of renewed confidence in the euro zone.

Cyprus

The confidence instilled by the ECB announcement was subsequently undermined by events in Cyprus. Cyprus had been hard hit by the exposure of Cypriot banks to Greek debt and the Cypriot government had requested a bailout in June 2012. After prolonged negotiations a bailout package was presented in March 2013. A controversial feature of this package was a levy on all deposits in Cypriot banks. After a public outcry this was amended to a levy on deposits of above €100,000, but the deal was still rejected by the Cypriot parliament. The agreement that was finally reached abandoned the levy but enforced the closure of the most troubled Cypriot bank. This demonstrated that the euro crisis was far from over.

Austerity

The troubled countries of the euro zone have been obliged to adopt "austerity" policies combining deep cuts in government spending with increases in taxes. Although the United Kingdom is not part of the euro zone, its government has also embraced an austerity program. It might be asked why the European governments appear to be so wedded to policies that cut living standards in a time of economic hardship. The case for austerity is that, while government spending cuts undoubtedly reduce GDP growth in the short run, they increase growth in the long run by reducing government debt. Countries with lower debt levels will then be able to borrow from financial markets at lower interest rates. It is also argued that the short-run negative effects on growth of cuts in public spending will be at least partly offset by increases in spending by the private sector on consumption and investment. Critics of austerity point out that, while theoretically possible, there is no evidence that public-sector spending cuts are actually associated with increases in private-sector spending. In fact, the experience of the troubled European economies shows that fears over job security as a result of cuts in the

144 Chapter 7

public sector, especially when private-sector debt is very high, cause the private sector to decrease spending at the same time as the public sector. The resulting severe recession reduces tax revenues. Since debt depends on the gap between revenues and expenditures, this makes it harder to reduce public debt.

Financial Regulation

Tighter regulation of the European banks is undoubtedly needed, but the problems associated with austerity have arguably been made worse by the way in which financial regulation has been implemented. The Brussels Agreement of October 2011 started the process of tightening regulations by imposing a mandatory level of 9 percent for bank capitalization within the European Union. Critics of these regulations have pointed out, however, that requiring banks to improve capital ratios without injections of capital from governments is likely to cause banks to cut down on loans, thereby squeezing credit at the same time as governments are implementing tight fiscal policies.

The Deeper Problem

The deeper problem with the euro zone is not that southern governments have been profligate. It may be true that Greek governments have lacked responsibility but other indebted countries, notably Ireland and Spain, had low budget deficits and moderate levels of public debt before the crisis. Their problem was one of large increases in private-sector debt, fueled by the low interest rates that initially accompanied adoption of the euro, though some of this private-sector debt later changed into budget deficits when governments bailed out banks. The increases in southern country debt were partly a result of high levels of savings in Germany and other northern countries. These countries were producing more than they consumed, which enabled them to sell exports to consumers in the southern countries, which then paid for them with surplus savings loaned to them by investors from the northern countries. The economies of both northern and southern countries were unbalanced: Countries such as Germany were producing too much and consuming too little, while countries such as Greece were producing too little and consuming too much. It is not possible to restore balance by cutting spending in the deficit countries while surplus countries continue to produce more than they are willing to consume. In a regime of flexible exchange rates balance would be restored through a fall in the external values of the currencies of deficit countries relative to those of surplus countries. With a common currency, equilibrium requires not only that deficit countries cut spending but also that surplus countries such as Germany reduce their savings and increase consumption, something they appear unwilling to contemplate. The adjustment cannot entirely be on one side.

One way in which pressure could be reduced on the weaker countries of the euro zone would be to introduce a Eurobond, which would be jointly issued by the euro zone countries. This would enable heavily indebted countries (often referred to as the southern countries) to borrow at lower rates of interest and would improve their chances of climbing out from under their mountains of debt. It would also, however, see countries with stronger economies (the northern countries), such as Germany, facing increases in interest rates. Many in the northern countries see this as a step toward a "transfer union" in which "prudent" countries effectively subsidize "profligate" countries. The reality is, however, that successful monetary unions, such as those between different regions in large countries, invariably require substantial transfers between richer and poorer regions.

Finally, some analysts have suggested that the best solution to the problems of the euro zone would be to split it in two. Germany and other euro zone countries with strongly positive current accounts, such as the Netherlands and Austria, could withdraw and form a separate monetary union, perhaps a deutschmark union. There would then be two European currencies (or three, counting the pound sterling). The German-led bloc would follow the very strict inflation-targeting advocated by Germany, while the remaining euro bloc, perhaps led by France, would be able to keep interest rates low, depreciate the euro to help their export industries, and pursue expansionary fiscal and monetary policies to counter recession.

Until recently it seemed inconceivable that the euro zone would break up. It was believed that euro zone governments would do whatever is necessary to preserve the common currency since the costs of ending it would be too high. The smaller countries using the euro know that if they were to reintroduce their old currencies those currencies would rapidly depreciate. This would dramatically increase the real value of government and bank debt, which is mostly denominated in euros, and cause a massive banking crisis. Other euro zone countries, such as Germany, would also suffer from the end of the common currency since their exports would be hard hit as Germany's exchange rate sharply appreciated. The countries with the means to resolve the crisis, however, seem unable or unwilling to make available the necessary resources or permit the adoption of policies needed to preserve the euro, while the troubled countries are unable or unwilling to make their economies more competitive. Imposing seemingly endless austerity on the debtor countries is no solution. The disintegration of the euro zone is not inevitable, perhaps not even likely, but it is no longer inconceivable.

Brexit

In 2013 the British Prime Minister David Cameron announced that a Conservative government would hold a referendum on EU membership if elected in 2015. Apparently he hoped that this promise would placate the right wing of his Conservative Party and counter the electoral threat posed by the anti-EU United Kingdom Independence Party (UKIP). After the Conservatives won the election the referendum was held on June 23, 2016, and resulted in a vote of 52 percent to 48 percent in favor of the United Kingdom leaving the European Union. This came as a shock to David Cameron, to the financial markets, and, apparently, to most of the British population in spite of the fact that many opinion polls had been predicting just such a result.

146   Chapter 7

In the leadup to the referendum the campaign in favor of remaining in the EU, led by Cameron, emphasized the economic costs of an exit. Although these costs are real and substantial, the "remain camp" were accused, with some justice, of exaggerating them. Unfortunately little effort was spent on presenting positive arguments for the EU, such as its role in promoting trade and supporting democracy in Europe or the bargaining leverage available to a large bloc of countries when negotiating international trade deals or imposing regulations on large multinational corporations.

Those who wished for Britain to leave the European Union were motivated by a variety of concerns.

1. *Immigration.* There was widespread belief that large-scale immigration was putting pressure on social services, including the National Health Service (NHS). The anti-immigration case was made all the more effective by statistics released shortly before the referendum which revealed that net long-term international immigration into the United Kingdom was expected to reach 323,000 in the year ending September 2016, though only half of this was migration from EU countries. A counterargument could have been made that the majority of immigrants are young, fully employed, and are therefore not a burden on the social services, while the NHS depends on immigrants for much of its personnel. Nevertheless, there were legitimate concerns about over-population as well as less valid concerns driven by a rose-tinted nostalgia for an imagined past and, in some cases, outright hostility to foreigners. Perhaps the most important of the many weaknesses of the "remain" campaign was its failure to ad-dress the immigration issue.

2. *Reassertion of national control.* There was a widespread view that too many decisions were being made by a bureaucracy in Brussels without any democratic accountability. In addition, exaggerated claims were made by the "leave" campaign about the large sums that would be saved if the United Kingdom did not have to contribute to the EU budget and about possible gains in efficiency available to British firms as a result of the dismantling of EU regulations. It was also argued, somewhat implausibly, that a Britain outside the EU would quickly be able to enter advantageous trading deals with other countries. Only time will tell if these claims are justified. Disillusion with Brussels was also fueled by the perceived harshness and incompetence with which the Eurozone crisis was being managed.

3. *A desire to register a protest against the political establishment.* There was a wide-spread frustration about globalization and a feeling that the legitimate concerns of or-dinary people were being ignored by the "political elites," which is a feeling by no means confined to the United Kingdom. While trade liberalization has brought about an increase in incomes worldwide, it has also had its casualties. A significant part of the population in the United Kingdom, as in other countries, has experienced stagnat-ing or even falling incomes over the last several decades and their plight has not been adequately addressed by the traditional political parties of either the Right or the Left.

For many people in the United Kingdom the EU had apparently come to symbolize globalization and a general sense of helplessness. It may also be that some people who voted "leave" did so thinking that it was a harmless way of sending a protest to London elites, not expecting the vote to actually succeed. This is supported by the fact that there seems to have been some "buyer's remorse" in the immediate aftermath of the vote.

The days following the vote to leave the EU saw a dramatic fall in the value of the pound, which fell to a thirty-year low relative to the U.S. dollar, and equally dramatic swings in the stock market, though the situation stabilized after a few days. The longer term effects of "Brexit" on the health of the British economy will depend on the results of negotiations between the United Kingdom and the European Union. Provision for leaving the European Union is established in Article 50 of the Lisbon Treaty (2007). Once this article has been invoked by the member state wishing to leave, a two-year period begins during which the terms of departure are negotiated. The final terms of departure are established by a majority vote on the Council without the departing country having a vote. Article 50, however, covers only the exit. Future trade relationships will have to be negotiated separately, will almost certainly take much longer than two years to reach, and will then require the approval of the parliaments of all twenty-seven member countries plus the European Parliament. The supports of the "leave" campaign have suggested that the United Kingdom will be able to negotiate an agreement in which it retains complete access to the European market, while regaining control over immigration. Such a deal is theoretically possible but it seems unlikely that European legislators would agree to such a generous deal. It is, of course, impossible to know at the time of writing (July 2016) what the terms of any final agreement will be but it will probably resemble one of three alternative models which have been widely discussed.

1. *The "Norway option."* From the point of view of the British economy this would be the best outcome but it is also the least likely to be achieved. Norway and a number of other countries that belong to the European Economic Area (EEA) have access to the European single market but in return have to make payments to the EU budget and observe all the single market regulations, including free movement of labor, without having any say in the making of those regulations. The EEA option, if agreed to, would allow the United Kingdom to set its own policies with respect to agriculture, fisheries, and taxation. It could therefore be sold as returning some control to the United Kingdom over its own affairs but not in the crucial area of movement of labor. The "Norway option" would therefore have the advantage of preserving access to the EU market for goods and services but would probably be unacceptable to the advocates of Brexit since it would continue to allow free migration. In any case it is hard to see how an agreement under which Britain has to continue implementing most EU regulations while no longer having any say in setting those regulations represents an advantage over full EU membership.

2. *The "Canada option."* Canada has negotiated a free trade deal with the EU which would eliminate most tariffs on goods but not on services, including financial services.

148   Chapter 7

3. *The "WTO option."* The third and least desirable outcome would be to have no special agreement with the EU but simply to rely on the trade rules set by the World Trade Organization (WTO). Like the Canada option this would exclude trade in services and, unlike the Canada option, would mean that trade in goods would be subject to the common EU tariff.

Whatever the form of the final agreement, Brexit will undoubtedly have a major impact on both the United Kingdom and the European Union. The "Norway option" would have the least damaging effect on the British economy but even with this option there would likely be some reduction in investment because of the danger that future policy changes within the EU would adversely affect Britain. Foreign investors might find it safer to invest in countries that are full members of the EU rather than in an offshore subsidiary. As indicated, however, the issue of immigration makes it unlikely that the "Norway option" would be accepted by the British supporters of Brexit. A more likely outcome is some variant of the "Canada option" but this does not guarantee access to trade in services, which account for over 40 percent of British trade with the EU. Estimates of the negative effect on British GDP vary but most are in the range of a cut in GDP growth of between 1 and 2 percent.[8]

These estimates are based on the effect of reductions in investment as a result of increased uncertainty and a weak pound, but they probably underestimate the full costs to the British economy of Brexit since they do not take full account of its potential effects on the City of London, Europe's financial center. As long as Britain is a member of the European Union financial institutions based in London have "passports" to do business in all EU countries without needing to set up local branches. Once Britain leaves the EU there is no guarantee that passporting will be retained, particularly if Britain refuses to sign on to an agreement that allows labor mobility in return for access to the European market. In that case financial firms might choose to move from London to other financial centers such as Frankfurt, Paris, or Dublin. Since financial and related firms currently have 730,000 employees in London the effect of a loss of passporting could be substantial.

The effects of Brexit on the remaining EU countries is even more difficult to predict. The immediate economic effects will undoubtedly be negative, though to a much smaller degree than will be the case for Britain; and these effects might be offset by gains at the expense of London if financial firms relocate to countries still within the EU. The long-term political effects are potentially more significant. An optimistic view is that greater progress toward integration may occur within the EU once it is free of its most awkward and obstructive member. A pessimistic view is that the success in Britain of a right-wing anti-EU party such as UKIP might provide an impetus to other right-wing anti-EU parties in continental Europe, such as the Front National in France, and possibly lead to the breakup of the EU. That seems unlikely at present but concerns about the danger of this happening may well cause the EU governments to adopt a hard line toward the United Kingdom when it comes to negotiations over market access.

---

[8] For example, Morgan Stanley predicted a reduction of 1.5 percentage points off the United Kingdom growth rate. *The Economist*, July 2-8, 2016, p. 21.

MERCOSUR

Mercosur (from the Spanish *Mercado Común del Sur*) is an association of South American countries formed by the Treaty of Asunción in 1991. It currently includes four countries, Brazil, Argentina, Uruguay, and Venezuela. Originally the membership of Mercosur included Paraguay and excluded Venezuela, but in 2012 Venezuela was admitted as a full member, one month after Paraguay's membership was suspended. This was a result of the impeachment of its president in a process regarded as undemocratic by the other members.

As can be seen from Table 7.6 Mercosur is similar to NAFTA but different from the European Union in that one of its members, in this case Brazil, is far larger than the others in terms of both population and GDP. Mercosur differs from both NAFTA and the EU, however, in that its members have similar levels of economic development with the exception of Paraguay, which, in 2010, accounted for only 2.5 percent of its population and 1 percent of its GDP.

While NAFTA is a free trade agreement and the European Union is an economic union, Mercosur is a customs union. The full members of Mercosur have free trade with each other and impose a common external tariff on nonmembers, though there are also five associate members, Chile, Bolivia, Colombia, Ecuador, and Peru, that receive tariff reductions but are not required to impose a common external tariff. While both NAFTA and the European Union

TABLE 7.6. Population and GDP for Mercosur Countries, 2010

Country	Population	GDP (US$ billions, PPP)	GDP per Capita (US$)
Brazil	190.7	2,169	11,374
Argentina	40.1	642	16,010
Uruguay	2.4	48	14,118
Paraguay (suspended, 2012)	6.2	33	5,323
(Venezuela, admitted 2012)	(30.0)	(375)	(12,500)
Total	240.4	2,892	12,030

Source: World Bank (GDP).

appear to have had largely beneficial effects in terms of trade promotion and increased income growth for their members, the effects of Mercosur are more controversial. As seen earlier, the costs and benefits of regional trade agreements are often analyzed on the basis of trade creation and trade diversion. On this basis Mercosur does not perform well. In a study of the customs union Yeats (1998) found that for Mercosur there is a greater likelihood of trade diversion than trade creation. This is due to the fact that trade between the member countries was growing most quickly in terms of goods for which outside countries had a comparative advantage. In other words, the members of Mercosur were buying from each other products that they should have bought from countries outside of the association. It is possible that, apart from trade creation, economic associations might benefit countries by giving some of them access to more advanced technology, but the scope for this is very limited in the case of Mercosur. Since its member countries are at similar levels of economic development there are unlikely to be major benefits from a wider transmission of technology, such as can occur in trade associations between industrialized and less-developed economies.

References

Books

Gerber, J. (2011). *International economics*. Boston: Addison-Wesley.

Södersten, B., and Reed, G. (1994). *International economics* (3rd edition). London: Macmillan.

Van den Berg, H. (2004). *International economics*. New York: Irwin.

Van Der Wee, H. (1986). *Prosperity and upheaval: The world economy 1945–1980*. Los Angeles, CA: University of California Press.

Articles

Helliwell, J. F. (2001). Canada: Life beyond the looking glass. *Journal of Political Economy*, *15*(1).

Krueger, A. (1999). Are preferential trading arrangements trade—Liberalizing or protectionist? *Journal of Economic Perspectives*, *13*(4).

Mundell, R. A. (1961). A theory of optimum currency areas. *American Economic Review*, *51*(4).

Trefler, D. (2001). The long and short of the Canada-U.S. Free Trade Agreement. *NBER Working Papers 8293*.

Yeats, A. J. (1998). Does Mercosur's trade performance raise concerns about the effects of regional trade arrangements? *The World Bank Economic Review*, *12*(1).

Chapter 8

The Soviet Union and the Socialist Economies of Europe

When the Bolsheviks (Communists) seized power in Russia in 1917 they found themselves in control of a country that was poor and underdeveloped compared to the other major powers. Since those powers were hostile to the new Russian regime the Bolshevik leaders felt they had little time to industrialize the country to the point that it would be able to resist foreign invasion. That they were correct in this assessment is confirmed by the German invasion of Russia in 1941 and its defeat by the newly industrialized Soviet Union.

Given the urgency in developing strong manufacturing industries traditional economic measures were deemed inadequate and, in any case, they were inconsistent with Marxist-Leninist ideology with its opposition to capitalism. After a short period of experimentation and debate a system of centralized planning was developed. This model was also implemented by Communist regimes imposed by the Soviet Union on several Eastern European countries after World War II. Central planning was undoubtedly successful in converting an overwhelmingly agricultural country into a major industrial power in a remarkably short period of time. Industrialization in the Soviet Union was, however, achieved at an enormous human cost. In time it also became clear that although the central planning model was able to create a heavy industrial base it was much less effective as a mechanism for producing the wide variety of high-quality products demanded by modern consumer societies. Consequently, the socialist economies of Europe came under serious strain in the 1970s and, almost without exception, collapsed in the late 1980s.

Historical Development of the Soviet Economic System

When the Bolsheviks seized power in Russia in 1917 they acquired control of a country that already had significant manufacturing industries. On the eve of the First World War the Russian Empire was the world's fifth largest industrial power. This gives, however, a misleading impression of Russia's economic status. Imperial Russia was still a predominantly agricultural country with very low productivity and on a per capita basis the country's GDP was by far the lowest of all the major powers. This is not to deny that the country had experienced substantial progress in recent decades. The 1880s and, to an even greater extent, the 1890s had seen substantial growth in industry. During the 1890s industrial production had grown at an annual average rate of 8 percent, much of this due to the major railway building program promoted by the government at the time. In the early 1900s it was agriculture that saw progress. The Stolypin reforms, beginning in 1906, promoted private ownership of land as an

151

alternative to the predominant form of collective farming. This led to the emergence of a more entrepreneurial class of relatively prosperous farmers. These "kulaks" (rich peasants) were later to be vilified and persecuted during the Stalinist era but they introduced more modern farming techniques. Despite such innovations, however, the Russian empire remained far behind the advanced Western economies. This fact was to play a large part in Russia's defeat in the First World War, setting the stage for the revolutions of 1917.

By 1917 the war, which had been expected to be of short duration, had caused great loss of life and wrecked the economy. Strikes and riots broke out in March of that year. The protesters were supported by the soldiers sent to suppress them and in several cities, including the capital, Petrograd, soviets (councils of workers and soldiers) were set up. Within days the Tsar had abdicated and the Russian Duma (or parliament), which up to that point had little power, established a provisional government. The new government, of which the most prominent member was the moderate socialist Alexander Kerensky, promised to enact land redistribution, social reforms, and various liberal measures such as freedom of speech. The provisional government was never able, however, to control the Petrograd soviet and made the fatal mistake of pledging to continue the war against Germany. It was because of this decision that the German government connived at the return to Russia of Vladimir Lenin, the exiled leader of the Bolsheviks, the most radical of Russia's socialist parties. Lenin soon gained control of the Petrograd Soviet and worked to undermine the provisional government. Finally, in the "October Revolution" in late 1917, supporters of the Bolsheviks seized the seat of government, the Winter Palace, and Lenin formed a government. This did not, however, bring about peace. One of the first

Vladimir Lenin.

actions of Lenin's government was to end the war with Germany but it then had to fight a civil war against opponents of the new regime. These opponents, known as "White Russians," were sometimes supported by foreign governments.

It was during this period that the Bolsheviks, now known as Communists, adopted the drastic emergency measures known as "war communism." The Bolsheviks based their ideology on the ideas of nineteenth-century German theorist Karl Marx, as expounded in his celebrated work "Capital: Critique of Political Economy," but when they seized power and established the Soviet Union they found little guidance from Marx on how to organize a postcapitalist economy. In developing his revolutionary theories Marx had focused on the destruction of capitalism rather than what would follow it. In addition, he had believed that the socialist revolution would first occur in an advanced capitalist economy such as that of Britain or the United States, not in a backward, mostly rural economy such as that of Russia in 1917. In so far as he did predict the aftermath of the revolution, he believed that a temporary system referred to as "the dictatorship of the proletariat" would guide the transition to a

The Soviet Union and the Socialist Economies of Europe   153

"socialist economy." Once a socialist economy was established there would still be a need for some economic incentives but people would be paid the "value" of their work rather than what they could extract by "exploiting" others. Ultimately, after some unspecified period of time, a "communist" society would emerge in which incentives would no longer be needed. Instead, production would presumably be achieved through voluntary cooperation. Since everyone would now be working together in harmony the state would "wither away" because there would no longer be any need for repression by the state. None of this provided a very clear blueprint as to how capitalism would be replaced by socialism, particularly in a predominantly rural economy. The dictatorship of the proletariat presupposed the existence of a large, politically conscious industrial working class or "proletariat," something that barely existed in the Russia of 1917.

During the era of "war communism" (1918–1921) the authorities simply requisitioned from the peasants the grain and any other goods needed to feed the factory workers and prosecute the war against the "White Russians." Not surprisingly this created a serious disincentive to production in both agriculture and industry. Industrial output fell to 14 percent of prewar levels. The situation was made worse by very low rates of investment due, at least in part, to the collapse of foreign investment as a result of the repudiation by the Bolshevik government of debts incurred by the former Tsarist regime. There was also hyperinflation, as the government desperately created money to finance war expenditures.

By 1921 the Communists had established firm control over most of the former Tsarist territories, which were now reorganized as the Union of Soviet Socialist Republics (USSR) or Soviet Union. At this point the economy was in a state of chaos. Faced with this dire economic situation, Lenin introduced the New Economic Policy (NEP). A tax in kind on agricultural output replaced food requisitions and peasants were allowed to sell their surpluses at market prices. Outside of agriculture the "commanding heights" of the economy (large-scale industries, transportation, banking, and foreign trade) remained in the hands of the state but firms employing fewer than twenty workers could be privately owned. The NEP was successful in rebuilding the economy. By 1927 output had returned to its prewar levels, though the recovery came too late to prevent a massive famine in 1921. There was considerable debate within the Soviet leadership about what would be the next step. The ultimate intention was to develop an industrialized state-controlled economy without depending on foreign investment, but the question was whether this would best be achieved coercively, by enforcing high levels of savings in order to achieve high rates of investment in capital goods, or voluntarily, by continuing to produce consumer goods with which to buy peasant cooperation.

After Lenin's death there was a short period of competition for power between his principal lieutenants but by 1928 Joseph Stalin was in full control of the Communist Party and the Soviet Union. In contrast to his rival Leon Trotsky, who advocated international revolution, Stalin believed in a policy of "socialism in one country." This meant that, faced with a largely hostile world, it was essential for the USSR to build up its industries as quickly as possible to make the country powerful and self-sufficient. Stalin felt that the way to achieve this was through economic planning and in 1929 he launched the first of several five-year plans. The success of this plan was mixed. Output grew remarkably quickly in some industries but lagged in others. Results were particularly poor in agriculture, which was to remain a problem area throughout the history of the Soviet Union. To ensure state control over the food supply Stalin had insisted that the peasants be organized in collective farms but they bitterly resisted collectivization, often burning their crops and slaughtering their livestock to avoid handing them over to the authorities. The result was a collapse of agricultural output and the great famine of 1932–1933. The fall in agricultural output was blamed by the regime on sabotage by the "kulaks," or so-called rich peasants. It reacted with a policy of brutal repression. Millions of peasants died either directly from the famine or through mass executions and deportations. Conditions were also grim for industrial workers as urban wages were suppressed and millions of political prisoners were incarcerated in labor camps.

Communist Party supporters carrying a poster of Stalin.

The second five-year plan, introduced in 1933, continued the emphasis of the first plan on capital goods and military supplies and, like the first, had mixed results. Its chances of success were not improved by the Great Purge of 1936–1938, during which thousands of people, ranging from ordinary workers to high civilian and military officials, were executed. The purge was initiated by Stalin as a means of getting rid of his political rivals within the Communist Party but it soon spread to all sections of society. Naturally it had a seriously disruptive effect on the workings of the five-year plan. Nevertheless, the first two five-year plans did achieve their fundamental objective. Industrialization was achieved at enormous human cost but it was achieved. During the 1930s the Soviet Union was transformed from an agrarian society to one of the world's leading industrial producers.

After the death of Stalin in 1953 his successors proved to be much less ruthless but the Soviet system of economic planning remained substantially in place. Agriculture remained a problem area and successive five-year plans continued to emphasize heavy industry and neglect consumer goods industries. The next two sections will describe in more detail the collectivization of agriculture and the central planning mechanism.

Collectivization of Agriculture in the USSR

Soviet agriculture was relatively unproductive in part because only 10 percent of land in the Soviet Union was arable but also in part because of inadequacies in economic management by the state. More specifically, labor productivity in agriculture had been low since the collectivization of the 1930s and the sector suffered from inadequate infrastructure. The practical purpose of collectivization of agriculture was to increase the food supply for urban workers, the supply of raw materials for manufacturing, and the quantity of exports as a source of foreign exchange with which to buy capital equipment. State grain procurements would be increased through preventing peasants from withholding produce. There was also an ideological

The Soviet Union and the Socialist Economies of Europe   155

goal to collectivization. During the later years of the Tsarist period and the years of the New Economic Policy (NEP) a gap had developed between the wealthier and poorer peasants. Although this gap was quite small, a reliance on income disparities as incentives was seen as inconsistent with Marxist ideology. In addition the Soviet leaders regarded the wealthier peasants, the "kulaks," as opponents of their policies. When a serious grain shortage occurred in 1928 Stalin claimed it was due to hoarding by the kulaks and authorized state requisitioning of grain. Since, not surprisingly, the peasants resisted these grain seizures, the Soviet authorities had decided by 1929 to introduce a program of collectivization, which would give them greater control over the peasants and, it was hoped, bring about increased agricultural productivity through allowing the adoption of large-scale farming methods. Small landholdings would be consolidated into large units that could be farmed using modern, large-scale equipment. It was believed that this would increase agricultural output. Since they were regarded as potential leaders of resistance to the new policies, "kulaks," including women and children, were deported to agricultural labor camps, where many of them died. These measures did not prevent the remaining peasants from resisting collectivization by slaughtering their animals rather than handing them over to the collective farms. As a result there was a massive reduction in livestock.

The immediate effect of collectivization was a large fall in agricultural production though, admittedly, this was made worse by a bad harvest in 1932–1933. There followed a massive famine in the countryside. The catastrophe hit all of the Soviet Union but was particularly severe in the Ukraine. Rather than modifying the collectivization program, however, Stalin continued to blame the kulaks for the catastrophe, claiming that they had been hoarding grain in anticipation of higher prices. The number of deaths resulting from collectivization is difficult to estimate but was probably between 6 million and 13 million.[1]

Throughout the remainder of the Soviet era collectivization remained in force, though without the loss of life associated with the Stalinist period. The agricultural sector was organized into *kolkhozes* (collective farms) and *sovkhozes* (state farms). Although it was collectively owned, some land in rural areas was allocated to individual households. It was not their property but they had some rights to its use. This might have provided incentives for increased production but for the fact that in both kolkhozes and sovkhozes it was usual to rotate individual farming lots with collective lots. This practice acted as a disincentive to effort since individuals who carefully cultivated their assigned lots would find that after five to seven years these lots would be swapped for collective lots, which often had exhausted soil due to intensive large-scale farming.

Agriculture remained a problem area for the economy of the Soviet Union despite periodic attempts to increase food production. In 1954, Khrushchev, Stalin's successor as leader of the Soviet Union, attempted to increase agricultural output by launching the "virgin lands" campaign. The intention was to bring into production the arid lands of Soviet Asia but, though the campaign was successful in substantially increasing grain production between 1954 and 1956, output subsequently declined. The campaign was ultimately unsuccessful partly because of the harsh climate of the virgin land areas but also because of shortages in

---

[1] Livi-Bacci (1993).

fertilizers and agricultural machinery and, above all, because of the failure to provide adequate incentives to the farmers.

Economic Planning in the Soviet Union and the Other Socialist Economies

For most of the period from 1928 until the fall of the Soviet Union its economy was based on state ownership of the means of production and central planning. A major limitation of this system was that the planners depended for their information on lower-level enterprise managers, who tended to overstate their input needs or underestimate their output potential. From their point of view it was safer to have some slack in the system so as to ensure that their targets were always met. This was a problem in any case but was made worse by the fact that in a pre-computer age the information on which the planners depended was often unreliable or outdated. The system was cumbersome and much of the time could only function through enterprise managers exchanging raw materials and equipment without the knowledge of the higher authorities. This acquired habit of bending the rules could very easily degenerate into outright corruption and this did in fact occur during the later decades of the Soviet Union.

Crop sowing on a collective farm in the Ukraine.

Under the Soviet system of central planning, economic planning was conducted through the "material balance method," which involved the following series of steps.

1. The Communist Party leadership and the central planning body (Gosplan in the case of the Soviet Union) would set production targets for the coming year.

2. These broad targets would be forwarded to the ministries responsible for the various industries which would then assign specific targets to individual enterprises.

3. The enterprises would indicate to the ministries the resources and intermediate goods needed to achieve the targets. The ministries would collate the information and pass it on to Gosplan.

4. The planning agency would then check the demand for and supply of inputs and final goods. If demand was not equal to supply the planning agency would revise the targets and pass them on to the industrial ministries.

5. In principle this process would be repeated until demand and supply balanced for all goods.

In practice there never was full convergence between demand and supply but shortages in some areas and surpluses in other. The material balances method was inevitably inefficient

The Soviet Union and the Socialist Economies of Europe 157

because of the need to process vast quantities of data, a lack of incentives, soft budget constraints, and the absence of capital markets.

Data Requirements

The material balances method required the gathering and collating of far more information than was required for a market system and more time than was ever available would have been needed to achieve full convergence between demand and supply, particularly in an era before the development of modern information technology. The system was able to operate reasonably effectively during the early years of the Soviet Union when the task was to produce a limited number of manufactured goods. As the economy became more complex and diversified, the planning system became less and less efficient.

Lack of Incentives

A major weakness of the central planning system was a lack of incentives. The system provided full employment and job security but, since promotion depended more on political loyalty than on technical ability, there was little incentive for workers to do more than the minimum necessary to retain their jobs. For managers the incentives were not so much lacking as perverse. It was in their interests to hoard labor and capital to ensure that they would be able to meet their production targets. During the period of Stalin's domination (1924–1953) a strategy of terror, achieved through mass executions and imprisonment, substituted for more positive incentives but under his less brutal successors the effects of the lack of incentives became very evident.

Soft Budget Constraints

By the 1960s concerns began to arise about a slowing of economic growth. It was hoped that the problems associated with centralized planning would be reduced by moving to a more decentralized system but this failed to improve the economic performance of the socialist economies. During the 1970s Kornai argued that the economic problems of these countries were the consequence of what he called "soft budget constraints."[2] Firms in market-based economies operate under "hard budget constraints" since they cannot long survive if they produce more goods than they can sell. This is because, in order to earn a profit, they have to keep their expenditures less than their revenues. In the socialist economies, however, enterprises were able to spend more on inputs than they received in revenues. In other words, they had "soft budget constraints." The concept of the soft budget constraint strongly influenced Gorbachev's "perestroika" reforms, which were introduced in the Soviet Union in 1987. These reforms included the State Enterprise law (1987), which stated that all state enterprises should cover their costs from their revenues as a result of sales. The state enterprises would not receive subsidies but, instead, any profits earned would be reinvested in the enterprise rather than siphoned off by the state. The reform was, however, largely ineffective because of the failure to follow through with the logical conclusion that enterprises operating at a loss should be closed. Consequently, the state-owned enterprises did not really face hard budget constraints.

---

[2] Kornai (1979).

158   Chapter 8

Absence of Capital Markets

Paradoxically, the rich endowment of the Soviet Union in energy resources and raw materials was a factor in causing the socialist economies to lag technologically behind the Western market-based economies. The capitalist economies responded to the oil shocks of the 1970s by developing new methods of production designed to economize on energy. These included high-value-added technologies such as computers and semiconductors. The Soviet Union and its central and eastern European partners, with their access to relatively cheap Russian energy resources, had less incentive to develop these technologies. The lag in technological progress was also a consequence of the fact that the central planning agencies, which guided the economic development of the socialist economies, were primarily organizations to coordinate plans rather than develop new technologies. Certainly there were research and development institutions tasked with responsibility for innovation but, in the absence of hard budget constraints, their focus was less on economic efficiency than on promoting growth in the size of their enterprises.

Attempts at Reform

Postwar Period

Central planning worked well during the three decades following the Second World War. During these years the problem was to rebuild Russia's economy after the destruction of the war. In many ways the task facing the Soviet Union was similar to that of the 1930s—a need to concentrate investment in a limited number of industrial sectors. Once this had been achieved, however, the planning system proved inadequate in managing a complex economy with a need for a vast array of consumer goods. This had become evident by the 1980s. Soviet GNP grew at a very respectable average rate of 6.5 percent per year from 1965 to 1980 but then fell to 1.8 percent per year between 1980 and 1985. The economy had chronic surpluses of some consumer goods and shortages of others, while the quality of goods was often very low.

Some economic reforms were introduced during the period of Brezhnev's leadership (1964–1982). During this period enterprises were reorganized to allow for a greater reliance on profitable methods of production but the planned economy was too inflexible to adjust to the demands of a complex modern economy and the Soviet economy stagnated during the 1970s. At the same time corruption became endemic, though the scale of the problem was obscured by bureaucrats manipulating data to hide their inability to reach their production targets. The security service, the KGB, became aware of the problem, however, through its network of informants. In 1982 Yuri Andropov, a former director of the KGB, succeeded Brezhnev as leader of the Soviet Union and launched a series of moderate reforms. These reforms stalled with Andropov's death in 1984.

In an effort to renew and accelerate economic reform the last leader of the Soviet Union, Mikhail Gorbachev (1985–1991), introduced the concepts of *glasnost* and *perestroika*. Through *glasnost*, or "openness," Gorbachev hoped that by exposing corruption and inefficiency he would be able to recruit the support of the Russian people against a Communist bureaucracy opposed to change. With this support he would implement *Perestroika*, or "restructuring," which meant implementing fundamental changes in the structure of the economic system. These changes included:

1. Changing the planning system to one more closely resembling the indicative planning which had been applied in a number of Western European countries, notably France, after the Second World War. The planning authorities would make recommendations as to broad targets rather than provide detailed prescriptions.

2. Profits would become the indicator of success in the management of state-owned enterprises.

3. The managers of these enterprises would be able to sell products and buy resources freely.

4. Small private businesses would be allowed and even encouraged.

5. Collective farms would make more land available for private plots for farm households.

These reforms fell, however, between two stools. They were opposed by both economic reformers, who felt that they did not go far enough in the direction of free markets, and "conservative" communists who preferred to maintain the system of centralized planning.

The Socialist Economies of Central and Eastern Europe

At the end of the Second World War Soviet troops occupied most of the countries of Eastern Europe and, despite promising to allow free elections, imposed communist regimes on them. Even without having to drastically change their economic systems these countries would have faced severe adjustment problems. The occupation forces dismantled capital equipment and shipped it back home to the Soviet Union. At the same time the eastern bloc countries were forced to make payments to the Soviet Union to cover reparations and occupation costs. The situation was the reverse of that in Western Europe, which received substantial aid from the United States under the Marshall Plan.[3] By 1948 those countries of central and eastern Europe in the Soviet sphere of influence had adopted the Soviet economic model. While this model was quickly introduced into the industrial sector it was not so easily implemented in agriculture. Changes were certainly made. In all of the socialist states large landowners were dispossessed and their holdings distributed among the peasants. The difficulty arose when it came to implementing the next step envisaged, which was to organize the peasants into collective farming units. While this was achieved in the majority of the socialist countries, in Poland and Yugoslavia, where there was strong resistance by the peasants to collectivization, private ownership and control of farms remained the normal practice.

In other economic sectors central planning was implemented but with mixed results in terms of economic development. The emphasis during the first two postwar decades was on achieving industrialization and growth through increasing factor inputs, especially the capital

---

[3] Under this plan, announced by the American secretary of state, George Marshall, in 1947, the United States gave $13 billion to help rebuild the war-devastated economies of Western Europe.

160   Chapter 8

input. The plans tended to neglect the need for technical change and the proportion of GDP spent on science and technology was generally less than in Western countries. The emphasis on "extensive growth" appeared to succeed in the 1950s, when domestic output in Eastern Europe as a whole grew at 7 percent per year.[4] This impressive rate of growth was, however, at least partly due to recovery from the devastation of the war years and in the 1960s most of the socialist countries experienced lower rates of growth. Even in the 1950s the benefits of high growth rates were offset by serious imbalances arising from an emphasis on heavy industry and a neglect of the consumer goods sector. A further weakness was that extensive growth relied on increasing output through expanding inputs of capital and labor rather than through increasing productivity. The result was a wasteful use of resources and a decline in economic efficiency which became evident in the 1960s. Wasteful practices were, in any case, almost inevitable in the system of central planning practiced by the countries of the Soviet bloc in which the need to achieve targets set by the planners encouraged managers of factories and other enterprises to hoard labor and capital.

Concern about the slowing rate of growth led to reforms in a number of countries in the 1960s, though there was substantial variation from country to country in the extent to which the planning system was modified. Within the Soviet bloc Hungary and Czechoslovakia moved furthest in the direction of reform, while East Germany, Romania, and the Soviet Union itself adhered more closely to the Stalinist model. Although the details varied from country to country the reforms generally included some or all of the following features.

1. Greater autonomy was given to the managers of individual enterprises. Some compulsory targets were still set but there was greater reliance on broad indicative planning rather than the setting of detailed directives, and enterprises were allowed greater flexibility in setting prices and wage rates.

2. Measures were introduced to increase the efficiency with which capital was used. These measures included capital charges as opposed to providing free capital equipment to enterprises, which were allowed to retain a proportion of their earnings with which to finance investment.

3. A limited role was allowed to free markets, though most of the economy still remained under state ownership. In agriculture there was greater emphasis on private plots and agricultural prices were increased.

4. Controls over foreign trade were relaxed. In some cases individual enterprises were allowed to trade directly in foreign markets as opposed to all international transactions being conducted through state trading agencies.

---

[4] Aldcroft, p. 208.

Comecon

History

From 1949 until the collapse of the Soviet Union in 1991 economic relations between the socialist countries of Eastern Europe and other close allies of the Soviet Union operated under the umbrella of the Council for Mutual Economic Assistance (CMEA), better known as "Comecon." Although these countries, with their centrally planned economies, sought to achieve self-sufficiency as far as was feasible, some intercountry exchange was unavoidable. Comecon was

Former Comecon secretariat building, Moscow.

established shortly after World War II to coordinate this intercountry exchange. Within the organization the Soviet Union was clearly dominant, producing about 70 percent of the total output of Comecon members. The European members were subsequently joined by Mongolia (1962), Cuba (1972), and Vietnam (1978).

Trade between Comecon members was very limited during the first decade after World War II. During this period each country pursued its own internal planning agenda with little reference to the national plans of other member countries of Comecon. Clearly this was not conducive to international trade and at first the Comecon played a very minor role in economic policy. After Stalin's death in 1953, however, the members of Comecon adopted policies to promote a greater degree of specialization and trade within the organization. A step in this direction was an expansion in the role of the Soviet currency, the ruble. During the years of the so-called New Economic Policy (NEP), Lenin had introduced *chervonets*, which were convertible into gold, but after 1932 the ruble was nonconvertible and remained so until the eve of the Soviet collapse in the late 1980s. In 1964, however, the "transferable ruble" was adopted as a medium of exchange between member countries. This followed closely upon the creation of the International Bank for Economic Cooperation (IBEC) (in 1963). Despite this, however, the process of economic integration between Comecon countries proceeded only slowly during the 1960s. This was largely due suspicion on the part of the smaller countries toward the Soviet Union, which accounted for about 70 per cent of the output of Comecon, as can be seen from Table 8.1. Nevertheless a pattern of trade evolved in which the Soviet Union relied heavily on exports of resources in the form of fuels, metals, and timber, while it imported manufactured goods from the neighboring Communist states of Europe.

It was in the 1970s that Comecon had its largest impact. During a decade of high energy costs in the non-Communist world, the members of the association benefitted from their access to low-priced fuel from the Soviet Union. Generally foreign trade was a state monopoly for the member countries of Comecon. World market prices served as a guideline for the rates at which goods were exchanged but they were only infrequently adjusted. There was also a tendency in the association's later years to underprice raw materials, including

162   Chapter 8

TABLE 8.1. Share of Total Comecon GNP Produced by Each of the Member Countries (%)

Country	1975	1990
Soviet Union	69.5	73.7
Bulgaria	2.3	1.8
Cuba	1.0	1.2
Czechoslovakia	4.9	4.9
German Democratic Republic	5.8	3.0
Hungary	2.7	2.5
Mongolia	0.1	0.1
Poland	8.8	7.2
Romania	3.6	3.0
Vietnam (joined 1978)	(1.5)	2.6

Source: Calculated from GNP statistics in the CIA World Factbook.

Soviet-produced oil and natural gas, which worked to the benefit of those member countries that produced and exported manufactured goods. It is not clear whether this represented a deliberate subsidy from the Soviet Union to its fellow Communist states or was merely the unintended consequence of the fact that Comecon prices adjusted slowly at a time when world energy prices were sharply rising.

The energy crisis of the decade also provided a short-run indirect boost to the socialist economies as Western banks, swamped with petrodollars, provided them with cheap credit, though in the long run this was to do them more harm than good. Unfortunately much of the capital flowing from the West was used to support consumption rather than productive investment. When the capital flows dried up in the 1980s, as a consequence of credit tightening by Western central banks, the Comecon countries found themselves burdened with heavy debts.

The final phase of Comecon's history began in 1985 when the Soviet Union under the leadership of Mikhail Gorbachev attempted to improve the international coordination of the socialist economies by increasing the authority of Comecon over its member countries. The policy was largely unsuccessful and in June 1988 Comecon countries were permitted to negotiate individual trade deals with the European Union. This marked the effective end of the association, though it was not formally abolished until June 1991.

Failure of the Socialist Economies

Western economists generally attribute the failure of the socialist economies to underlying flaws in the central planning model. More long-standing issues were, however, at least as important in explaining why the central and eastern European economies lagged behind those of western Europe. The economic gap in Europe between the more developed West and the less developed East existed from at least the sixteenth century and arguably existed from as early as the ninth century.[5] The dividing line between the two Europes, which ran close to the Elbe River, corresponded closely with the so-called Iron Curtain, which marked the boundary between the "socialist" economies of the East and the more market-based economies of the West from the end of World War II until the disintegration of the Soviet bloc in the 1980s. The "socialist" countries attempted to close the gap in economic development between the two parts of Europe through implementing central planning and, for a time, they appeared to be successful. In the 1970s, however, they were tempted by the cheap loans available as a result of the energy shocks, which flooded the international banks with petrodollars. Their intention was to switch from import substitution industrialization (ISI) strategies to import-led growth strategies. Technology and capital would be imported from the West, used to promote manufacturing, and then paid for by exporting manufactures to the West. This was not very different from the export-led growth strategies which had been successfully implemented in the newly industrialized economies of East Asia. The "socialist" countries were, however, less fortunate than the East Asian countries in their timing. It proved difficult to increase exports in the recessionary conditions of the international economy in the late 1970s. As a result the "socialist" countries built up large foreign debts to the West. This accumulation of debt was part of a wider international pattern. Several Latin American and Asian countries which adopted the same strategy of borrowing were afflicted by the debt crisis of the 1980s, following the sharp recession and the tightening of international credit in 1979–1982.

Deteriorating conditions in the international economy also played a major role in the timing of the collapse of the Soviet Union, although its economy had already been showing weakness for some decades. The Soviet Union, although it did not accumulate debt, was affected indirectly by the economic downturn of the 1980s through its dependence on the other socialist economies for manufactured goods. Additional blows to the Soviet economy at this time were a decline in the prices of gold, oil, and gas, beginning in 1981, and an increase in military expenditures as a result of the acceleration of the arms race by the U.S. president, Ronald Reagan. This was not the decisive factor in the fall of the Soviet Union, as is sometimes claimed, but it certainly increased Soviet economic difficulties coming at a time of declining foreign exchange earnings.

While the immediate cause of the revolutions of 1989 in Eastern Europe and the breakup of the Soviet Union was the world economic downturn in the late 1980s, long-term inefficiencies in the centrally planned economies also played a role. The rigidity of the planning structures of the European socialist countries and the Soviet Union made their economies less flexible than those of countries with more market-based systems. As a result they were less

---

[5] As pointed out by A.G. Frank (1998).

164   Chapter 8

able to engage in the economic restructuring that occurred elsewhere. The most important test of any economic system is how well it performs when economic conditions are unfavorable.

References

Books

Aldcroft, Derek H. (1978). *The European economy 1914-1980* (chap. 6). London: Croom Helm.
Cameron, Rondo. (2003). *A concise economic history of the world* (4th edition, chaps. 10, 14, 15). New York: Oxford University Press.
Heilbroner, Robert. (1993). *The making of economic society* (9th edition, chap. 9). Englewood Cliffs, NJ: Prentice Hall.
Nove, Alec. (1989). *An economic history of the U.S.S.R.* Reading, Berkshire: Cox and Wyman.

Articles

Frank, André Gunder. (1998). What went wrong with the "socialist" east? *Humboldt Journal of Social Relations, 24*(1/2), 171–193.
Kornai, Janos. (1979). Resource-constrained versus demand-constrained systems. *Econometrica, 47*(4).
Livi-Bacci, Massimo. (1993). On the human costs of collectivization in the Soviet Union. *Population and Development Review, 19*(4).

Chapter 9

Emerging Economies: The BRICS Countries

As the economic woes of the industrialized countries of the West have worsened, more prominence has been assumed by the "emerging economies," which are increasingly seen as the driving forces in the expansion of the global economy. The emerging economies may be described as those countries that are going through a process of rapid growth and industrialization but have not yet attained the status of rich industrialized countries.

The largest of the emerging economies now hold regular meetings to discuss economic and political issues. In 2006 the foreign ministers of Brazil, Russia, India, and China (which came to be known as the "BRIC" countries) met to organize the first of a series of official summits, beginning in 2009. In 2010 South Africa was admitted to the group, which was now renamed "BRICS," with the "S" standing for South Africa. The BRICS countries will be discussed below individually. They are obviously important because of their large economies and prominent role in world affairs but each is individually interesting for other reasons. An account of the recent experience of Russia and China gives some insight into the difficulties faced by economies that are or have been in transition from Communist centrally planned systems to market-based economies. India and China are two Asian giants playing an increasingly important role in the world output of manufacturing and services. Many of the challenges that have been faced by Brazil are common to other Latin American countries. Finally, South Africa is the economic powerhouse of the African continent and, like Brazil, has prospered as a result of the rise in natural resource prices, driven by the economic expansions of China and India.

Russia

Russia, the largest component of the Soviet Union until it dissolved into fifteen separate republics in 1991, was ruled by the Communist Party and had a centrally planned economy throughout most of the twentieth century. The origins of the Soviet system of central planning have already been described at some length in chapter 8. As indicted in that chapter, central planning was developed as an attempt to deal with the Soviet Union's inability to compete

166   Chapter 9

with other European countries. In 1921 the Soviet Union adopted the New Economic Policy, which allowed some free markets and private ownership of property, but this led to only modest growth and benefited urban entrepreneurs and prosperous peasants who were seen as hostile to the Communist Party. Given the regime's quite legitimate sense of being surrounded by enemies, it appeared that the Soviet Union did not have time to rely on the market system to develop a modern economy. In 1928–1929, therefore, Joseph Stalin introduced a command economy, with the collectivization of agriculture and a series of national plans directing almost all economic activity.

The resulting system, Stalinism, was authoritarian, with the means of production (labor, capital, factories) and foreign trade almost entirely controlled by the government and the Communist Party. Stalinism was successful in bringing about a rapid growth in heavy industry, but this was accomplished at an enormous human cost. The collectivization of agriculture, which involved the state taking control over decision making in farming out of the hands of the peasant farmers, resulted in famines causing millions of deaths during the 1930s. Nevertheless, through the forcible transfer of resources into manufacturing, the Soviet Union developed a major industrial economy during a remarkably short period of time.

In the 1950s, after Stalin's death, the inherent weaknesses of the Soviet system of central planning began to emerge. Central planning in a country as large as the Soviet Union involved an enormous, cumbersome, and often corrupt bureaucracy. Guaranteed employment without any financial reward for excellence meant that workers tended to do only the necessary minimum, while promotion of managers depended more on political connections than on managerial or technical skill. Stalin, through mass political purges and executions, had terrorized the population and the managers into achieving his goals, but his successors were unwilling to adopt such brutal measures. Finally, while central planning could rapidly increase production in a limited number of economic sectors by shifting unused or poorly used resources into heavy industry, it was much less efficient in organizing the production of consumer goods. Essentially the Soviet economy was a permanent wartime economy. Under Leonid Brezhnev in the 1970s and early 1980s the command economy was rife with corruption and bureaucratic sclerosis.

After the death of Brezhnev in 1982 there were some attempts at increasing efficiency by decentralizing decision making, but serious reform really began with Mikhail Gorbachev, who became leader of the Soviet Union in 1985. Gorbachev recognized that the Soviet Union needed to reduce its concentration in heavy industry and move toward production for mass consumption. He also saw that the country was lagging behind the West in the high technology information–based industries, which were becoming increasingly important.

The program of Gorbachev and his fellow reformers is associated with two movements. *Perestroika* ("restructuring") was a movement for economic reform, while *glasnost* ("openness") was a movement aimed at promoting openness and transparency in government operations. The two programs were linked; in launching *glasnost* Gorbachev hoped to win public support against the bureaucracy, which was resisting his economic reforms. Initially these reforms did not mean the adoption of capitalism but rather were intended to make the socialist economy work better. The earliest reforms simply involved a transfer of some decision-making powers from the central planners in Moscow to lower-level state functionaries such as managers of state enterprises, but in 1988 a more radical step was taken when private ownership of some businesses was allowed.

A major issue that was not effectively tackled during the Gorbachev years was price reform. Under central planning, prices and production levels of goods were set arbitrarily by the planners, and prices bore little relationship to the demand for goods. This meant that there would constantly be surpluses of some goods and shortages of others. Generally, the prices of basic necessities were set at low levels with the result of excess demand for those goods. Allocation would then be either through formal rationing or through queuing, as in a wartime economy. Reforming the price system was bound to be painful as the adoption of a system of market prices would immediately result in sharp rises in the prices of necessities relative to other goods. This would eventually result in the increased production of those goods, but in the short run, those on lower wages (most of the population) would suffer severe hardship as many products were priced out of their reach.

Not only would there be changes in relative prices, but price reform would also ignite a general inflation. Decades in which official prices were low but there were few goods to buy meant that the people of the Soviet Union were holding large, unusable money balances. Once prices were allowed to adjust to market levels, these money balances would be spent, pushing up average price levels. Fearful of igniting inflation and imposing economic hardship on a large section of the population, the reformers of the Gorbachev era failed to implement an effective system of market prices. Without such a system, however, the economy continued to be weak.

Economic failure was accompanied by political unrest. *Glasnost* undermined support for the Communist Party by revealing widespread corruption and inefficiency and allowed an explosion of ethnic tensions among the different nationalities living in the various republics of the Soviet Union. In this way *glasnost* undermined central control and led to breakdowns in the distribution of goods and services. The economy deteriorated rather than improved. Finally, in 1991 the central government was dismantled and the Soviet Union split into fifteen separate states. By far the largest of these successor states is Russia, which in 1991 had a population of 147 million, comprising 51.4 percent of the total population of the Soviet Union.

The Yeltsin Era

After the breakup of the Soviet Union, Russia faced severe problems. The old system had almost collapsed. Inept fiscal and monetary policies had left a legacy of huge budget deficits and inflation (which reached 365 percent in 1991), though the effects of inflation were partly disguised by price controls.

Boris Yeltsin.

168   Chapter 9

Russia therefore sought guidance and assistance from the IMF and the Western countries in developing a market-based economy.

TABLE 9.1. Russia. Annual Rate of Increase in the Consumer Price Index 1991-2001

Year	Rate of Inflation (%)	Year	Rate of Inflation (%)
1991	160.4	1997	11.0
1992	2508.8	1998	84.5
1993	840.0	1999	36.6
1994	214.8	2000	20.1
1995	131.6	2001	18.8
1996	21.8		

Source: Inflation Rate in Russian Federation, http://inflationinrussia.com/inflation_table.aspx

The first problem to be tackled was price inflation, which reached over 2,500 percent in 1992. Since this was fueled by excessive money creation, it was necessary to reduce the rate of monetary growth to stabilize the economy. The IMF and Russia's other foreign advisers, however, failed to give sufficient recognition to the lack of an efficient central bank or effective tax system in Russia and imposed unrealistic targets with respect to the speed at which price stabilization should be achieved. Lacking other policy levers, Russia relied exclusively on reducing the rate of growth of the money supply to tackle inflation. Since the tax system was inefficient, the government's budget remained in deficit, the gap being filled by heavy borrowing, including foreign borrowing. The result was a large inflow of foreign capital and a sustained appreciation of the real exchange rate, which reduced the competitiveness of Russian goods.

A number of economists, the most prominent being Joseph Stiglitz, believe that the IMF, in advocating the rapid adoption of a market economy, failed to recognize the importance of simultaneously transforming the societal and political components of the Russian polity. When Western countries moved from wartime to peacetime economies in 1945, there had been concerns about the difficulties of making the transition. Some controls remained in place for several years and the transition occurred gradually. This occurred in countries that, unlike Russia, already had the basic market institutions. In the case of Russia, the country's Western advisers advocated an immediate market revolution. Stiglitz believes that these "market fundamentalists" were motivated by the belief that institutions are irrelevant or that the necessary institutions would simply materialize once a market economy was established.

"Shock Therapists" and "Gradualists"

The various advisors to the Russian government differed in their views about how to best maintain the progress of economic transformation. Some experts advocated a kind of "shock therapy." They supported the rapid privatization of state assets in the belief that this was needed to create a class of people with a vested interest in capitalism. Without such a class there was a danger that the country might revert to Communism. Others favored a more "gradualist"

Emerging Economies: The BRICS Countries **169**

approach. They believed that if reforms were introduced too quickly there would be economic failures leading to a backlash against reform. These advisers emphasized the importance of "sequencing" reforms to make sure that the appropriate institutions, such as credit rating institutions and social security, were in place in advance of privatization and price liberalization.

The new government, headed by Boris Yeltsin, attempted to reform everything at once. Prices were immediately freed, except for basic food and fuel, and there was a rapid privatization of state-owned enterprises. The reforms were certainly successful in allowing a type of market system to emerge. A market-based exchange rate linked Russia to the world economy and a large part of the economy was privatized within a very short period. By 1995, 62 percent of GDP was produced in the private sector. At the same time, however, there were severe disruptions in the economy and in society. The breakdown in the command economy resulted in severe shortages of goods which, in combination with budget deficits, caused hyperinflation. As seen earlier, inflation reached over 2,500 percent in 1992. This high rate of inflation was partly a result of disagreements between the different centers of authority. The *duma* (parliament) and the central bank undermined the policies of the executive branch of government. Even within the executive realm there were sharp divisions between reformers, conservatives, and populist reactionaries. War in Chechnya further weakened the position of the government. With the decline of state power official corruption and organized crime flourished.

A notable feature of the Yeltsin era was the way in which the few prospered at the expense of the many. The economic reforms, combined with a climate of official corruption, led to a drastic increase in income and wealth inequality. This was in part due to the rapid rate of privatization, which favored insiders with political connections. Social and political tensions were made worse by a sharp rise in unemployment. Many state-owned enterprises were unable to compete in a market economy or could survive only through massive layoffs.

Failures of the 1990s

Critics of the policies of the 1990s focus on the following issues.

1. *Inflation.* While it was necessary to eliminate inflation, this should have been done more gradually. The high interest rates associated with a rapid tightening of monetary policy stifled new investment and contributed to the overvaluation of the exchange rate.

2. *Privatization.* This was implemented rapidly with little care as to how it was done. A lack of laws ensuring good corporate governance led to managers stealing assets from shareholders. Another problem was that the privatizations reduced the power of the central government but not that of local and regional governments, which could now use a host of taxes and regulations to extort "rents" from firms operating in their jurisdictions.

3. *Social capital.* The transition eroded what economists call "social capital," the glue that holds society together. People were seen to get rich not by working hard but by using political connections to buy state property cheaply.

4. *Shock therapy.* The sequencing of reforms is important, as China's more successful transition has shown, but little attention was paid to this in the Russian case.

5. *Dismantling of capital controls.* The liberalization of capital account transactions and the replacement of multiple exchange rates by a unified rate between 1991 and 1994 contributed to the problems the Russian economy was to face in 1997–1998. Many economists, including some who formerly advocated a rapid liberalization, now believe that the removal of controls over capital flows was premature, given the failure to put in place the institutions necessary for an efficiently running market economy. This was especially serious for a country in which corruption and lawlessness had become a major problem. For example, the lack of effective regulation made it easy for illegal arms merchants and the Russian mafia to transfer funds internationally.

Collapse of the Ruble in 1998

In 1997–1998 the Russian economy, already weak, was hit by two shocks. The first was the East Asian Crisis of 1997, which undermined market confidence in all the emerging economies. The second was a decline in oil and nonferrous metal prices, which reduced Russia's foreign exchange earnings. As a result, the current account balance turned negative and there was a flight of foreign capital from Russian government bonds. By August 1998, the government lacked the reserves needed to redeem the foreign share of the debt falling due in December 1998. The banks also had unsustainable foreign exchange liabilities. The Yeltsin administration saw itself faced with two options. It could borrow directly from the central bank to pay its domestic bills but this would increase the rate of growth of the money supply and wreck the price stability, which had been so hard won. Alternatively, it could force a nonvoluntary restructuring of the short-term debt. It chose the latter option. In August 1998 the Russian government devalued the ruble, defaulted on its domestic debt, and with the approval of the IMF declared a 90-day moratorium on payments by commercial banks to foreign creditors.

Putin's Russia

In 1999 and 2000 the situation improved: First, there was more stable political leadership. A centrist Duma was elected in 1999 and Vladimir Putin assumed the presidency in 2000. This reflected a desire on the part of the Russian electorate for strong, stable leadership. The new

Emerging Economies: The BRICS Countries   171

regime improved the efficiency of the taxation system and higher oil prices boosted government revenues. Second, the balance of payments improved. The depreciation of the ruble favored domestic producers, and higher world oil prices boosted export earnings as well as government revenues. During the following decade, under Putin's leadership, Russia's nominal GDP doubled, growing at an average rate of 7 percent per year. By 2007, GDP finally surpassed that of 1990, indicating that the economy had at last recovered from the recession associated with the transition to a market-based system. Russia also coped well with the global crisis of 2008. In 2008-2009 the country experienced a severe recession, but the recession was short lived. In 2009-2010, real GDP resumed its growth, while inflation was moderate and the ruble remained stable.

Nevertheless, there are still reasons for concern about the stability of the Russian currency. The economic success of Russia in the first decade of the twenty-first century was partly due to sound fiscal policies but it also owed much to high resource prices. The Russian economy remains heavily dependent on exports of commodities, particularly oil. One of the more unfortunate legacies of the transition from central planning to a market-based economy is that Russia has been transformed from a major manufacturing power into primarily an exporter of natural resources. The fiscal position also depends on the resource sector, with customs duties and taxes on fuel and energy accounting for nearly half of the federal government's revenues. Russia's continuing prosperity is therefore extremely vulnerable to a downturn in commodity prices. Other economic weaknesses are the income gap between rich and poor, which has grown even wider during the Putin years, and a lagging agricultural sector, which results in a heavy dependence on food imports.

TABLE 9.2. Russia. Rate of Growth of Real GDP Per Capita 1993-2016

Year	GDP Per Capita Growth (%)	Year	GDP Per Capita Growth (%)
1993	-8.8	2005	6.7
1994	-12.7	2006	8.4
1995	-4.0	2007	8.7
1996	-3.5	2008	5.5
1997	1.6	2009	-7.8
1998	-5.1	2010	4.5
1999	6.7	2011	4.0
2000	10.4	2012	3.5
2001	5.5	2013	1.2
2002	5.2	2014	0.7
2003	7.8	2015	-2.9
2004	7.6	2016	-0.2

Source: GDP Per Capita/Statistics from IMF, https://knoema.com/pjeqzh/
gdp-per-capita-by-country-statistics-from-imf-1980-2022

172   Chapter 9

China

China has the largest population and third largest land mass of the world's countries. It was characterized by chronic political instability from the collapse of the last imperial dynasty, the Qing, in 1912 until the Communist reunification of the country in 1949. After the establishment of the Communist government a system of centralized planning was put in place, which remained in operation until the introduction of market reforms. A series of plans were issued and directed by the State Planning Commission, under the supervision of the State Council and (ultimately) the Central Committee and Politburo of the Chinese Communist Party. The State Planning Commission controlled, or sought to control, the economy through a variety of levers, including the following:

1. Production targets were set for each farm and factory.

2. Supplies of raw materials and machinery were controlled by the state.

3. Workers were directed to specific factories or farms.

4. The prices of many commodities were kept artificially low and the goods rationed, while for other products consumption levels were manipulated through varying the prices at public retail outlets.

5. Factory wage rates were set directly by the planners.

6. Profit on the farms was divided up among households through a system of work points and total farm income was controlled by varying the price paid for quotas of output which were required to be sold to the state. These prices were generally kept low as a way of effectively taxing agriculture to support industrialization.

All this, of course, involved a monumental amount of paperwork. Even at the best of times central planning would have resulted in inefficiencies, as is evident from the experience of the Soviet Union. In a centrally planned economy the inability of consumers to signal demands through the price system inevitably means surpluses of some goods and shortages of others. This problem tends to be especially acute in large countries like China since it is difficult to collect the vast amount of information needed by the planners. As with the Soviet Union, the most serious weakness of the system was the lack of an effective incentive system. Workers faced no incentive to work hard since wages were fixed (they remained constant between 1957 and 1977) and there was job security, while managers had no incentive to exceed production targets or economize on resources.

In the case of China the above weaknesses of the planning system were made worse as the economic and political system was subjected to violent disruption during the Great Leap Forward (1958–1960) and the Cultural Revolution (1966–1976). Major changes in policy create problems for investors, producers, and workers even in a market economy, but the problems are much worse in a centrally planned economy. During the "Great Leap Forward," China's leader, Mao Zedong, launched a "Maoist" strategy, which included combining agricultural cooperatives into communes, emphasizing small-scale rural industrial production at the expense of urban manufacturing, eliminating private plots on the farms, and abolishing rural free markets. The result was disastrous. Grain output fell by 20 percent between 1957 and 1960 and the resulting famine caused 30 million deaths between 1958 and 1962, though a severe drought (1959–1961) certainly made the situation even worse than it would otherwise have been. During the Cultural Revolution (1966–1976), Mao seized power by encouraging young people, known as the "Red Guards," to attack his rivals within the party and the government. Skilled administrators and factory managers were replaced by ideologues, bonuses for factory workers and private plots for peasants were eliminated, and 16 million urban dwellers were relocated to the countryside. The economic consequences of these policies were disastrous. Even in good times, however, economic performance was generally mediocre in both the agricultural and industrial sectors.

Poster during the cultural revolution.

Problems with Agriculture and Industry

Agriculture

After 1957 agriculture was a major problem area. Grain production increased, but this increase barely exceeded the growth in population. Positive features were rural electrification and the introduction of agricultural machinery, but the effects of these developments on labor productivity were offset by the fact that, due to population growth and the reduction of rural idleness, the rural labor force grew by 100 million between 1957 and 1975, while there was no significant increase in the area under cultivation. An additional factor was the spread northward of rice cultivation (which is twice as labor intensive as wheat cultivation). As a result there was a decline in output per worker-day of 15 to 36 percent between 1957 and 1975. Peasant consumption remained at low levels because the small surplus was siphoned off by the state to finance industrial development. That a lack of incentives in agriculture, as in industry, hampered attempts to improve agricultural performance was evident from the difference in productivity between private plots and collective output in the communes. Each individual family in an agricultural commune had its own private plot, which it tended with loving care. Only a tiny proportion of farmland was in the form of private plots, but these generated about 30 percent of total agricultural output.

Industry

The Communist government was successful in achieving high rates of investment (in excess of 20 percent of GNP in most years) and the capital–labor ratio rose fivefold between 1952 and 1979. During the same period, however, output per worker increased only 2.8 times. This poor performance was partly due to the political turmoil associated with the Great Leap

174   Chapter 9

Forward and the cultural revolution. Between 1966 and 1976 (which included the cultural revolution) output per worker rose by only 11 percent, while, in contrast, it rose by 87 percent between 1962 and 1965. An overemphasis on heavy industry also contributed to the poor performance. An example of the effects of this can be seen from the experience of the steel industry. In 1979 China produced 34.5 million tons of steel at a time that 20 million tons of steel were lying unwanted in warehouses.

Economic Reforms in China Since 1978

In 1978 the Communist Party, now headed by Deng Xiaoping, announced a ten-year program of economic development. During the next three decades reforms were introduced in the following areas.

Agriculture

The program aimed for agricultural growth of 4 to 5 percent annually over the period 1978–1985. To provide peasants with an incentive to increase production the former collective lands were allocated to farm families, and by 1983 most collective agricultural activity had been replaced by household farming. In order to alleviate the shock of an abrupt transition from controlled (below market) prices to market prices, a dual-price system was established. Production quotas continued to be fixed and sold to the state at low, controlled prices but any surplus produced above the quota could be sold on free markets at free market prices. The policy was a resounding success in that growth rates of agricultural output rose from an annual average of 4 percent in 1971–1978 to 13 percent in 1982–1986. Since then there have been cuts in the compulsory state quotas and a growing proportion of China's food supply is provided through the free market. Nevertheless, a dual-price system remains, with some food provided at controlled prices much lower than the market prices. Unfortunately, this has contributed to a growth in corruption: Officials are tempted to sell price-controlled produce illegally on the free market, especially since official salaries have lagged behind inflation.

Population Control

Population growth was to be reduced to less than 1 percent per year within a three-year period. The "one child policy" was adopted to force a rapid decrease in China's rate of population growth.

Promotion of Foreign Trade

Increased exports would be required to pay for imports of technology. Prior to the reforms, international trade was controlled by twelve foreign trading corporations (FTCs). The reforms gradually opened trade by removing price controls and ending export subsidies. In order to minimize disruption to the domestic economy China created special economic zones (SEZs). Within these zones provincial and local governments were allowed extensive freedom to experiment with economic and trade policies. As part of the new emphasis in foreign trade China applied to join the GATT in 1986 and after difficult negotiations it was able to join the World Trade Organization (the successor of the GATT) in 2001.

Emerging Economies: The BRICS Countries   175

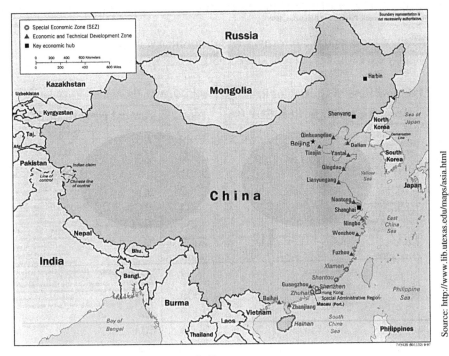

Map 9.1. China. Special Economic Zones

Industry

It was hoped that overall industrial growth of more than 10 percent per year would be achieved. Initially the emphasis was on the development of light consumer goods industries and large-scale projects to relieve bottlenecks in basic industries, such as fuel, electric power, metallurgy, and transportation but in more recent years there has been a focus on high technology industries. The education system, which now graduates more than 325,000 engineers each year, has concentrated on producing a labor force with the skills most relevant to high technology. A measure of the success of this strategy is the fact that China's exports grew eightfold between 1990 and 2003, and China now accounts for about a third of Asia's electronics exports. Ironically, in view of the political tensions between the Chinese and Taiwanese governments, a large part of this growth is due to Taiwanese companies moving their operations to the mainland to

Shenzhen, China.

176   Chapter 9

take advantage of cheaper labor. China has also benefited from Japan's continuing economic difficulties.

The effect of the economic reforms was extraordinary, with annual rates of growth of real GDP frequently exceeding 9 percent since 1980, as can be seen from Table 9.3.

TABLE 9.3. China. Rate of Growth of Real GDP 1980-2016

Year	Annual Growth of Real GDP (%)	Year	Annual Growth of Real GDP (%)
1980	7.9	1999	7.6
1981	5.3	2000	8.4
1982	9.0	2001	8.3
1983	10.9	2002	9.1
1984	15.2	2003	10.0
1985	13.5	2004	10.1
1986	8.9	2005	11.3
1987	11.6	2006	12.7
1988	11.3	2007	14.2
1989	4.1	2008	9.6
1990	3.8	2009	9.2
1991	9.2	2010	10.6
1992	14.2	2011	9.5
1993	13.9	2012	7.9
1994	13.1	2013	7.8
1995	10.9	2014	7.3
1996	10.0	2015	6.9
1997	9.3	2016	6.7
1998	7.8		

Source: GDP by Country/Statistics from IMF, knoema.com/tbocwag/
gdp-by-country-statistics-from-imf-1980-2022?country=China

In introducing these reforms, Deng had no intention of replacing Communism with capitalism but rather aimed to introduce a form of market socialism. This involved separating the ownership of the means of production from the control of production. Since there was no obvious model for China to follow, Deng and his supporters tended to proceed by trial and error. They would experiment by introducing a reform in a certain region or enterprise and, if it proved successful, extend the reform to the rest of the country. Since China is far from homogeneous, reforms that worked in one part of the country sometimes gave rise to unforeseen problems in other regions. The result was a frequent need to reverse policies.

A further complication was that authority in China was much more decentralized than in other Communist countries. Partly for strategic reasons and partly because he believed in local self-sufficiency (for ideological reasons) Mao had favored dispersing industry, especially heavy industry, away from existing industrial centres. As a result of this policy and because of an inadequate transportation system China was becoming a collection of segmented local economies that were largely self-sufficient. It was inevitable that much of the economic planning would be in the hands of provincial and municipal governments so that while China before 1978 had a government-controlled economy, this economy was only partly controlled by the *central* government. This fact has contributed to the difficulties faced in recent years by the Beijing government in maintaining control over the provinces, particularly those that have prospered most as a result of economic reform. A major feature of the reforms has been giving state enterprise managers more responsibility for day-to-day decisions relating to prices and production. Very frequently, however, powers relinquished by the planners in Beijing have been taken up not by enterprise managers but by local governments, which have proved very reluctant to surrender their power over local economies. This is understandable since the provincial and municipal authorities are faced with great demands which make them reluctant to give up opportunities for gaining revenues. Overpopulation has caused an exodus from the land and local governments are required to provide nonagricultural employment and social support to growing urban populations.

Continuing Challenges

Demographic Issues and Unemployment

Clearly all has not been plain sailing and a number of problems have emerged, either as a result of the reforms or because the reforms have been only partial. Major problems already challenging China's rulers and people include a growing urban–rural income gap, rising unemployment, overinvestment, and high levels of debt. Another problem, which will have to be addressed in the not too distant future, is the challenge of providing for an aging population. This is a side effect of the dramatic fall in birth rates as a result of the one-child policy. By 2030 a quarter of the country's population will be over age sixty-five. This could be an especially serious problem for China since, unlike the industrialized countries of the West, it does not have pension funds.

Now that guaranteed employment is a thing of the past, a social security system is also needed to provide for the unemployed. Unemployment has grown as a result of massive layoffs in state-owned companies since 1998. These layoffs have not been matched by growth in employment in private firms, which has been limited by the fact that credit by the state-owned banks is still directed mainly toward state-owned enterprises. The proportion of loans made by the state-owned banks has, however, been declining relative to lending by new commercial banks, which is a promising development since these new commercial banks are more likely to favor the private sector. In an effort to reduce unemployment China has encouraged inflows of foreign direct investment (FDI) but this has been made more difficult by China's inability or unwillingness to enforce intellectual property rights. Some foreign firms refuse to invest out of a fear that their products will be copied.

Overinvestment and Underconsumption

On the other hand, if China were to have more success in attracting FDI it might create as many problems as it solved. It would increase the danger of overinvestment in capital-intensive

178   Chapter 9

production, which in turn would lead to high debt levels, declining profit rates, and bankrupt-cies. Overinvestment already exists in part because of the success of China's export industries. The resulting buildup of foreign exchange reserves has increased the rate of growth of the country's money supply with the result that an increased availability of credit has encouraged domestic firms to overinvest. In neighboring Asian countries similarly high rates of investment played a role in triggering the Asian crisis of 1997. That crisis was a result of foreign financing, which led to very high levels of foreign debt. Such a situation is unlikely to afflict China, for which domestic investment has been overwhelmingly financed by domestic savings rather than foreign capital inflows, but this does not mean that very high levels of investment will not create problems. As investment increases there is the natural tendency for returns on new investment to decrease. Eventually this leads to inefficient investment, with very low marginal returns on capital. Making this problem worse in China's case is the fact that investment is biased toward inefficient state-owned enterprises as a result of the state-dominated banking system being directed to channel funds to those enterprises.

An already high rate of investment increased still further when the Chinese government adopted policies to raise it in reaction to the global financial crisis between 2007 and 2011. This was an appropriate course of action at the time and, in the short run, was successful in reducing the severity of the crisis. In the longer run, however, it contributed to a situation in which Chinese firms and households have dangerously high levels of debt. In the first quarter of 2016 the debt–GDP ratio reached 237 percent.[1] This means that credit has to grow at an accelerating rate just to pay interest on existing loans and finance sufficient new investment to maintain current rates of economic growth, while the low marginal returns on capital referred to previously means that China now needs higher and higher levels of new investment just to generate this constant rate of growth. In an IMF Working Paper in 2012, Lee, Syed, and Liu estimated that the contribution of investment to growth would soon need to reach 60 to 70 percent of GDP to avoid a slowdown in the economy.[2] They also pointed out that with consumption declining to about 40 percent of GDP, the investment-led growth model has failed to adequately improve living standards.[3] After all, what is the point of a high rate of economic growth if it does not raise consumption levels?

The Chinese government is aware of this problem and is seeking to rebalance the economy by slowing investment growth and promoting competition. This is not, however, an easy task. One difficulty in bringing about the necessary shift is the high national saving rate, due in large part to the lack of a reliable social safety net to tide Chinese individuals through economic downturns and support them in retirement. An additional factor has been the one-child policy that came into force in 1980. This policy increased the need for saving since it undermined the tradition in which the elderly were supported in retirement by their children. The problem should become less acute in the future since the one-child policy will be replaced by a two-child policy beginning in 2017 but it may be years before the change has a significant impact on the rate of saving.

---

1. *Financial Times*, April 24, 2016.

2. Lee, Syed, and Liu (2012), p. 6.

3. Ibid., Lee, Syed, and Liu (2012), p. 7.

Emerging Economies: The BRICS Countries **179**

Other Challenges: State-Owned Enterprises, Regional Disparities, the Environment, and Exports

Other continuing problems relate to state-owned enterprises, regional disparities, environmental destruction, and the danger of increased foreign resistance to Chinese exports. Each of these issues is briefly described now.

1. By the year 2000, non-state firms were producing 75 percent of China's manufactures but the state-owned enterprises, which generally remain very inefficient, still provide much of the manufacturing employment in China and are badly in need of restructuring.

2. Regional disparities in income have widened considerably as a result of the reforms. As noted earlier, special economic zones (SEZs) have been created to promote development in promising regions, such as the Guangdong and Fujian provinces. Within these zones foreign investors are given tax advantages and local governments are permitted to keep a larger share of tax collections to finance infrastructure improvements. The result has been remarkable economic growth in the coastal provinces, especially Guangdong, which received half of all the foreign investment in China between 1978 and 1987. This has created resentment on the part of the inland provinces and also a great deal of interregional migration, although this is discouraged by the central government, which ties access to housing, education, and health services to place of employment.

3. Another problem of increasing concern is the deterioration of the environment. Industrial expansion in China has caused environmental destruction and severe pollution, especially, though not exclusively, in Chinese cities. China currently has sixteen of the twenty most polluted cities in the world. If the costs of environmental destruction were subtracted from its GDP, as perhaps it should be, China's rate of economic growth would fall from about 10 percent per year to about 2 percent.

4. The principal motive for China joining the World Trade Organization (WTO) in 2001 was to reduce the danger of restrictions on exports. Since China has emphasized labor-intensive exports and has become a center of low-wage manufacturing, it is seen by other countries as a threat to employment. There are also other developments that may threaten Chinese trade. For example, Western countries have outsourced production to China and at the same time cut back on health and safety restrictions on imports. As a result there have been some widely publicized cases of goods that do not meet Western safety standards being imported from China. Unless China raises and more effectively enforces tighter health and safety standards on its products there may be a backlash against its exports. This is made more difficult to achieve by the high levels of corruption among Chinese administrators.

180   Chapter 9

Impact of China's Expansion on the International Economy

China's economic rise has influenced the international economy through its effects on international payments, on the funding of U.S. government budget deficits, and its impact on the economies of other emerging economies. Each of these influences will be discussed in turn. With respect to international payments, China's persistent trade surpluses have resulted in claims by other countries that it has maintained an undervalued exchange rate, but this criticism now has less validity than it once had. Before 2005 the renminbi (RMB) was pegged to the U.S. dollar but in that year China adopted an exchange rate band using a trade weighted index of currencies instead of a dollar peg.[4] As a consequence the RMB can now appreciate relative to the U.S. dollar as the dollar declines in value in world markets. Between 2005 and 2011 the RMB has appreciated by 26 percent against the U.S. dollar (from ¥8.1917 per $1 in 2005 to ¥6.4718 per $1 in 2011).

China is a large funder of U.S. government debt. China's huge current account surplus and large inflows of foreign direct investment means that it has the largest foreign reserves of any country. It uses part of these reserves to buy foreign bonds, being currently responsible for about 15 percent of net purchases of U.S. government bonds. While this by itself may not seem sufficient to pose an overwhelming threat, it nevertheless raises concerns because any change in Chinese willingness to buy U.S. bonds will be very visible to the financial markets and might cause a snowball effect on other buyers of bonds.

Finally, China's spectacular growth has had both positive and negative effects on the economies of other emerging markets. Countries such as Mexico and Brazil, which used to count on low wage rates as an advantage in capturing foreign markets, can no longer do so because China can outcompete them in this regard. When China joined the WTO, for example, Mexico's export industries lost a large share of the clothing market. China has an advantage not only because of low wage rates but also because of its huge domestic market that enables it to gain economies of scale even before venturing into foreign markets. In terms of natural resources, however, China's growth has been very beneficial to resource producers in Latin America and Africa. Resources such as oil, iron ore, platinum, and aluminium have seen sharp rises in world prices, at least partly because of growing Chinese demand.

China and Russia: "Shock Therapy" versus "Gradualism"

Russia and China followed very different paths to reform. The Russian reformers moved quickly, trying to reform everything at once. In order for such a strategy to work, however, it was crucial that the economy be stabilized to prevent the emergence of unsustainable budget deficits and hyperinflation. The reformers were not successful at achieving this stability, partly because of the political turmoil associated with the breakup of the Soviet Union and ethnic tensions within the Russian Federation, but also because of stresses created by the process of economic reform itself. With the end of guaranteed employment there was a need to create social safety nets, while new financial markets needed new regulatory systems. Perhaps the most difficult task was the privatization of state-owned enterprises. Privatization is a complicated procedure even when it involves only one industry, but in Russia's case it involved

---

4. The renminbi (BMB) means "people's currency" and is the official currency of the People's Republic of China. Its primary unit is the *yuan*.

most of the economy. The end result was that a small group of insiders, the "oligarchs," gained the lion's share of the privatized assets.

This reform strategy had catastrophic effects in the short run and uncertain effects in the long run. In 1996 Russia's GDP was at 64 percent of its 1990 level.

In contrast to Russia, China adopted a strategy of piecemeal reforms. These were initially concentrated in agriculture and were then extended in the 1980s to various special economic zones. The policy was to implement a "gradualist" or "dual track" strategy. Reforms were initially limited to certain geographical areas or economic sectors while central planning remained in force in the rest of the economy. Gradually the market reforms were extended to more and more sectors and regions. In this way the structures of the market economy were introduced without bringing about a premature collapse of the centrally planned economy. The result was that China's economy did not contract at all throughout the reform years.

The "shock therapy" approach adopted in Russia has, however, its defenders. Supporters of the more rapid reform strategy believe that China's success was due not so much to the gradual nature of those reforms as to the fact that prior to the adoption of its reforms the bulk of its population was employed in low productivity agriculture. Since over 70 percent of the labor force was employed in agriculture in 1978, China was able to introduce reforms into the rural economy, which led to a large exodus of people from rural to urban areas with virtually no loss in output. It had a large reserve of surplus labor to staff the new urban-based industries. In Russia there was no such surplus of labor. Staffing the new industries meant withdrawing labor from existing manufacturing operations.

India

India, like China, has begun to exert an increasingly powerful impact on the global economy. India's impact on world trade, while substantial, however, is less than that of China, not only because it has a lower overall growth rate but because its manufacturing sector is much smaller and trade plays a smaller role in its economy. Since 1980 real GDP growth has averaged 6 percent per year in India, compared with 10 percent per year in China.

For the first thirty years after independence the economic policy of successive Indian governments was to promote industrialization in the hope that this would help to trigger progress in agriculture. In fact, however, the agricultural sector remained a drag on the overall economy. Small landowners and rich peasants acted together as a powerful pressure group opposing land reforms or increases in land taxes, which remained very low. Lacking alternatives, the government relied heavily on regressive indirect taxes for revenue. This benefited the higher income groups in both urban and rural areas at the expense of the poor. The industrial sector also failed to achieve its potential. A series of five-year plans was implemented which invariably emphasized the production of investment goods, which were seen as crucial to further economic growth. The result was an overemphasis on heavy industry.

There were signs of improvement in the 1980s when the growth rate increased with gains in industry especially notable in coal, oil, and automobile production. There were also promising signs in agriculture, largely due to an expansion of irrigation and the decade saw rapid growth in the production of both wheat and rice. These improvements were associated with

182   Chapter 9

changes in economic policy initiated by Rajiv Gandhi when he became prime minister in 1985. New policies included the introduction of a long-term fiscal plan intended to make future budgets more predictable and to generate a surplus in the government's budget. It was anticipated that such a long-term budget would, first, make long-term planning easier for the private sector and, second, eliminate inflation. Though the policies succeeded to the extent that there was an increase in growth in the 1980s, further progress was hindered by the opposition of powerful interest groups to necessary reforms. It took a crisis to provide the impetus for the more radical economic policies that have set India on the high growth path of the last two decades.

The Crisis of 1990

In August 1990 the Iraqi occupation of Kuwait pushed up oil prices and forced the evacuation of 150,000 Indian workers. The resulting crisis was particularly severe for India because of the nature of its balance of payments. In the past, trade deficits had been offset by surpluses on "invisibles" due to the funds sent home by Indians working in other countries. Disruption in the Middle East reduced the value of India's exports to West Asia and increased the cost of oil imports while at the same time the exodus of Indian workers from Kuwait reduced the value of repatriated incomes from Indians working overseas. The negative effects on India's current account triggered fears about the stability of the rupee and caused a withdrawal of funds by nonresident Indians. This had the effect of eroding India's foreign exchange reserves.

The crisis forced major changes in both economic policies. Manmohan Singh (at that time minister of finance) introduced a series of radical measures in the budget of July 1991. Major changes were made to policies affecting government expenditures and revenues, and foreign exchange. Subsidies were cut to reduce expenditures. The price of fertilizer, for example, was increased by 30 percent. On the revenue side, taxes were raised and it was announced that selected public enterprises would be privatized. Finally, the rupee was devalued by 18 percent in two steps and an IMF loan was requested to stem the loss of foreign exchange reserves. These measures were successful in coping with the immediate crisis. India's foreign exchange reserves increased from 25 billion rupees (in June) to 95 billion rupees (by the end of the year).

More generally, 1991 saw a shift away from import substitution industrialization toward an outward-oriented, market-based economy. In 1990 India's economy was highly regulated. A system of permits, sometimes known as the "License Raj," protected Indian businesses from both domestic and foreign competition.[5] Larger firms were often state owned. The losses of these generally inefficient state-owned enterprises were covered by government expenditures that might have been better devoted to improving the health, education, and transportation systems. As part of the 1991 reforms a new trade policy was implemented. Import licensing procedures were simplified, where they were not abolished outright, and firms engaged in foreign trade could now open foreign exchange accounts and borrow from foreign lenders. Quotas on imports were abolished and tariffs reduced from an average rate of 87 percent in 1990 to an average of 33 percent in 1994. Restrictions on foreign borrowing by firms were

---

5. The term "License Raj" was a reference to the centralized system of government in operation during the "British Raj," the period of British rule in India.

reduced and, as already seen, the rupee was devalued. The result was a dramatic increase in economic growth, as can be seen from Table 9.4.

TABLE 9.4. India. Rate of Growth of Real GDP 1980–2016

Year	Annual Growth of Real GDP (%)	Year	Annual Growth of Real GDP (%)
1980	5.3	1999	8.5
1981	6.0	2000	4.0
1982	3.5	2001	4.9
1983	7.3	2002	3.9
1984	3.8	2003	7.9
1985	5.3	2004	7.8
1986	4.8	2005	9.3
1987	4.0	2006	9.3
1988	9.6	2007	9.8
1989	5.9	2008	3.9
1990	5.5	2009	8.5
1991	1.1	2010	10.3
1992	5.5	2011	6.6
1993	4.8	2012	5.5
1994	6.7	2013	6.5
1995	7.6	2014	7.2
1996	7.6	2015	7.9
1997	4.1	2016	6.8
1998	6.2		

Source: GDP by Country/Statistics from IMF, knoema.com/tbocwag/
gdp-by-country-statistics-from-imf-1980-2022?country=India

To some extent the shift away from import substitution industrialization was forced on India by the crisis of August 1990, since it had reduced the ability of India to import the inputs of capital goods needed to support industrialization. The collapse of the Soviet Union played an even larger role, however, in forcing a rethinking of economic policy. This was partly because it had served as a model for India's version of central planning and partly because the Soviet Union had previously bought a variety of goods from India that could not easily be sold elsewhere.

The biggest gains were in output since 1991 have been in outsourcing and automobile production. India has become an exporter of services such as call centers and data processing firms, taking advantage of a large, relatively well-educated, English-speaking labor force. The automobile industry has also flourished, with labor productivity tripling in the 1990s. Backward industries remain, however. Restrictions on trade and foreign investment still stifle competition in industries such as banking and retailing. Productivity in Indian supermarkets is only 20 percent of the level in the United States, due to the persistence of small-scale, inefficient shops. India also has problems with its infrastructure (roads, electric power generation, airports and sea ports). China has invested heavily in infrastructure projects but India's infrastructure has fallen behind the needs of a rapidly growing economy.

A train in Delhi.

Brazil

Import Substitution and the Lost Decade

After World War II, Brazil adopted an import substitution industrialization (ISI) strategy, promoting the development of manufacturing industries for the local market. This strategy included the use of exchange controls to protect selected domestic industries and overvalued exchange rates to enable them to import equipment cheaply in terms of local currency. The ISI strategy was successful in promoting rapid growth in Brazil's economy for several decades. The average rate of economic growth during the 1950s was over 9 percent per year and, after a slowdown in the mid-1960s, economic growth was even more spectacular between 1968 and 1973. During that period the average rate of growth of GDP was 11.1 percent and annual growth in manufacturing output was 13.1 percent. Growth slowed during the 1970s as a result of the first oil shock of 1973, but still remained high at almost 7 percent per year between 1974 and 1980.[6] During those years, however, the foreign debt rose sharply as Brazil succumbed to the temptation to borrow large sums at the prevailing low interest rates. At this time, as a result of their greatly increased export incomes, the oil-exporting countries were flooding world financial markets with cheap "petrodollars."

There followed the "lost decade" of the 1980s when Brazil was hit simultaneously by a further sharp rise in the cost of oil imports (with the second oil shock of 1979) and by sharply increased interest rates on its foreign debt as central banks tightened monetary policy to counteract high inflation. Between 1981 and 2003 the rate of economic growth averaged less than 2 percent per year, which was below the rate of growth of the labor force. This low rate of economic growth, which reflected a very low rate of growth of labor productivity, kept down growth in tax revenues and deprived the state of the means to maintain transportation infrastructure, healthcare, and public education. Brazil's performance was particularly poor during

---

6. During the first oil shock the posted price of oil rose by almost 400 percent within the space of a few months.

the 1980s, when the annual growth in labor productivity was negative (–0.2 percent) but it was not very good in the 1990s, either.

Brazil's poor performance in terms of labor productivity, which was the primary cause of low economic growth, was a result of low rates of investment and low growth in total factor productivity. Total labor productivity depends on increases in the stock of physical capital (such as machinery or tools) and improvements in total factor productivity (TFP), the efficiency with which labor uses that capital. TFP, in turn, depends on technological change and improved worker training, referred to by economists as "human capital." Brazil's poor record in terms of TFP is not surprising given its very low rates of spending on education. It ranked very low in terms of university education even compared to low-income countries in Latin American.

In the absence of significant improvements in human capital, economic growth depended on increases in the stock of physical capital but this declined after 1990. Between 1965 and 1989 the rate of gross capital formation averaged 22.4 percent of GDP and labor productivity grew by 2.6 percent per year largely as a result of this high rate of investment. Between 1990 and 2003, however, capital formation was an average of 19.5 percent of GDP. The rate of investment would have been even lower if there had not been a high rate of foreign direct investment in Brazil during this period.

Inflation was also a major problem during the "lost decade," rising to more than 1,000 percent at the start of the 1990s, but was brought under control through the introduction of a stabilization plan known as the *Plano Real*, which included the introduction of a new currency, the *real*, pegged to the U.S. dollar. By pegging its currency to the dollar Brazil ensured that its price level could not deviate too far from that of the United States.

Brazil and the IMF

Brazil sought assistance from the IMF in 1998. Inflation, which fell from 1,927 percent in 1993 to 7 percent in 1997, had already been tamed and the economy was growing at a rate of 3 percent per annum but there were other problems. Brazil faced large budget deficits and a federal-provincial split in responsibility for government spending which made it difficult to bring deficits under control. The stabilization program recommended by the IMF had short-term and medium-term goals. A rise in interest rates was introduced to accomplish the short-term goal of stemming a capital outflow. The medium-term goal was to restore credibility to the management of public finances and it was believed that this would be best achieved through fiscal tightening. The IMF package failed, however, to accomplish even its short-term goal. Capital outflows continued and Brazil was forced to float the *real* in January 1999. At the same time inflation rose sharply.

On the recommendation of the IMF, austerity measures were then introduced, including lower social security payments and the privatization of state assets, to reduce inflation. Procedures were also introduced to increase fiscal transparency. The austerity program was successful in temporarily reducing inflation and bringing about a budget surplus in 2000 but Brazil's exports performed poorly and there was a current account deficit of 4.7 percent of

GDP in 2001. This brought about a further depreciation in the *real* and revived inflationary pressures.

When Luiz Inácio Lula da Silva assumed office as president of Brazil in 2003 he inherited an economy with low growth, high levels of government spending, and an unsustainable level of borrowing. As a left-wing politician he was regarded with suspicion by domestic and foreign investors. This suspicion turned out to be unfounded. During Lula's term of office the economy began to grow rapidly with growth rates ranging from 3.2 percent (in 2005) to 7.5 percent (in 2010), as shown in Table 9.5. The economic success of this period benefited from the policies of both Lula and his predecessor as president, Fernando Henrique Cardoso. First, exports increased as a result of the depreciation of the *real* in 1999. Second, Lula continued the anti-inflationary and liberalization policies of his predecessor. Interest rates were kept high to ensure a low rate of inflation. Third, his redistribution policy, the *Bolsa Familia*, strengthened social cohesion and increased human capital. The *Bolsa Familia* consisted of four programs that provided social security for previously marginalized groups and gave them improved access to primary education. Fourth, the accelerated growth program, a four-year program introduced in 2007, provided an estimated R504 billion in funding for infrastructure.

Luiz Inácio Lula da Silva.

TABLE 9.5. Brazil. Rate of Growth of Real GDP 1991–2016

Year	Annual Growth of Real GDP (%)	Year	Annual Growth of Real GDP (%)
1991	1.0	2004	5.8
1992	−0.5	2005	3.2
1993	4.7	2006	4.0
1994	5.3	2007	6.1
1995	4.4	2008	5.1
1996	2.2	2009	−0.1
1997	3.4	2010	7.5
1998	0.3	2011	4.0
1999	0.5	2012	1.9
2000	4.4	2013	3.0
2001	1.4	2014	0.5
2002	3.1	2015	−3.8
2003	1.1	2016	−3.6

Source: GDP by Country/Statistics from IMF, knoema.com/tbocwag/gdp-by-country-statistics-from-imf-1980-2022?country=Brazil

The achievements of the last decade are impressive, but Brazil's continuing success depends on the successful introduction of reforms in social security and business regulation. Brazil spends 5 percent of its GDP on pensions. If the social security system was in balance, without a cash flow deficit, this 5 percent would be available for spending on education and infrastructure or tax incentives for private sector investment. Strong public-sector unions, however, make reform of the public-sector pension system very difficult. There are also continuing problems in the terms of ease of doing business in Brazil. Reforms of the regulatory environment would go a long way toward improving long-term growth prospects.

South Africa

South Africa has the largest economy in Africa, accounting for almost one-quarter of the continent's total GDP. After South Africa received its independence from Britain in 1910, the ruling white minority imposed a system of racial domination on the black majority, which was formalized in 1948 as the apartheid system. Apartheid aroused widespread opposition both within South Africa and in the wider world. It led to internal unrest and the imposition of international sanctions. Eventually these internal and foreign pressures resulted in the end of apartheid and multiracial elections in 1994.

The government elected in 1994, headed by Nelson Mandela, inherited an economy weakened by many years of international sanctions and internal unrest. In an effort to increase economic growth the government introduced the Growth, Employment and Redistribution (GEAR) strategy in 1996. This was a neoliberal strategy aimed at imposing fiscal discipline and enticing foreign direct investment. The policy was successful in reducing the fiscal deficit but unemployment remained high. In 2000 Mandela's successor, Thabo Mbeki, accelerated economic liberalization, easing restrictive labor laws and privatizing state assets. The success of these policies can be seen from Table 9.6. Subsequently South Africa's GDP grew by 2.7 percent in 2001 and over the next seven years economic growth ranged between 2.9 and 5.4 percent per year. Growth was interrupted by a recession in 2008–2009 but resumed in 2010 and 2011.

Copper mine at Palabora, South Africa.

188   Chapter 9

TABLE 9.6. South Africa. Rate of Growth of Real GDP 1994-2016

Year	Annual Growth of Real GDP (%)	Year	Annual Growth of Real GDP (%)
1994	3.2	2006	5.6
1995	3.1	2007	5.4
1996	4.3	2008	3.2
1997	2.6	2009	-1.5
1998	0.5	2010	3.0
1999	2.4	2011	3.3
2000	4.2	2012	2.2
2001	2.7	2013	2.5
2002	3.7	2014	1.7
2003	2.9	2015	1.3
2004	4.6	2016	0.3
2005	5.3		

Source: GDP by Country/Statistics from IMF, knoema.com/tbocwag/
gdp-by-country-statistics-from-imf-1980-2022?country=South%20Africa

South Africa's success since 1994 is due both to sound macroeconomic policies and to the growth in commodity prices as a result of China's extraordinary industrial growth. South Africa is rich in natural resources and agriculture.

The country has yet, however, to overcome the following economic and social problems.

1. *A shrinking labor force and high unemployment.* The number of individuals in the formal economy has declined since 1994 and at the same time unemployment has risen, reaching 24.8 percent in 2010, according to IMF estimates.

2. *Income inequality.* The high rate of unemployment has added to an already high rate of income inequality. There has been some decrease in income inequality between the races since the end of apartheid but this has been offset by an increase in intra-racial inequality associated with the rise of an African elite.

3. *Low levels of education.* Only 15 percent of South African students move on to higher education. As a result the country has a severe shortage of skilled labor.

4. *Low rates of saving.* Savings and investment rates are constrained by uncertainties associated with high levels of crime and corruption.

5. *Energy supply.* The growth in the supply of electricity has lagged behind the growth in demand.

6. *Health issues.* South Africa has very high rates of HIV.

References

Books

Bagchi, A. K., and D'Costa, A. P. (Eds.). (2013). *Transformation and development: The political economy of transition in India and China.* New Delhi: Oxford University Press.

Brainardi, L., and Martinez-Diaz, L. (Eds.). (2009). *Brazil as an economic superpower?* Washington, DC: Brooking Institution Press.

Chang, Y.-W., and De Haan, J. (Eds.). (2013). *The evolving role of China in the global economy.* Cambridge, MA: MIT Press.

Eichengreen, B., Gupta, P., and Kumar, R. (Eds.). (2010). *China and India in the world economy.* Oxford: Oxford University Press.

Eichengreen, B., Park, Y. C., and Wyplosz, C. (Eds.). (2008). *China, Asia and the new world economy.* Oxford: Oxford University Press.

OECD. (2010). *Economic survey of South Africa.* Paris: OECD.

Rothermund, Dietmar. (1993). *An economic history of India* (2nd edition). London: Routledge.

Articles

Desai, Padma. (2003). The ruble collapses in August 1998. In *Financial crises, contagion, and containment: From Asia to Argentina* (pp. 136–161). Princeton, NJ: Princeton University Press.

Stiglitz, Joseph E. (2002). Who lost Russia? In *Globalization and its discontents* (pp. 133–165). New York: W.W. Norton and Co.

Stracke, Christian. (2004). Structural weaknesses and country risk: The case of Brazil. In Sam Wilkin (Ed.), *Country and political risk: Practical insights for global finance.* London: Risk Books.

Online Articles

Carvalho, Laura. (2017). Facing unemployment, austerity and scandal, Brazil struggles to keep it together. The Conversation, https://theconversation.com/facing-unemployment-austerity-and-scandal-brazil-struggles-to-keep-it-together-71663

FocusEconomics. (2017). Economic forecasts from the world's leading economists. China economic outlook, http://www.focus-economics.com/countries/china

Ilnu, Ayush. (2012). Globalization & its impact on Indian economy: Developments and challenges, http://www.legalservicesindia.com/article/article/globalization-&-its-impact-on-indian-economy-developments-and-challenges-1018-1.html

Chapter 10

East Asia: The Development State

The "development state" refers to an economic and political system, characteristic of several countries in East Asia, in which the economy is generally market based but the state provides a strong guiding hand. This definition is sufficiently broad to encompass several countries that are quite varied in terms of their economic experience. For this reason it is convenient to place the "development states" of East Asia into four categories.

1. China, the largest of the East Asian countries—a country in the process of transition from a centrally planned system to a market-based economy.

2. Japan, the second largest East Asian country—the first to industrialize and, to some extent, a model for the others.

3. The newly industrialized countries (NICs)—which consist of South Korea, Taiwan, Hong Kong, and Singapore. They have achieved high-income status within the last forty years.

4. The high-performing Southeast Asian countries—Indonesia, Malaysia, the Philippines, and Thailand have more recently been following, with varying degrees of success, the path established by the NICs. In contrast to Japan and the NICs, these countries tend to be relatively well endowed with natural resources.

China, as a special case, has already been covered in chapter 9. This chapter will describe the economies of Japan and the small and midsize East Asian countries.

Economic Growth and Exports

In 1997, the region experienced a devastating economic crisis. In the preceding years, however, few were predicting disaster for East Asia. Rather the attention of most observers was focused on the "Asian miracle." In some respects the term "miracle" was an exaggeration (as was the expression "Asian meltdown," later used as a description of Asia's experience at the end of the twentieth century), but there is no doubt that in the decades immediately before 1997 the economies of the region experienced remarkable growth. The overall economic growth of the NICs, the Southeast Asian countries, and the People's Republic of China averaged 7.7 percent per annum between 1971 and 1992, although this average disguises significant national variations. These high rates of growth were accompanied by high savings and investment rates. During the 1980s savings rates were generally above 30 percent (43 percent in the case of Singapore).

190

Map 10.1. East Asia

This remarkable economic growth during the later years of the twentieth century was accompanied by major structural changes in the East Asian economies. This is not surprising since countries going through a period of rapid growth generally experience major changes in their economic structure. Rising incomes bring about an increase in the share in consumption of goods for which demand is income elastic, meaning that an increasing proportion of rising incomes is spent on manufactured goods and services, while the share of income spent on basic foodstuffs decreases since demand for them is relatively unresponsive to changes in income. On the supply side of the economy improvements in technology increase labor productivity substantially in agriculture and manufacturing but less so in services. Consequently, employment in the services sector increases as the growing demand for the output of that sector can only be satisfied through increasing the proportion of the labor force employed in services.

The expected structural shifts occurred to a greater or lesser degree in the East Asian economies. In almost all the countries of the region the share of agriculture in employment and output shrank between 1970 and 1993, the major exceptions being Hong Kong and Singapore, where the agricultural sector was already small to begin with. The decline in the

192   Chapter 10

share of agriculture was especially marked in South Korea but was also notable in Indonesia and Thailand. The expected increase in the share of services also occurred in the East Asian economies with the exception of South Korea, which saw a slight shift away from services toward manufacturing.

The industrialization of East Asia was fueled by exports. In this respect the economies of the region differed from emerging economies in other parts of the world, such as Latin America, which had promoted industrialization by producing manufactured goods for their domestic markets. Between 1965 and 1989 exports from the East Asian region grew at an annual average rate of 15.5 percent for the newly industrialized countries and an average rate of 7 percent per year for the high-performing economies of Southeast Asia. During the last two decades of the twentieth century there was also a large increase in the Asian share of world foreign direct investment (FDI). Between 1985 and 1990 Japan's share of outward flows of FDI increased from 11.1 to 22.1 percent, while that of the NICs increased from 0.7 to 3 percent. If we look at inward flows the most striking result is the increased share of the Southeast Asian countries. Their share of inward flows of FDI rose from 2.5 to 4.3 percent at a time when there was a substantial increase in FDI worldwide.[1]

Since 1970 intraregional trade (trade of Asian countries with other Asian countries) has grown even more quickly than trade between the Asian region and the rest of the world, in contrast to trends in the earlier part of the twentieth century. A regional bias is also evident in the dominance of Japanese banks in foreign lending to the East Asian economies, while recent decades have seen an increase in labor mobility between the countries of East Asia. There are several reasons for this increasing concentration of trade and investment within the region. One explanation is that it is simply a restoration of a long-standing historical pattern. In 1938 intraregional trade accounted for about 59 percent of total international trade for the Asia-Pacific region, about the same as its present share. After World War II, however, there was a sharp decrease in the share of intraregional trade, for two major reasons. First, after the war Japan's economy was in ruins so that countries which had previously imported Japanese manufactures now had to find alternative sources of manufactured goods outside the region. Second, as a result of the Cold War the United States provided massive amounts of foreign aid to South Korea and Taiwan. Much of this aid had military purposes, but it naturally resulted in the recipient countries importing more American goods. In the late 1950s, however, Japan resumed its status as an industrial giant and in the 1980s the Cold War ended. More recently, the extraordinary growth of China's economy has had the effect of accelerating the tendency for a growing share of world trade to be concentrated within Asia.

Various explanations have been proposed for this remarkable growth in the East Asian economies. In particular, attention has been focused on the degree to which government policies helped or hindered growth in output and exports. In addressing these issues it is appropriate to start with an account of the economic development of Japan, the first Asian country to industrialize.

---

1. Islam and Chowdhury (1997) provide details of FDI inflows and outflows in their Table 1.10.

Japan

As the first Asian country to industrialize, Japan merits special attention. The "Flying Geese" model, developed by Kaname Akamatsu, saw the East Asian economies as following, at different times, a pattern of development originated by Japan (which he regarded as the leading "goose"). In this scenario the NICs followed the path set by Japan a generation or so earlier and were themselves imitated at a later stage by the Southeast Asian countries.

The implication of the "Flying Geese" model is that the origins of the Asian "development state" lie in nineteenth-century Japan. In 1854 the American Commodore Perry sailed into Tokyo Bay with a fleet of warships and forced Japan's rulers to open up their country to the outside world. Aware of how neighboring countries were being conquered or dismembered by Western powers, a group of young samurai overthrew the ruling shogunate in 1868 in the name of the Emperor Meiji and began the era of radical reforms known as the Meiji Restoration (1868–1912).[2] This was essentially a period of authoritarian military government. It was believed that national independence could be maintained only with a strong, modern army, which would require a modern economy, hence the slogan "Strong economy, strong army." Since the reformers believed that time was against them, Japan would need to modernize quickly but, as it was a poor country lacking capital and entrepreneurs with experience in operating modern technologies, only the government had the resources and personnel to achieve this goal. This marked the beginning of a long tradition of government intervention in the economy. The emphasis at the time was naturally on the expansion of industries directly related to military needs, such as iron and steel, and on labor-intensive industries in which Japan, with its low wages, would have a comparative advantage, such as textiles.

Another tradition was established when, for financial reasons, the government sold state assets on a large scale in the 1880s. These assets, including factories, were picked up by a small number of individuals who usually had connections with the government leaders. Giant industrial conglomerates, known as *zaibatsu*, with close links to the state, emerged, while small businesses and farms also began to flourish as the economy picked up steam. This pattern of large firms and small firms coexisting side by side, known as "dualism," has persisted to the present day.

The militaristic state which subsequently developed in the twentieth century led Japan into disaster in World War II but much of the economic system created during the Meiji period was revived in a modified form after the war. The military emphasis is no longer in place but the tradition of large corporations with close government ties has continued, though the conglomerates are now known as *keiretsu* rather than *zaibatsu*.

The Japanese Economic "Miracle"

It took time to recover from the devastation of the Second World War and Japan's GDP did not return to its prewar level until 1954, but the country then entered a period of economic expansion. An upturn in the economy in 1955 was followed by thirty-five years of high growth with

---

2. Prior to 1868 the Emperor had become a primarily religious figure and political power was exercised by a ruler known as the "Shogun."

only brief interruptions. In 1961 the government announced a plan which anticipated future growth of 7.2 percent per year, but this turned out to underestimate the long-term average growth rate between 1950 and 1973, which averaged 10.5 percent per year. In comparison, the annual growth rate of world GDP in this period averaged only 4.7 percent. Reasons that have been put forward to explain the spectacular growth rate of the Japanese economy include a "dualist" economic structure, high rates of saving and investment, industrial policies, and an emphasis on international trade. Each of these will now be considered in turn.

Dualism

Rural Japan.

To a greater extent than in most other industrialized countries, Japan's economy has long been characterized by the persistence of "dualism." Alongside large modern corporations with high levels of productivity there exists a sizeable small business sector with much lower levels of productivity. For decades these small firms benefitted the large corporations in three ways. First, they provided a pool of inexpensive labor that could be drawn upon if the big firms wished to expand their labor forces. Second, the smaller, less technologically advanced firms bought old equipment from the more modern firms, thus creating a secondhand market for capital goods. This effectively reduced the cost to the corporations of replacing old machinery. Finally, the small firms acted as a buffer against the business cycle. In good times the large corporations would contract out work to the small firms, while in bad years it would be the small firms that would shut down.

The existence of a buffer against the business cycle enabled the large firms to develop worker loyalty by providing stable employment to their workforces. Until recently it was generally believed that a strong tie between firms and their employees was one of Japan's major economic strengths. Firms guaranteed lifetime job security, which was obviously desirable to employees but also had advantages from the point of view of the firm. The major advantage was that workers were more likely to cooperate in the introduction of new and improved methods of production since these represented no threat to their job security. There were also potential disadvantages, however, as lifetime employment required constant retraining of the labor force, which became less specialized than was true in other industrial countries, while promotion tended to be based on seniority rather than talent. Over the last twenty years the seniority system and lifetime employment have declined in importance because of enormous changes in production processes, including the introduction of industrial robots and widespread restructuring of industry. Increasingly Japanese firms have emphasized financial incentives (payment by merit). At the same time, the small business sector, heavily protected by regulations and subsidies, has come to be seen as a drag on the economy because of its low productivity levels.

Savings and Investment

Japan has very high savings rates and correspondingly high investment rates. By the late 1980s capital formation amounted to about 25 percent of GNP in spite of the fact that investment opportunities in Japan were diminishing as the rate of economic growth slowed. Much Japanese investment in this period flowed to other countries, notably to the United States with its large current account deficits, but there was also overinvestment domestically, and this was to be a factor in the recession of 1991–1994. Several explanations for Japan's high savings rates have been put forward, most of which apply equally well to the other high saving countries of East Asia. First, growth rates in income were very high, since consumption patterns generally lag behind changes in income. A "virtuous cycle" emerged in which Japanese consumers were constantly basing their consumption levels on last year's income, which was much lower than this year's. This resulted in high levels of saving, which led to high levels of investment and continuing high rates of income growth, so that consumption continued to lag behind income. The argument is plausible but is obviously not the whole story since Japanese savings continued to be high even after growth started slowing down in the 1980s. A second explanation for high rates of saving and investment is that the taxation system favors savings. Japanese taxes tend to be indirect, hitting consumption more than income. Finally, in common with other East Asian countries, Japan has an inadequate social security system. Since the Japanese system of social welfare is far from generous, people have to save in order to provide for themselves in case of old age or sickness, though to some extent the lack of state provision is made up for through generous company pension plans and health benefits.

Factory in Kawasaki.

Industrial Policy

In the 1950s the Japanese government, as part of a strategy to reduce current account deficits, imposed a wide range of controls on foreign exchange and imports and introduced policies to promote exports. Initially, preference was given to basic industries, such as iron and steel, heavy industries, and chemicals, and involved mainly importing and copying old technology from overseas in a process known as "improvement engineering." Later in the decade the emphasis shifted to more advanced industries, such as shipbuilding, televisions, and radio-optical equipment. In the 1960s the Japanese government promoted higher technology industries,

196   Chapter 10

including consumer electronics, machine building, and automobiles. In the 1970s and 1980s the emphasis was on computer hardware.

These government policies accorded with the tradition of close cooperation between the government and the private sector established since the Meiji period. The means used to influence the economy evolved over time. During the 1950s government intervention was very direct, including the use of exchange controls and import quotas. In the 1960s its intervention became more subtle, involving provision of some subsidies and "administrative guidance," which meant proffering "advice" to firms, backed up with some government pressure. The effectiveness of such policies remains the subject of controversy. Japan's economy undoubtedly performed extremely well for thirty-five years, but there are different opinions about to what extent this was due to government policies. It is likely that government intervention was sometimes useful but was not the sole cause of Japanese economic success and sometimes played a negative role.

An example of an apparently successful industrial policy was the promotion of the semiconductor industry. Until the mid-1970s the industry was largely a U.S. monopoly but by the late 1970s Japanese producers were capturing a growing share of the world market. The industry was supported by the government, partly with small direct subsidies, but mainly by more subtle methods, such as joint government–private sector research projects and state encouragement of a "Buy Japanese" policy. The direct returns on investment in semiconductors is relatively low, which implies that government support was necessary for the growth of the industry. Such support was worthwhile since the semiconductor industry is dynamic, with technological spinoffs that are beneficial to other industries.

While an argument can be made for industrial policy as having been helpful in some industries, however, there are also counterexamples, and the negative features of Japanese government intervention became more apparent as the economy slowed down. Some of the most successful Japanese companies have thrived without official support or even in the face of government opposition. It is also clear that overregulation has contributed to inefficiency in some sectors, notably agriculture and services. Japan's agricultural sector is highly protected and Japanese food prices are about twice as high as those in neighboring Asian countries. This has led to demands for trade liberalization from countries that hope to increase food exports to Japan. At the same time, regulations are hampering progress in the service sector. A well-known example was the prohibition, until 1998, of self-service at gasoline stations, which, because of the high wages of service station attendants, added considerably to consumer gasoline prices.

International Trade

In the 1950s Japan began with little to export and substantial import needs to rebuild industries destroyed during the war. Raw materials and machinery would have to be imported but since Japan had few natural products and its manufacturing industries were badly damaged, it was difficult to get foreign exchange to pay for these imports. This was one of the reasons for Japan's adoption of controls over imports and foreign exchange at the time. In the 1960s, however, things turned around and there began a long period of export-led growth, as is evident from Table 10.1, which indicates the increase in exports by value between 1955 and 1970.

East Asia: The Development State **197**

The growth rate of Japanese exports in the 1960s averaged 16.9 percent per annum, twice the growth rate of world trade in general.

TABLE 10.1. Japanese Exports by Value (1955–1970)

Year	Value of Exports (in U.S. dollars)
1955	$2 billion
1960	$4.1 billion
1970	$19.3 billion

One result of this success was that other countries became less tolerant of Japanese trade restrictions. In response to pressure from other countries there was some liberalization during the 1960s but progress was slow and largely consisted of a shift from tariffs to nontariff barriers. There was somewhat more progress during the 1970s and 1980s, when further liberalization resulted in significant reductions in tariffs. At the same time the yen appreciated, which should have led to an increase in imports. Japan's import/GDP ratio nevertheless remained low compared to that of other industrial countries. Studies of the Japanese economy in the 1980s usually attributed this either to government policies, notably nontariff barriers, or to Japanese consumer resistance toward foreign goods. Things only began to change after the Plaza Accord (1985), which caused a sharp appreciation of the yen. Japanese imports then rose from US$129 billion in 1986 to US$237 billion in 1991.

Economic Setbacks

As can be seen from Table 10.2, the Japanese economy appeared to be performing well throughout most of the 1980s, but it was then that the seeds of Japan's later problems were sowed. Difficulties began with the Plaza Accord of September 1985. At that time the Group of Five (G5) large industrial countries (the United States, Japan, West Germany, France, and Britain) agreed to a readjustment of exchange rates. As a result the yen appreciated by 92 percent against the U.S. dollar between 1985 and 1988. This resulted in the "high yen" (*endaka*) recession when the growth of the Japanese economy slowed in 1986. The recession proved to be brief, lasting only a year, but the policies adopted to fight it helped to bring about fundamental changes in Japan's economy. A postrecession boom lasted from 1986–1991 but, unlike earlier booms, it was based not on exports but on domestic demand, which proved to be fragile. The boom was the result of the monetary policy adopted to counteract the recession. The Bank of Japan lowered interest rates to support investment in high technology industries. Because of the high value of the yen, however, these industries found it more profitable to produce for the domestic market than for export. The emphasis on domestic consumption was also supported by a rise in the real incomes of consumers as the yen appreciated, causing a decrease in the price of imported goods.

At the same time, the combination of rising real incomes and low interest rates led to speculation in real estate and the stock market, giving rise to a "bubble economy." From 1985–1989

198   Chapter 10

stock prices rose 212 percent, while land prices increased 196 percent. It was the bursting of this bubble in 1991 that marked the beginning of a severe recession followed by prolonged economic stagnation. The Nikkei stock market index fell by 62.3 percent between December 1989 and August 1992. Land prices held up longer but then fell in 1991 by 15 percent.

The collapse in stock and real estate prices was triggered by a change in monetary policy. In 1989 the government and the central bank became concerned about asset inflation and the monetary stance was tightened sharply in May 1989. Over the next two years asset values went into a tailspin, causing a severe recession between 1991 and 1994. Since then the Japanese economy has experienced low rates of economic growth and even this less-than-impressive result has been achieved only through a sustained fiscal expansion that raised the public debt to 233 percent of GDP by 2011, the largest proportion for any industrialized country.

TABLE 10.2. Japan. Rate of Growth of Real GDP 1980-2016

Year	Annual Growth of Real GDP (%)	Year	Annual Growth of Real GDP (%)
1980	3.2	1999	-9.3
1981	4.2	2000	2.8
1982	3.4	2001	0.4
1983	3.1	2002	0.1
1984	4.5	2003	1.5
1985	6.3	2004	2.2
1986	2.8	2005	1.7
1987	4.1	2006	1.4
1988	7.1	2007	1.7
1989	5.4	2008	-1.1
1990	5.6	2009	-5.4
1991	3.3	2010	4.2
1992	0.8	2011	-0.1
1993	0.2	2012	1.5
1994	0.9	2013	2.0
1995	2.7	2014	0.3
1996	3.1	2015	1.2
1997	1.1	2016	1.0
1998	-1.1		

Source: GDP by Country/Statistics from IMF, knoema.com/tbocwag/
gdp-by-country-statistics-from-imf-1980-2022?country=Japan

A combination of factors accounts for the recession and the subsequent underperformance of the economy. The collapse of asset values when the bubble economy burst reduced the level of wealth and caused a drop in consumer spending. This was made worse by a credit crunch caused by the collapse of the real estate market, which left the banks with nonperforming loans and made them reluctant to engage in new lending. Recovery was made more difficult by the fact that low interest rates had caused overinvestment in the late 1980s and left the economy with an excess capacity. Finally, Japan is facing a demographic crisis. A high birth rate during and immediately after the Second World War, combined with a very low birth rate since then, has meant that Japan has the world's most rapidly aging population with over 20 percent of its people over the age of 65, a proportion that is continuing to grow. An aging population places greater strain on the health system and social services and reduces the proportion of adults in the labor force.

The Emerging Economies of East Asia

In Akamatsu's "Flying Geese" model the smaller countries of East Asia followed the path of economic development previously laid out by Japan. This was partly a result of investment by Japanese firms in neighboring countries and partly a result of the impression made on the governments of these countries by the evident success of Japanese economic policies. The newly industrialized countries were the first to follow the example of Japan during the 1960s and the high-performing Southeast Asian countries subsequently followed the NICs in the 1970s and 1980s.[3] The impressive rates of growth achieved by some of these countries are indicated in Table 10.3. Interest in the East Asian economies has long been focused on the role of public policy in promoting economic development. The major arguments for and against the interventionist policies characteristic of the "development state" will be discussed below. More recently attention has also been drawn to issues related to the financial sector. Weaknesses in the financial sector and in regulatory systems, which bear at least part of the blame for the crisis of 1997, will also be discussed.

Everett - Art/Shutterstock.com

---

3. Hong Kong is an exception among the NICs in that its government has largely avoided the openly interventionist policies characteristic of Japan and the other East Asian countries.

Table 10.3. Selected East Asian Countries. Rates of Growth of Real GDP 1980-1996

Year	South Korea	Thailand	Malaysia	Indonesia
1980	-1.7	4.6	7.4	9.9
1981	7.2	5.9	6.9	7.6
1982	8.3	5.4	5.9	2.2
1983	13.2	5.6	6.3	4.2
1984	10.4	5.8	7.8	7.6
1985	7.8	4.6	-0.9	3.9
1986	11.2	5.5	1.2	7.2
1987	12.5	9.5	5.4	6.6
1988	11.9	13.3	9.9	7.0
1989	7.0	12.2	9.1	9.1
1990	9.8	11.6	9.0	9.0
1991	10.4	8.4	9.5	8.9
1992	6.2	9.2	8.9	6.5
1993	6.8	8.7	9.9	8.0
1994	9.2	8.0	9.2	7.5
1995	9.6	8.1	9.8	8.2
1996	7.6	5.7	10.0	7.8

Source: GDP by Country/Statistics from IMF, knoema.com/tbocwag/gdp-by-country-statistics-from-imf-1980-2022?

Public Policy: The "Development State"

Prior to 1997 economic analysis of the East Asian economies was generally concerned with explaining the very high rates of economic growth that had been enjoyed by most of the countries of the region since the 1960s. Some explanations of this "economic miracle" have deemphasized the role of government policy, stressing instead other characteristics of the NICs and Southeast Asian countries. The first of these was the advantages of "backwardness," by which countries could grow through a process of "catching up." Since it is obviously easier to modify or improve existing technology than to invent that technology in the first place, countries in the early stages of industrialization can achieve very rapid rates of economic growth by simply copying the practices of already industrialized countries. Once the imitator's economy has "matured" (or caught up), however, growth

rates will inevitably slow down. While catching up may be part of the reason for high growth rates in Asia, it is clearly not the whole story since not all developing or partly industrialized countries experience high rates of economic growth.

The Asian "miracle" has also been attributed to rapid capital accumulation associated with high rates of savings. Discussions of the role played by capital accumulation usually begin with the growth accounting identity in which the expansion in output of an economy (Q) is a result of the contribution of physical capital, such as machinery (K), the contribution of labor (L), and growth in total factor productivity (TFP):

Growth in Q = Contribution of K + Contribution of L + Growth in TFP

The contribution of capital is the result of savings and investment, the contribution of labor is due to growth in the size and skill levels of the labor force, while growth in total factor productivity refers to any growth in output not directly attributable to changes in the quantity and productivity of either labor or capital. It reflects such factors as improvements in organization, institutions, and technology. As a result of growth accounting exercises, Alwyn Young (1992) and Paul Krugman (1994) came to the conclusion that growth in total factor productivity is not particularly high for the East Asian economies when compared with TFP in other regions of the world. Instead, most of the growth in the Asian economies can be attributed to their very high saving and investment rates. This is not a universally held view. The statistics have been challenged and even if Asian growth rates can be explained by high saving and investment rates, these may themselves be a result of government policies. Economists who believe that public policies have been important, however, do not necessarily agree on which policies have had the most positive effect. On this issue there are two major schools of thought. The "neoclassical" approach emphasizes outward-oriented policies, while the "functional" approach emphasizes a variety of policies, including (but not limited to) trade policies.

The "orthodox" or "neoclassical" view is that the success of the East Asian economies was due to outward-oriented policies, particularly open trade policies. These were beneficial not because of the principle of comparative advantage described in chapter 1, but because of the dynamic effects of freer trade. Advocates of outward-oriented policies stress productivity growth resulting from openness to international competition, the advantages of economies of scale as a result of selling to world rather than just domestic markets, and the advantages of greater access to foreign technology that comes from openness to international trade and investment. On the other hand, critics of the neoclassical approach have pointed out the NICs and Japan, usually cited as the best examples of the benefits of open trade policies, have not consistently pursued such policies. Japan, South Korea, and Taiwan have all, at least until very recently, tended to combine promotion of exports with the protection of domestic producers.

Supporters of more openly interventionist economic policies propose a "functional approach," which emphasizes both "policy fundamentals" and "selective intervention." Policy fundamentals are policies designed to create a favorable environment for the private sector and include sound macroeconomic policies and investments in human capital through promoting education. Selective intervention describes industrial policies, which are designed to promote specific industries or sectors of the economy considered to be strategic. An example of selective intervention would be export incentives for specific industries. Clearly such government

202   Chapter 10

intervention can only be successful if policies are well designed. Consequently, advocates of the functional approach place a great deal of emphasis on institutional frameworks. More specifically, supporters of industrial policies emphasize deficiencies in the market system, while critics of such policies emphasize deficiencies in government decision making.

Market Failure and Government Failure

After the crisis of 1997 the East Asian countries came under pressure to reduce the degree of government intervention in their economies, and it is clear that inefficiencies had emerged in a number of countries. Prior to 1997, however, the NICs in particular were often recommended as models of sound economic management. The extensive government intervention that characterized most of them was justified on the grounds of "market failure," a term describing a situation in which private (market) decisions are not socially optimal. Market failures may arise as a result of "externalities," which occur when the activities of one consumer or producer affect the welfare of others in ways not reflected in market prices. They may be either positive or negative. An example of a positive externality would be when a firm provides training for workers later employed by other firms, while a negative externality would occur if a company discharges effluent into a river, which provides a water supply for others. The point is that the producers of positive externalities are not sufficiently rewarded for these activities and therefore underproduce, while the producers of negative externalities do not bear the full cost of their activities and therefore overproduce. There is therefore a case for government intervention to subsidize providers of positive externalities and tax or impose restrictions on producers of negative externalities. In this way firms would be encouraged to undertake activities with beneficial side effects and discouraged from activities with undesirable side effects.

Externalities are not the only possible causes of inefficiency. Market failure may also occur because of the existence of imperfect markets, such as monopolies, which enable inefficient firms to survive and accumulate excessive profits. Imperfect information, especially with respect to capital markets, may also cause market failures since producers and consumers need to be fully informed if they are to make efficient decisions. Finally, there may be concerns that the operation of a free market will result in an inequitable distribution of income.

While market failures can undoubtedly occur, critics of government intervention point out that there may also be "government failures." Potential causes of such failures include the following:

1. *Rent-seeking activities.* In this context the term "rent" refers to unearned income gained at the expense of others as a result of special privileges or government favors. When the government intervenes in the market to provide subsidies, discriminatory tax breaks, or protection from competition from imports, firms have an incentive to spend resources on lobbying politicians and civil servants, on publicity campaigns designed to sway the public, or simply on outright bribes to get policies that benefit their interests. From the point of view of society these resources are wasted and would be better spent on improving the quality of products or finding cheaper ways to produce them.

2. *Predatory behavior of state officials.* Rent-seeking activities occur when individuals or firms in the private sector try to gain advantages at the expense of society as a whole. Public sector officials may also seek to maximize their interests at the expense of society by promoting unnecessary regulation. In this way they maximize their own power and privilege. Once a government bureau or agency is established it tends to create work for itself by widening as far as possible the scope of its activities.

3. *Vote-seeking politicians may generate or worsen business cycles.* It has been argued that business cycles tend to reflect electoral cycles. In election years there may be a tendency for governments to overspend or undertax in the hope of buying popularity. This generates an unhealthy boom in the economy so that in the years between elections deflationary policies have to be introduced to counter the inflation triggered during election years.

4. *Moral hazard.* By providing explicit or implicit guarantees to firms, governments may encourage high-risk behavior on the part of investors. The frequently substantial profits earned on risky investments when they pay off are retained by the investors, while losses that accrue when these investments fail are absorbed by the taxpayers.

The Structure of the State

Until they suffered the crisis of 1997, the East Asian countries had a reputation of being able to reduce market failures without generating government failures. This was especially true of the NICs. Three characteristics common to most of these countries were close partnerships between government and business, the creation of elite bureaucracies, and the existence of authoritarian governments. Close partnerships between government and business (especially big business) were said to promote efficiency by ensuring a flow of information between the main agents in the economy. There is always a danger, however, that such partnerships might develop into "crony capitalism," in which the powers of the state are placed at the disposal of corporate interests with ties to the political elite, even when these interests conflict with the needs of society as a whole. The governments of Indonesia, under Suharto, and the Philippines, under Marcos, were notorious for favoring business interests owned by relatives and friends of the president.

The East Asian countries, particularly Japan and the NICs, also benefitted from having efficient civil services. Government officials, especially those employed in the departments making the most important economic decisions, were capable and well trained. Employment in such agencies as the Economic Planning Board in South Korea carried great prestige and

204   Chapter 10

attracted capable people, in contrast to the situation in other countries where the civil service is less esteemed.

Finally, authoritarian political systems were said to promote an emphasis on long-term planning. Until recently most East Asian governments were not particularly democratic. Since authoritarian governments are less responsive to lobbyists than democratic governments the technocrats in the economic and technical ministries of these governments were able to focus on the long-run interests of their country without needing to appease the selfish or short-term interests of pressure groups, or so it was argued. A weakness in the case of supporters of such technocratic rule, however, is that authoritarian systems, lacking broad-based, political institutions, are very sensitive to the abilities and benevolence of the leader (or leaders) of the state. A benevolent dictator may be succeeded by a corrupt or incompetent leader and even if the leadership is capable and well intentioned, authoritarian regimes tend to be associated with limits on human rights and the exclusion of labor from decision making because of an emphasis on keeping down labor costs. It may be possible to get away with excluding from power the bulk of the population for quite long periods of time, but this often leads to a pent-up explosion of industrial unrest, such as occurred in South Korea in the 1980s.

The Financial System

Recent developments, such as the subprime mortgage crisis, have raised questions in the industrialized countries of the West about the extent to which markets, particularly financial markets, have been deregulated during the last twenty years. Throughout that period, policy makers and the majority of economists were generally enthusiastic about the virtues of financial liberalization as an ultimate goal, though some believed that it should be adopted only gradually and cautiously. The mainstream view was that free financial markets are beneficial because they reward savings and channel them toward the most efficient investments. Some economists, however, believed that since there are potentially many market failures in the financial sector, a strong regulatory framework is essential for financial markets to function efficiently. Recent developments in the United States and elsewhere have provided support for this view.

Prior to the 1990s, the absence of a sound regulatory framework in the majority of the East Asian countries seemed not to matter since the lending policies of financial institutions in the region were largely subject to state direction, either directly or indirectly. It was only in the late 1980s and the 1990s that the banks of these countries were effectively freed from state direction as a result of pressure from Western governments and the IMF. Once financial institutions were able to set their own lending practices the need for a sound regulatory system to prevent irresponsible lending soon became evident. It was not, however, simply the case that a state-controlled financial sector had acted as an imperfect substitute for a well-regulated but otherwise free banking system. The financial practices in place prior to the liberalizing reforms were sometimes justified as contributing directly to the high rates of growth in the East Asian economies. Apart from the dangers of market failure, two major arguments were frequently put forward in defense of a state-directed system. One was based on alleged efficiencies of a credit-based financial system, while the other was based on possible advantages of internal capital markets.

East Asia: The Development State 205

Credit-Based Financial Systems

A "capital market-based" financial system is one in which the principal source of finance for firms is the sale of securities (stocks and bonds), while a "credit-based" system is one in which firms depend mainly on bank credit. Supporters of credit-based systems argue that they avoid the bias toward short-term profitability that is characteristic of stock market-based systems, where it is crucial to maintain share prices in the short run in order to raise funds through sales of stock. Consequently, in a credit-based system, firms are able to adopt a long-term focus. On the other hand, an obvious disadvantage of an emphasis on credit as a means of financing investment is that it leads to firms being highly leveraged. This was clearly the case in those East Asian countries that were most severely affected by the crisis of 1997. High leverage is manageable while growth is rapid but becomes unsustainable when growth slows, and some reduction in growth is inevitable as economies mature.

Internal Capital Markets

"Internal capital markets" provide a mechanism with which to avoid the asymmetries of information between borrowers and lenders, which can be a source of market failure. Borrowers usually know more about the projects in which they wish to invest than do the institutions from which they wish to borrow. This means that lenders are at least partially dependent on borrowers for the information on which they base their lending decisions. Unfortunately, they cannot tell how honest the lenders are or how accurate the information is that they provide. As a result, credit may not be optimally allocated and even when loans are made, lenders may charge risk premiums to compensate for the riskiness of lending. A way of avoiding this situation is for firms to rely on their own retained earnings (their "internal capital markets") rather than trying to borrow from poorly informed lenders. An argument used to justify state-dominated credit-based systems was that they operated like nationwide internal capital markets. Because of a close relationship between the government and the firms requiring credit, the state had access to much better information than private banks and other financial institutions. Since the government ultimately determined where the banks would lend their money the asymmetry of information problem did not arise and a better allocation of credit occurred than would otherwise have been the case.

The Regulatory Framework and the Financial Sector

Recurring financial crises in recent decades have highlighted the importance of a suitable regulatory framework to minimize market failure in financial systems. The Asian financial crisis of 1997 exposed serious deficiencies in financial regulations. With the lifting of controls on international capital flows during the 1990s it became essential that effective systems of financial regulation be put in place to prevent irresponsible lending behavior on the part of financial institutions. In several Asian countries, notably Thailand, Malaysia, South Korea, and Indonesia, banks and other financial institutions borrowed large sums overseas short term and lent them long term locally, often to finance high-risk investments.

For this reason the IMF, the World Bank, and Western governments in their analyses of the Asian crisis focused on inadequacies in prudential regulations such as minimum capital

206   Chapter 10

requirements, which are designed to preserve the safety and soundness of individual financial institutions. Undoubtedly there was much room for improvement in these areas and the recent experience of the United States and other Western countries has underlined the importance of such regulations in reducing the risk of instability in financial markets.

Recovery from the Asian Crisis

The effects of the Asian Crisis of 1997 were severe, with sharp rises in both inflation and unemployment and cuts in social services. Fortunately, however, they were short lived. Serious inflation emerged as a result of the sharp currency devaluations. In 1998 the price level was increasing at a rate of 40 percent in Indonesia and 9.5 percent in South Korea. The austerity measures imposed by the International Monetary Fund in response to the financial crisis resulted in significant cuts in public services, including health and education. Finally, unemployment rose sharply. Statistics are often unreliable but the unemployment rate for South Korea, which has reasonably reliable statistics, was 6.5 percent in March 1998, having been less than 3 percent throughout the earlier 1990s. Estimates of layoffs in Indonesia range between 2.5 million and 6.6 million, but these figures probably greatly underestimate the true scale of the problem because they do not include the informal sector. Rising unemployment exposed the inadequacies of the social safety net in East Asian countries, which was not previously an obvious concern.

Nevertheless, the East Asian countries recovered remarkably quickly, as can be seen from Table 10.4. With the exception of Indonesia, they began to recover in early 1999, while Indonesia also returned to a high growth path after 2002. The annual rate of economic growth for the East Asian countries, excluding China and Japan, exceeded 6 percent between 1997 and 2006. While less than the pre-crisis rate, this is considerably higher than the annual growth rate for the world economy as a whole. Clearly the crisis did not have the prolonged negative impact that had been anticipated. The immediate recovery was helped along by currency depreciations, which gave a boost to exports, and once confidence was restored in financial markets, foreign capital began to flow back into the region. The longer term return to high growth was due to a number of factors. First, the high savings rates and emphasis on education, which had played such a major role in promoting growth before 1997, remained in place. Second, financial market reforms and economic liberalization policies were adopted which enhanced economic efficiency. Finally, the region benefitted from the continued high rate of growth of China's economy. As in the decades before 1997, the rapid growth in the East Asian economies is being driven by export expansion, but increasingly trade is within the region and particularly with China, as opposed to Europe and North America.

East Asia: The Development State 207

TABLE 10.4. Selected East Asian Countries. Growth in GDP Per Capita 1996-2006 (%)

Year	South Korea	Thailand	Malaysia	Indonesia
1996	6.6	4.6	7.2	6.6
1997	4.9	-3.7	4.6	3.5
1998	-6.2	-8.5	-9.7	-14.1
1999	10.5	3.6	3.5	-0.4
2000	8.0	3.7	6.0	3.8
2001	3.7	2.5	-2.1	2.2
2002	6.8	5.2	2.8	3.0
2003	2.4	6.2	3.3	3.3
2004	4.5	5.4	4.4	3.6
2005	3.7	3.3	2.7	4.2
2006	4.6	4.2	4.2	4.0

Source: GDP Per Capita by Country/Statistics from IMF, knoema.com/pjeqzh/gdp-per-capita-by-country-statistics-from-imf-1980-2022?

References

Books

Argy, V., and Stein, L. (1997). *The Japanese economy*. New York: Macmillan.

Frankel, J., Stein, E., and Wei, S.-J. (1997). *Regional trading blocs in the world economic system*. Institute for International Economics.

Hamada, K., Kashyap, A. K., and Weinstein, D. E. (Eds.). (2011). *Japan's bubble, deflation, and long-term stagnation*. Cambridge, MA: M.I.T. Press.

Islam, I., and Chowdhury, A. (1997). *Asia-Pacific economies*. London: Routledge.

Tinbergen, Jan. (1962). *Shaping the world economy: Suggestions for an international economic policy*. New York: Twentieth Century Fund.

Articles

Akamatsu, Kaname. (1962). A historical pattern of economic growth in developing economies. *Journal of Developing Economies, 1*(1).

Lee, Chung H. (1992). The government, financial system and large private enterprises in the economic development of South Korea. *World Development, 20*(2).

Quah, Danny. (2010). Post 1990s East Asian economic growth. In Takatoshi Ito and Chin Hee Hahn (Eds.), *The rise of China and structural changes in Korea and Asia*. Cheltenham, UK: Edward Elgar.

Chapter 10

Online Articles

Aghevli, Bijan B. (1999). The Asian crisis causes and remedies. International Monetary Fund, http://www.imf.org/external/pubs/ft/fandd/1999/06/aghevli.htm

Hiroshi, Murayama. (2017). South Korea, Taiwan face "high-income trap," https://asia.nikkei.com/Politics-Economy/Economy/South-Korea-Taiwan-face-high-income-trap

Okazaki, Tetsuji. (2015). Lessons from the Japanese miracle: Building the foundations for a new growth paradigm, http://www.nippon.com/en/in-depth/a04003/

Chapter 11

The Middle East and Africa

The term "Middle East" is here used to refer to Western Asia and the Arab countries of North Africa. It is one of the most volatile regions of the world and one of the most strategically important. Its importance is partly due to its oil reserves, but also to its geographical location and its significance to major world religions. Since the influence of the Middle East on the global economy was greatly increased by the increase in oil prices as a result of the activities of OPEC, the cartel of oil exporting countries, the role of OPEC will first be described, though not all of the members of OPEC are Middle Eastern countries and not all Middle Eastern countries are members of OPEC.

OPEC and the Oil-Exporting States

The decades after the Second World War saw both a rapid growth in energy consumption and an increase in the importance of oil as an energy source. As a result of a long economic boom enjoyed by industrialized countries, energy consumption grew at an average annual rate of 5.7 percent per year during the 1960s. During that same decade oil increasingly replaced coal as the source of this energy, though oil was, of course, important long before the 1960s. Prior to the Second World War it was already used as a fuel for road and air transportation and was a major input into the petrochemicals industry. Nevertheless, the prewar period was still primarily a world of coal and steel. Even as late as 1953 coal provided about 70 percent of the world's energy needs, while oil produced accounted for only about 20 percent. By 1970, however, oil provided about 40 percent of world energy needs. This large expansion in oil consumption did not have the effect on oil prices that might have been expected since the growth in the demand for oil was outstripped by increased supply as cutthroat competition between the oil companies ensured a supply of cheap energy. Oil prices actually fell by about 10 percent between 1955 and 1967. The experience of the 1970s was to be very different.

Given the growth in oil consumption, oil prices would eventually have increased but the increase that actually occurred early in the 1970s was extreme and occurred in a very short space of time, creating a need for rapid adjustments. That the price increase occurred in this way was due to political events in the Middle East and to the activities of an oil cartel, OPEC (the Organization of Petroleum Exporting Countries). OPEC had been formed in 1960 to manage the dealings of the countries owning oil resources with the Western companies which sold oil on world markets. During the 1960s OPEC had done little to raise the price of the resource but the cartel flexed its muscles to great effect in 1973–1974 during what came to be known as the first energy crisis.

209

To explain the events of 1973–1974, however, it is first necessary to describe how cartels function. A cartel, such as OPEC, is an organization of producers or sellers to fix prices and production of a resource or commodity. Any cartel, if it is to be successful in increasing the incomes of its members, must satisfy the following three conditions.

Oil pump jacks in Bahrain.

1. Demand for the commodity sold by the cartel must be "inelastic" with respect to price. In other words, the price increase imposed by the cartel must not reduce sales to the point that revenues actually fall. This condition is generally satisfied by goods which are necessities with few or no substitutes. This certainly describes oil, at least in the short run. Also important is the fact that the prices imposed by OPEC members on the oil companies (known as "posted prices") were not the same as the prices paid by the ultimate consumers at the petrol pump. Prices at the pump increased by a much lower percentage than posted prices because the posted prices represented only part of the cost of oil to the companies. This fact goes far in explaining why consumption declined so little in 1974 in spite of a massive increase in the price charged to the oil companies by the exporters.

2. Since cartels increase prices by reducing output, it is necessary for the members to be able to agree on the desired reduction in output and on how reduced production quotas should be allocated among them. Such agreement has proved elusive for many cartels, including OPEC for much of its history. Members of cartels naturally want to increase their production quotas at the expense of fellow members.

3. It follows that there must be an effective policing mechanism to ensure that individual producers do not undercut the agreed upon price and produce more than their quota. In the case of OPEC the oil companies actually provided the policing mechanism since they acted as distributors and tax collectors for the member countries of the cartel.

The OPEC Oil Crises (1973 and 1979)

During the late 1960s international inflation increased as a result of American government expenditures on the Vietnam War and the social programs launched in the United States as part of President Johnson's "war on poverty." As oil prices lagged behind general inflation the leaders of the OPEC countries naturally became discontented with the pricing system. They were able to impose a relatively modest increase in posted prices in 1970–1971 but it took a political crisis in the Middle East to galvanize the OPEC members into radical action. In 1973 a coalition of Arab states launched an attack on Israel during what came to be known as the Yom Kippur War (also known as the October War). During this war the Arab oil exporting countries imposed an embargo on oil exports to the United States, Portugal, and the Netherlands, which were viewed as Israel's strongest backers. To prevent the oil companies from getting around the embargo by redistributing oil deliveries between importing countries, there was also a cut in overall production of 20 percent. The embargo lasted for only six months but it had a long-lasting impact since it showed the oil exporters how powerful they could be when acting in concert.

Fortuitously for OPEC there was no international surplus of oil at the time. Oil importers rushed to replenish their oil supplies by purchases on the Rotterdam spot market, a market which normally provided only emergency stocks and accounted for 3 or 4 percent of world supply. The resulting drastic increase in the spot price acted as a signal to OPEC members to increase posted prices still further to keep pace. As a result, posted prices rose by 400 percent in a few months, though this represented a much smaller but still substantial increase in average prices at the pump of 20 percent to domestic consumers. There was little effort at rationing existing inventories on the part of the rich oil importing countries in 1973–1974 and, despite the large price increase, demand for oil fell by only 6 percent, demonstrating that demand for oil was extremely inelastic with respect to price in the short run. Although the crisis began as a political action by the Arab members of OPEC it soon became clear to all members, Arab and non-Arab alike, that under the right circumstances an oil cartel could substantially increase revenues while reducing output.

In the following years there were serious attempts by Japan and the Western European countries to conserve energy and find alternative energy sources, such as North Sea oil in the Atlantic, but there was little attempt at conservation by Canada or the United States. Since rising world inflation during the 1970s meant that by 1978 the terms of trade were moving against the OPEC producers, the stage was now set for the second oil crisis. As with the first crisis, this arose out of political events in the Middle East. The protests leading to the overthrow of the Shah of Iran in 1979 included a strike by oil workers. Disruptions in oil supplies continued with the Iran–Iraq War, which broke out in 1980 when Saddam Hussein, president of Iraq, tried to take advantage of the chaos in Iran following the Islamic revolution. As a result, posted prices increased by 140 percent between 1979 and 1981. The international effects of this second oil crisis were, however, very different from those of the previous crisis. As seen earlier, during the crisis of 1973 posted prices increased by 400 percent but demand for oil fell by only 6 percent. After the second crisis, however, during which posted prices increased by 180 percent, demand for OPEC oil fell by about 20 percent. The difference in price elasticity of demand was principally due to the fact that central banks adopted tougher counterinflationary policies than they had after the first crisis. These policies resulted in the most severe recession since the Second World War, drastically reducing world demand for oil. Also important was the greater availability of non-OPEC sources of oil. As a result of the earlier increase in oil prices it had become worthwhile to increase oil extraction in the North Sea, Alaska, and Mexico. Finally, the 1980s saw more serious efforts at conservation than had the 1970s.

212   Chapter 11

Although OPEC was less successful in increasing oil revenues during the second crisis than it had been during the first, there had been a permanent increase in the wealth and power of the oil exporting states of the Middle East, especially relative to the non-oil-exporting countries of the region. This became even more apparent after 1999 when OPEC was again able to assert its power as a result of increased global demand for oil.

Non-Oil-Exporting States

While the oil-rich states have flourished, the economic performance of the non-oil-exporting countries of the Middle East has slipped over the past quarter century. A major cause of this less than stellar performance is the demographic challenge faced by these countries in recent decades. In common with less-developed countries in other parts of the world, Middle Eastern countries are experiencing a combination of declining infant mortality rates, rising life expectancy, and a reduction in fertility rates. Since the decrease in fertility rates has so far occurred more slowly than the decline in mortality rates, the result has been a surge in population growth and a "demographic bulge" with the number of young adults growing faster than the rest of the population. Since demand for labor is growing more slowly than supply, unemployment is rising, particularly youth unemployment.

A second source of economic difficulty is a slowness to adapt to globalization. Apart from the oil sector, the Middle Eastern economies have been largely inward-looking, especially in terms of manufacturing. Governments of the region continue to rely on the import substitution industrialization (ISI) strategies that have been abandoned elsewhere. Exports of manufactures lag far behind those of Eastern Europe, South Asia, and Latin America. The situation is different for the oil-exporting countries, which rely heavily on exports, but the oil extraction industry has only limited linkages with other parts of the economy and draws into the extractive sector capital and labor which might otherwise be used in manufacturing. The inward orientation is promoted by high tariffs and quantitative restrictions on imports. Additional barriers to trade are inefficient bureaucracies, cumbersome regulatory systems, and an emphasis on state ownership or control of major manufacturing enterprises. State-owned banks control a large share of total financial assets in the region, with the result that a large proportion of funds is channeled into projects favored by governments, leaving only limited capital available for other enterprises.

A third problem facing the Middle East is the financial dominance of the oil-rich states, which worsens contagion effects from these states to other countries of the region. Not only is demand for foreign labor in the oil-rich states sensitive to fluctuations in world demand for oil but financial flows from these states into neighboring countries are also sensitive to oil prices.

Among the problems facing the countries of the Middle East, therefore, are weak links to the global economy, a lack of technology transfer (due to low levels of foreign investment outside of the oil sector), and high costs of doing business. Political resistance to economic reform, always a problem, is particularly difficult to overcome in the Middle East because of the uncertain future of a number of regimes and the possibility of abrupt transitions such as are now occurring with the "Arab Spring." Even before the Arab Spring, however, popular dissatisfaction with authoritarian regimes was undermining the confidence of foreign investors who might otherwise have promoted innovation.

The Middle East and Africa 213

Economic and Social Indicators

Despite the problems described above, the extent to which the economies of the non-oil-producing states are failing is sometimes exaggerated. The performance of these economies in recent decades has not been systematically worse than for many developing countries in other regions of the world and living standards have been rising in an absolute sense. There is nevertheless growing frustration because of a decline in *relative* prosperity as the region falls behind East Asia and India.

In the mid-twentieth century the Middle Eastern countries did a reasonable job in developing human capital from an admittedly low base and improving technological efficiency. This led to growth in total factor productivity (TFP), a term referring to that growth in output which derives from improvements in technology and organization, as opposed to increased inputs of labor and capital. During the 1980s the region shared with most of the rest of the world a slowdown in growth of total factor productivity. While the rest of the world saw a rebound in TFP in the 1990s, however, this was not true of the Middle East. The general picture is one in which economic performance was in line with that of developing countries in other regions up to and during the 1970s but there followed a significant relative decline in growth in TFP during the 1980s and especially the 1990s.

The picture is mixed for other economic and social indicators. Although the absolute number of poor people has grown in recent decades, Gini coefficients show that, with the exception of the oil-rich sates, inequality in the Middle Eastern countries is comparable to that in most other developing countries.[1] Inequality is much less severe than in Latin America or sub-Saharan Africa. There have also been continuing improvements in education. One area in which the Middle East does perform poorly, however, is in unemployment. Although unemployment data are limited, data that exist suggest that unemployment rates in the Middle East are greater than in any other region of the world apart from sub-Saharan Africa. This is a major driver of discontent. Even though past economic performance has been comparable to that in other parts of the world, there is a perception that employment opportunities are dwindling.

Explanations for the economic malaise of the region focus on social and institutional structures, of which three merit further attention: the demographic transition, religion, and the legal system.

Demographic Transition

As noted earlier, the persistence of high levels of unemployment is in large part a result of demographic factors. The labor force in recent years has been growing at a rate of about 3 percent per annum, too rapidly for all new entrants to be employed. This labor force growth has been driven by a high rate of population growth which, in turn, is caused by an initially high crude fertility rate, a rapid decline in infant mortality, and a general rise in life expectancy. Since the adjustment of birth rates to lower death rates takes time there has arisen a large age cohort bulge or "demographic bulge," which may last for many years. It is true that to some

---

[1] The Gini coefficient, as used in economics, is a statistical measure of inequality in the distribution of income.

214   Chapter 11

extent the problems caused by the bulge have been alleviated by cross-border migration since the non-oil economies tend to be net exporters of labor and the oil exporters of the Persian Gulf tend to be net importers of labor. There is, however, a limit to the labor needs of the Gulf states and their demand for immigrant workers varies with the highly volatile price of oil, which contributes to economic and political instability in the Middle East.

Religion

Given the strong religious beliefs of most of the people of the Middle East, the question naturally arises as to the role of religion in promoting or retarding economic development. Low inflows of foreign investment, other than in the resource-based sectors, are sometimes attributed to the role of Islam in the Middle East. This should not be overstated since some Islamic countries in other parts of the world, notably Malaysia and Indonesia, have experienced rapid economic growth in recent decades. Nevertheless, there are ways in which Islam affects the economy, particularly with respect to financial institutions. The Koran contains an injunction against *riba*, which has been variously interpreted as a ban on usury or a complete prohibition on the charging of interest. Other teachings of the Koran may restrict the use of financial instruments such as options, futures, and insurance contracts. It has also been suggested that inheritance rules based on Islamic practice may explain why commerce and finance in the Middle East have often been dominated by non-Muslim religious minorities.[2]

Concern about these issues has led to attempts to reconcile religion and economic development. Islamic banking developed in Egypt in the 1960s as a way of bringing financial practice into conformity with sharia (the religious law of Islam). This has not, however, resolved all the difficulties of the financial sector. The prohibition on *riba* has limited the use of bank loans and bonds and has encouraged a strong equity bias in the portfolios of Islamic financial institutions. Another measure designed to widen the scope of activities available to Islamic financial institutions was the introduction (in 2001) of *sukuks* (sharia-compliant bonds). These pay dividends through cash flows from tangible assets rather than interest.

Legal Systems

Economic development is influenced by secular as well as religious rules. In most Middle Eastern countries the system of commercial law is based on either British common law or the civil code system of France, though in some countries the system has been modified to make it more consistent with sharia law. The legal code formally adopted is, however, only part of the story. Also important is the extent to which it is applied. Is there a "rule of law" and are regulatory authorities efficient or slow and cumbersome in enforcing the rules? In these respects the Middle Eastern countries do not seem any worse than the majority of developing countries. Likewise corruption, while it exists, does not appear to be more severe than in most other regions of the world. In general the Middle Eastern countries score about average for developing countries in international comparisons of administrative malfeasance based on indices of corruption such as Transparency International.

---

[2] See Kuran, Timur (2003), "The Islamic Commercial Crisis: Institutional Roots of Economic Underdevelopment in the Middle East", *Journal of Economic History*, 62(3).

The Arab Spring

The authoritarian governments of the Middle East were long able to maintain control through a combination of economic redistribution and political repression. Government largesse took the form of subsidies, price controls, and other instruments of state economic control. This was supported by revenues from sales of natural resources, which increased the income of the oil-exporting countries directly and made it possible for

them to provide subsidies to the non-oil-producing countries of the region. Whenever redistributive policies failed to placate the population, governments could resort to the methods of the police state. In recent years, however, both repression and redistribution have become less effective. Repression by the police state has been undermined by the use of information technology, which rapidly spreads information that governments may wish to suppress and makes it easier for potential rebels to coordinate their activities. At the same time demographic pressures have increased the number of unemployed, dissatisfied youth. Ironically, improvements in education, an area in which the Middle Eastern states have been most successful, have actually increased their political difficulties. A wide gap has opened up between the aspirations of educated young people and the employment opportunities available to them in countries with little international trade other than in oil. The resulting wave of revolutionary protests has overthrown authoritarian regimes in Tunisia, Egypt, Libya, and Yemen, while Syria is in the midst of a civil war. Almost all the other countries of the Middle East have experienced protests of varying severity. Since there is no quick solution to the economic problems of the region, however, frustration is likely to continue for several years regardless of whether or not changes of regime occur.

Sub-Saharan Africa

At least until very recently it appeared that sub Saharan Africa was lagging behind other parts of the world in terms of economic development but this had not always been the case. In the 1950s Africa's level of development was comparable to that of the Southeast and East Asian countries (with the exception of Japan). In the second half of the twentieth century, however, it fell far behind. A major factor holding back the continent was a high level of risk due to frequent reversals of government policy, which

Johannesburg, South Africa.

216   Chapter 11

discouraged foreign investment. Other disadvantages included a relatively poor endowment of human capital resulting from low rates of literacy and import substitution industrialization (ISI) policies which favored urban areas at the expense of farmers, as did price controls on food. The situation has changed since the turn of the twenty-first century, with much of Africa experiencing rapid economic growth, though economic performance has varied considerably across the continent, as can be seen from Table 11.1. Some countries, such as Ethiopia and Angola, have achieved double-digit rates of growth, while others, such as Zimbabwe, have experienced very low or even negative rates of growth.

TABLE 11.1. Average Annual Growth Rates in Real GDP for Selected African Countries 2004–2013 (%)

Country	2004–2008	2009–2013	2004–2013
Angola	17.4	5.2	11.3
Ethiopia	11.7	9.2	10.5
Ghana	6.6	8.3	7.4
Kenya	5.2	4.3	4.7
Mozambique	7.8	7.3	7.5
Nigeria	7.1	7.1	7.1
South Africa	4.9	2.1	3.5
Tanzania	7.3	6.5	6.9
Uganda	8.3	5.1	6.7
Zimbabwe	−6.8	7.2	1.9

Source: African Economic Outlook, 2014.

The impressive economic growth rates achieved by the more successful African economies have been due to an expansion in international trade, driven in large part by the growth in demand by emerging economies, especially China and India, for African resources, which include petroleum, bauxite, industrial diamonds, and gold. This expansion in trade has not, however, been without its disadvantages. In particular it has resulted in unbalanced economies with a continued or even increased dependence on exports of natural resources. In Ghana and South Africa imports from China have displaced domestic manufactures of clothing and furniture. This continued dependence on resources means that Africa's export earnings are vulnerable to fluctuations in the prices of a limited number of commodities.[3] The African countries are conscious of the need to restructure their economies. In an effort to broaden trade, they

---

[3] See Padayachee, chapter 1, for the impact of Chinese imports on African manufactures.

The Middle East and Africa **217**

have sought to diversify their sources of export earnings by pressing for liberalization of agricultural trade by Western countries. High-income countries such as the United States, Canada, Japan, and the member countries of the European Union have been criticized for protectionist agricultural policies and subsidies, leading to world overproduction of foodstuffs which African countries might otherwise sell, such as dairy products and grains. So far, however, progress in fighting agricultural protectionism has been slow.

As an alternative strategy the African Union has sought to promote intra-African trade by advocating an African free trade area but so far progress here has also been slow. Protectionism, this time on the part of African countries themselves, has slowed growth in trade between these countries. More success has been achieved in developing regional economic organizations, which numbered eight in 2013.[4] Perhaps the most successful of these is the Common Market for Eastern and Southern Africa (COMESA). The ratio of intraregional trade to total trade for the nineteen member countries of COMESA grew from 5.1 percent during 1996–2000 to 6.7 percent during 2007–2011.[5] African attempts at regional cooperation have nevertheless been generally unsuccessful because political considerations have overwhelmed economic needs and mechanisms to enforce compliance with regional agreements have been lacking.

Even after the recent economic expansion, sometimes described optimistically as an "African Economic Renaissance," it remains true that in spite of being rich in resources, Sub-Saharan Africa is characterized by widespread poverty. As already indicated, this can be attributed to an overdependence on agriculture and on mineral exports. Attempts to overcome these limitations have included not only policies to widen trade but also plans to expand manufacturing for the domestic market. South Africa, in particular, has encouraged foreign direct investment in manufacturing industries. Despite some progress in increasing manufacturing production, however, there persists a lack of balance in the economies of the continent. Controversy surrounds the issue of why the economies of Africa remain so heavily dependent on the extraction and export of natural resources. One economic paradigm attributes the continent's prolonged economic difficulties of the late twentieth century to the disruptions inflicted on African economic structures during the era of colonialism. In this view the extensive trade routes which had crossed much of Africa for millennia were largely destroyed by European countries during their "Scramble for Africa" in the late nineteenth century. During the colonial period which followed new industries and new trade routes were developed to meet the needs of Western countries for African minerals and agricultural goods. The view that rich countries, known as "core" countries, enrich themselves by extracting resources from poor countries, which are thereby impoverished, is known as "dependency theory." It stands in strong contrast to an earlier paradigm known as "modernization theory," which attributes the poverty of low-income countries to weaknesses in their domestic institutions.

---

[4] The African Union has recognized the following eight regional economic communities: Arab Maghreb Union (AMU), Common Market for Eastern and Southern Africa (COMESA), Community of Sahel-Saharan States (CEN-SAD), East African Community (EAC), Economic Community of Central African States (ECCAS), Economic Community of West African States (ECOWAS), Intergovernmental Authority for Development (IGAD), Southern African Development Community (SADC).

[5] TradeMark Southern Africa, February 26, 2014.

218   Chapter 11

Dependency Theory

Those who advocate "dependency" theories argue that the low-income countries cannot develop their economies simply by imitating the already industrialized countries. The countries of sub-Saharan Africa were drawn into the global economy through colonialism, which created a system of international trade in which raw materials and agricultural goods were extracted from colonized territories for the benefit of the imperialist powers. In turn, the colonies served as captive markets for the manufactures produced by those powers. Even after the realization of independence the foreign trade of the former colonies continued to be characterized by exports of primary products and imports of manufactured goods. This pattern was all the more damaging, it is claimed, because the prices of primary products have tended to decline over time relative to the prices of manufactured goods, causing the terms of trade to move to the disadvantage of the developing countries. Dependency theorists agree that this pattern of dependency needs to be broken and this cannot be achieved through promoting globalization. They distrust foreign direct investment by transnational corporations, claiming that these corporations import managers and skilled workers, employing local people solely as unskilled labor. The transnational corporations are also said to repatriate their profits rather than invest them locally.

While dependency theorists largely agree on the origins of the difficulties facing the countries of sub-Saharan Africa, they hold a variety of views about the appropriate means to reduce dependency. Some theorists advocate inward-looking policies of import substitution industrialization, though this view has become less prevalent in recent times. Others advocate collective bargaining strategies, which can either take the form of resource cartels, such as OPEC, or lobbying through international organizations for policies favorable to low-income countries, such as the opening of rich country markets to exports from poorer countries.

Dependency theorists have their critics, who maintain that their distrust of globalization is unfounded for two reasons. First, some economies which are open to international trade and foreign investment have performed much better than others which are relatively closed. East Asian countries, such as South Korea, have flourished through promoting exports. Second, it is not clear that there is a tendency for the terms of trade to shift against primary products. Indeed, Africa's recent experience of rising export prices of natural resources suggests otherwise. It is also worth noting that until the 1960s the African economies had enjoyed relatively high rates of economic growth, high levels of investment, and rapidly growing exports. In 1960 Ghana had a per capita income equal to that of South Korea. It is only since the early 1970s that Africa stagnated relative to much of Asia. This was due not to distortions in international trade but to low literacy rates and low national savings rates, which had previously been made up for by high levels of foreign aid and foreign investment.

Modernization Theory

In contrast to dependency theory, modernization theory lays the blame for Africa's poverty at the door of the continent itself. According to modernization theory, barriers to economic development are created by the structures of "traditional societies," which are said to be mainly rural and dominated by rigid social structures that discourage innovation. For progress to occur in such societies there must develop some means of protecting property rights and rewarding innovation. Clearly, this implies that developing countries can only progress if they adopt the capitalist institutions of the industrialized countries. Since this can best be done through increasing interdependence between rich and poor countries, success will come to the poorer countries as a result of opening their economies to international trade and foreign investment.

Critics of modernization theory believe that it reflects an ethnocentric viewpoint. Anything that is not typical of European and North American economies tends to be labeled "traditional" and seen as an obstacle to progress. The critics also argue that the "modernization" approach is too optimistic about the benefits of closer ties between rich and poor countries and ignores potential conflicts of interest that may exist between them. One example of how the interests of rich and poor countries can diverge is the reluctance of the industrialized countries to open up their economies to agricultural imports. A second example is how, in the name of enforcing intellectual property rights, the high-income countries pressure low-income countries into purchasing drugs produced by the Western pharmaceutical companies instead of much cheaper generic drugs. Critics of modernization theory can also argue that, given the structures of African economies, the dismantling of long-established economic controls in the name of economic liberalization may have the unintended consequence of creating fiscal difficulties. Taxes on trade account for about a third of government revenues in Africa and liberalization therefore limits the ability of governments to raise tax revenues needed to finance improvements in infrastructure.[6]

Clearly both the dependency and modernization approaches are open to criticism. A compromise view might be that while neither modernization nor dependency theories provide completely satisfactory prescriptions for economic development, they both provide some useful insights. Modernization theory is correct in pointing out that traditional cultures and institutions sometimes need to be modified if economic development is to occur, while dependency theories underline the problems caused by disparities of power between rich and poor countries.

Future Prospects

Among the factors limiting the economic growth of African countries in the twentieth century were the demographic structure of the population, low levels of literacy, and low levels of investment. There are signs of improvement in all three of these areas. High birth rates had resulted in a disproportionately young population. Since birth rates are now falling, the age structure of the sub-Saharan population will change in the near future, with a larger proportion of this population consisting of young, working age adults. Literacy levels are also improving and considerable progress has been made in expanding primary and secondary education. Countries in sub-Saharan Africa have increased spending on education at an average annual rate of 6 percent over the last decade.[7]

Domestic investment remains relatively low, in large part because of inadequacies in the financial sector and government policies which have hindered domestic investment. Small,

---

[6] See Padayachee, chapter 1.
[7] UN News Centre, April 27, 2011.

220   Chapter 11

inefficient financial structures have failed to mobilize savings, while government controls over the financial sector have added to the difficulty of mobilizing domestic capital, particularly in the agricultural sector. Low levels of domestic investment are, however, being made up for by increasing foreign investment. The last decade has seen considerable investment in Africa by China, while the European Union has also shown increased interest in investment in African countries. This foreign investment has been concentrated in extractive industries but has also resulted in some growth of manufacturing. East Africa, for example, is now a leader in the use of computers and mobile telephones for financial services.

If this progress is to be maintained, however, there are obstacles to be overcome. Among these obstacles are poorly developed infrastructure and high levels of official corruption, which make sub-Saharan Africa an expensive region in which to do business. Other problems include political instability in several countries and high rates of HIV/AIDS.

References

Books

Kayizzi-Mugerwa, S. (1999). *The African economy: Policy, institutions and the future*. London, New York: Rutledge.

Lairson, T. D., and Skidmore, D. (1997). *International political economy*. Fort Worth, TX: Harcourt Brace and Co.

Noland, M, and Pack, H. (2007). *The Arab economies in a changing world*. Washington, DC: Peterson Institute for International Studies.

Padayachee, V. (Ed.). (2010). *The political economy of Africa*. London, New York: Rutledge.

Richards, A., and Waterbury, J. (2008). *A political economy of the Middle East* (3rd edition). Boulder, CO: Westview Press.

Articles

Abbey, J. L. S. (2012). Challenges and prospects of infrastructural development in an oil and gas economy. CEPA Presentation at Symposium on Poverty Reduction and Oil Revenue.

Kuran, Timur. (2003). The Islamic commercial crisis: Institutional roots of economic underdevelopment in the Middle East. *Journal of Economic History, 62*(3).

INDEX

NOTE: Page references in *italics* refer to figures, illustrations, photos, and tables.

A

Ad valorem tariffs, 4
Africa. *see also individual names of countries*
  "African Economic Renaissance," 217
  African Union, 217
  average annual growth rates in real GDP for selected countries, *216*
  colonialism in, 19
  dependency theory, 218
  economic growth, 216–217
  during "first era of globalization," 18–19
  future economic prospects of, 219–220
  modernization theory, 218–219
  sub-Saharan Africa, overview, 215–217, *215*, *216*
aggregate demand
  aggregate supply framework, 59, *59*, 60–61
  Bretton Woods System and, 80
  defined, 59
Agreement Concerning Automotive Products (Auto Pact), 121
agriculture
  collectivization of, in Soviet Union, 154–156, *156*
  Common Agricultural Policy (CAP), 130
  famine in China, 173, 174
  during "first era of globalization," 18
  Great Depression and, 53
  in India, 181
  post-WWI production, 43–44
Akamatsu, Kaname, 193, 199
Aldcroft, Derek II., 31
Algeria, 19
Allied Powers
  finances, 31
  Reparations Commission, 38
American Relief Administration, 33
Andropov, Yuri, 158
Arab Spring, 212, 215, *215*
Argentina. *see also* Latin America
  "hard peg" policy of, 102
  Mercosur, 116, *149*, 149–150
Article IV Consultations (IMF), 103

Asia. *see also individual names of countries*
  Asian Crisis of 1997, 96–97, 105, 110–113, *111*, *112*, 115, 203–204, 206
  "Asian miracle," 190, 201
  East Asia as "development state," 190, 200–204
  emerging economies of East Asia, 199–207, *199*, *200*, *203*, *207*
  during "first era of globalization," 18, 19–20
  post-WWI trade, 44–45, *45*
"austerity," European sovereign debt crisis and, 143–144
Austria, European financial crisis of 1931, 67
Austrian school of thought about Great Depression, 50–51
authoritarian political systems (Japan), 204
automobile industry, NAFTA and, 121

B

Bagwell, K., 93
Bahrain, oil pump jacks in, *210*
balance of payments
  capital account, 6
  current account, 5–6
  defined, 5
  financial account, 6–7
  fiscal policy and, 14–15
  overview, 7
Bank for International Settlements (BIS), 70, 99, 125
banking
  "first era of globalization" and banking crisis of 1907, 26
  Great Depression and banking panics, 55–57
  Great Depression and international monetary arrangements, 70
  Great Depression hypotheses, *61*, 61–63, *62*
  regulatory framework and financial sector, 205–206
Bank of Canada, 13
Bank of England, 13
Bank of Japan, 197
Basel Accords, 100–101, *101*
Basel Committee on Banking Supervision, 100–101
Belgium
  colonialism by, 19
  ESCS formation and, 127

221

222　Index

hyperinflation in Germany, following WW I, 35
　physical destruction from WW I, 31, *32*
Benjamin, D. K., 60
Bernanke, Ben, 58, *61*
Bessemer steel process, 17
Bhagwati, Jagdish, 99
bilateral trading agreements, 69–70
bimetallic standard (U.S.), 23
"Black Tuesday," 62
Bolivia, Mercosur and, 149–150
Bolsa Familia, 186
Bolsheviks, 151
Border Industrialization Program (BIP) (Mexico),
　124–125
Boxer Rebellion, 19
Brady, Nicholas, 108–109
Brazil. *see also* Latin America
　as BRICS country, 184–187, *186*
　Mercosur, 116, *149*, 149–150
Bretton Woods System, 75–94. *see also* General
　Agreement on Tariffs and Trade (GATT); Interna-
　tional Monetary Fund (IMF); World Bank; World
　Trade Organization (WTO)
　Bretton Woods Conference and Agreement, 80–84,
　　82
　EEC/EU issues and, 133
　as fixed exchange rate system, 12
　labor and environmental issues, 91–94, *92*, *93*
　legacy of WWII, 76, 76–77
　Marshall Plan and European Payments Union
　　(EPU), 77–80, *78*
　overview, 75
　rise and fall of, 86, 88–91
　rise and fall of (1947-1973), 88–91
　Triffin dilemma, 84–86, *85*, *86*, *87*
　World Trade Organization (WTO) creation, 88, *88*
Brexit, *145*, 145–148, *146*
Brezhnev, Leonid, 158, 166
BRICS countries, 165–188. *see also individual coun-
　try names*
　Brazil, 184–187, *186*
　China, 172–181, *173*, *175*, *176*
　as emerging economies, 165, *165*
　India, 181–184, *183*
　Russia, 165–171, *167*, *168*, *170*, *171*, 180–181
　South Africa, *187*, 187–188, *188*
British Commonwealth Preferences, 70–71
Broad Economic Policy Guidelines, 72
Buy Japanese" policy, 196

C

Cameron, David, 145–148
Canada. *see also* North American Free Trade Agree-
　ment (NAFTA)
　Brexit and "Canada option," 147, 148
　Canada-U.S. Free Trade Agreement (CUSTA), 118,
　　121, 122, 126
　"first era of globalization," 22–23
　post-WWI trade, 44–45, *45*
capital
　absence of capital markets in Soviet Union, 158
　balance of payments, 6
　Bretton Woods System and, 80
　capital goods, defined, 1–2
　capital market liberalization policy, 105
　"first era of globalization" and, 22–23, *23*
　internal capital markets, 205
　international financial crises and contagion, *96*,
　　96–97
　international financial crises, globalization, and
　　capital mobility, *97*, *97–100*
　socialist economies of Central and Eastern Europe,
　　160
capital controls dismantling, BRICS emerging econo-
　mies and, 169
Capital: Critique of Political Economy (Marx),
　152–153
Cardoso, Fernando Henrique, 186
cartels, 210
central banks. *see also* U.S. Federal Reserve
　Bank of Canada, 13
　Bank of England, 13
　European Central Bank (ECB), 13, *134*, 142–143
　monetary policy and, 13
　post-WWI restoration of gold standard, 41–42
Central Europe, socialist economies of. *see* Soviet
　Union and socialist economies of Europe
central planning system, of Soviet Union, 151, 154,
　156, 157, 165, 166
chain of debt, World War I and, *42*, *42–43*
Chechnyan war, 169
chemicals, during "first era of globalization," 18
chervonets, *161*
child labor, 92, *92*
Chile
　capital inflow restrictions, 100
　Mercosur, 149–150
China. *see also* Asia
　Bretton Woods System and, 86
　as BRICS country, 172–181, *173*, *175*, *176*

as East Asian "development state," 190
during "first era of globalization," 19–20
"first era of globalization," 23, 24
hyperinflation after WW II, 76
renminbi (RMB), 180*n*4
silver standard, 23
subprime mortgage crisis of 2007 and Great
   Recession, 114
classical gold standard, 23–25. *see also* gold standard
classical school of thought, about Great Depression,
   50–51
clearing agreements, 69–70
Clinton, Bill, 125
Cold War era, Bretton Woods System and, 76
collectivization, 154–156, *156*
Colombia, Mercosur and, 149–150
colonialism, in Africa, 217
Comecon (Council for Mutual Economic Assistance),
   161, 161–162, *162*
commercial banks, Federal Reserve System creation,
   26–27
commodity control schemes, Great Depression and, 71
Common Agricultural Policy (CAP), 130
Common Market for Eastern and Southern Africa
   (COMESA), 217
common markets, defined, 116
communism. *see also* Soviet Union and socialist
   economies of Europe
   China as BRICS emerging economy, 172
   "first era of globalization" and, 20–21
comparative advantage
   defined, 2–3
   dynamic comparative advantage, 4
compensation agreements, 69
Congo Free State, 19
consumption
   defined, 1–2
   hyperinflation following WWI, 39
   overinvestment and overconsumption in China,
      177–178
contagion, *96*, 96–97, 140
corporations
   Debt Crisis of 1980s and, 107
   Great Depression and, 52
   hyperinflation follow WWI and effects on, 39
   Japanese dualism and, 193, *195*
   socialist economies of Central and Eastern Europe,
      160
Council for Mutual Economic Assistance (CMEA)
   (Comecon), *161*, 161–162, *162*

Council of Ministers (EU), 128–129
"crawling peg," 101
credit
   Bretton Woods System and, 83–84, 86–88, *87*
   "capital market-based" financial system, 205
   credit-based financial systems, East Asia, 204–205
   credit hypothesis of Great Depression, 61, *61*
   second generation transmission, 97
Credit-Anstalt, 67
Crisis of 1990 (India), 182–184
Cultural Revolution, 172
currency
   Bretton Woods System and, 81–84
   dollar, 68, 82, 84–86, 89–91, 111
   EU and, 132–133
   euro zone creation, *134*, *134–136*
   exchange rates, 7–12, *8*, *9*, *10*
   Great Depression and, 66–69
   hyperinflation following WW I, 36, 37–38
   India (Crisis of 1990), 182–184
   "key currencies," post-WWI, 40 (*see also* gold
      standard)
   pound/pound sterling, 84–86, 89–91, 147
   real (Brazil), 185
   ruble collapse (1997-1998), 170
   Scarce Currency Clause, 81–82, 90, 104
   yen (Japan), 69, 197
   yuan, 180*n*4
current account, balance of payments, 5–6
current transfers, 6
customs union
   common markets and, 116
   defined, 116
Cyprus, European sovereign debt crisis and, 143
Czechoslovakia, as socialist economy, 160

D
Dawes, Charles G., 38
Dawes Plan, 38, 42
Debt Crisis of 1980s, 95–96, 106–109, *110*
debt-for-debt swaps, 108
debt-for-equity swaps, 108
deep integration regulations, 91
deflation
   Great Depression and credit hypothesis, 61
   Great Depression and deflationary expectations,
      49, 62
de la Madrid, Miguel, 123
Delors, Jacques, 131
Delors Report on Economic and Monetary Union, 131

224   Index

demand
    aggregate demand, *59*, 59, 60–61, 80
    changing patterns of production and demand,
        post WWI, 43–44
    Great Depression and, 53
    price elasticity, 210
Deng Xiaoping, 174, 176
dependency theory, 218
deregulation, international financial crises and, 98–99
Desai, Padma, 97
"development state"
    defined, 190 (*see also* East Asia)
    public policy and, 200–204
diminishing trade hypothesis, 47–48
discounting, 26, 66
Dispute Settlement Body (DSB) (WTO), 88
Doha Round, 88
dollar
    Asian Crisis of 1997, 111
    Bretton Woods System and, 82, 84–86, 89–91
    Dollar Area, 68
Dow Jones Industrial Average, stock market crash of
    1929 and, 62
dualism, 193, 194–495
Duma (Russia), 152, 169
dynamic comparative advantage, 4
dynamic effect, 62

E
East Asia, 190–207, *192*
    Asian Crisis of 1997, 96–97, 105, 110–113, *111*,
        112, 115, 170, 203–204, 206
    "Asian miracle," 190, 201
    "development state," defined, 190, 200–204
    economic growth and exports, 190–192
    emerging economies of, 199–207, *199*, *200*, *203*,
        207
    Japan, 193–199, *194*, *195*, *197*, *198*
Eastern Europe, socialist economies of. *see* Soviet
    Union and socialist economies of Europe
East Germany
    financial crisis of 1992 and exchange rate
        mechanism (ERM), 133–134
    socialist economies of Central and Eastern
        Europe, 160
Economic Planning Board in South Korea, 203–204
Ecuador, Mercosur and, 149–150
Eichengreen, Barry, 38, 49, 52, 55, 67, 72
electricity, during "first era of globalization," 18

emerging economies. *see* Africa; BRICS countries;
    East Asia; Middle East
Engel, Ernst, 47
Engel's law, 47
environmental issues
    Bretton Woods System and, 91–94, *93*
    in China, 179
    NAFTA, 126, *126*
equilibrium exchange rate, 9
Eurobond, 144–145
Europe. *see also* European Union (EU); World War
    I; World War II; *individual names of agencies;*
    individual names of countries
    European financial crisis of 1931, 67
    European sovereign debt crisis, 139–145
    Great Depression compared to Great Recession, 72
    post-WWI trade, 44–45, *45*
    socialist economies of. *see* Soviet Union and
        socialist economies of Europe
European Central Bank (ECB), 13, *134*, 142–143
European Coal and Steel Community (ECSC),
    127–128
European Commission, 128
European Council, 128–129
European Court of Justice, 129
European Economic Area (EEA), 147
European Economic Community (EEC), 116,
    128–129, 134. *see also* European Union (EU)
European Economic Cooperation (OEEC), 79
European Economic Recovery Plan (Marshall Plan),
    78. *see also* Marshall Plan
European Monetary Union, 72, 132–136, *134*
European Parliament, 129
European Payments Union (EPU), 77–80, *78*, 89
European sovereign debt crisis
    austerity policies, 143–144
    Cyprus events, 143
    European Stability Mechanism (ESM), 141–142
    financial regulation, 144
    fiscal union, 142
    implications, 144–145
    Maastricht Treaty and European Central Bank,
        142–143
    overview, 139–140, *140*
    "taking haircut" on Greek debt, 140–141
European Stability Mechanism (ESM), 141–142
European Union (EU), 127–138
    Brexit, *145*, 145–148
    Common Agricultural Policy (CAP), 130
    European Monetary Union, 132–136, *134*

expansion of, *136–138*, 136–137
institutions of EEC and, 128–129
NAFTA compared to, 119
overview, 116, 127–128
policy issues, 129–130
population and GDP for countries of, *136–137*
Single European Act (1987), 130–132
"Eurosclerosis," 131
euro zone
creation of, *134*, 134–136
European Stability Mechanism (ESM) and, 141–142 (*see also* European sovereign debt crisis)
Excessive Deficit Procedure (1992), 72
Exchange Control Area, 69
exchange rates
Bretton Woods System and, 90
defined, 7
European sovereign debt crisis, 144–145
euro zone creation, 135
exchange rate mechanism (ERM), 133–134
exchange rate model, 7–10, *8, 9, 10*
exchange rate policy and international financial crises, 100–102
fixed and flexible, 11–12
Great Depression and exchange controls, 69
Great Depression compared to Great Recession, 72
hyperinflation following WW I and, 38
managed, 12
monetary policy and, 15–16
stability of, and classical gold standard, *23*, 23–25
Exogenous Shocks Facility (IMF), 103
exports. *see* regional trade agreements (RTAs); trade
Extended Fund Facility (IMF), 103

F
Fetters of Gold and Paper (Eichengreen, Temin), 67
financial account, defined, 6–7
financial crisis of 1992, exchange rate mechanism (ERM) and, 133–134
financial leadership model (Kindleberger), 65–66
"first era of globalization," 17–28
defined, 17
exchange rate stability and classical gold standard, *23*, 23–25
globalization through imperialism, 18–21
international trade and, 21–22
mobility and, 22–23, *23*
monetary policy in era of gold standard, 25–27
second industrial revolution and, *17*, 17–18
First World War. *see* World War I

fiscal policy
balance of payments and, 14–15
defined, 12–13
EU and, 131
European sovereign debt crisis and, 142
Great Depression and fiscal expansion (Germany, Sweden), 71
Great Depression compared to Great Recession, 73
hyperinflation following WW I and, 38
monetary policy compared to, 13–14, 15–16
overview, 12
twin deficit hypothesis, 15
fixed exchange rates, 11–12
Fleming, J. Marcus, 16
flexible (floating) exchange rates, 11–12
"Flying Geese" model, 193, 199, *199*
food processing, during "first era of globalization," 18. *see also* agriculture
foreign direct investment (FDI), 6, 177, 192
foreign exchange markets, 99
foreign trading corporations (FTCs) (China), 174
France
colonialism by, 19
ECSC formation and, 127
European sovereign debt crisis, 139, 143
Great Depression and, 49–50, *50*
hyperinflation in Germany, following WW I, 35
physical destruction from WW I, 31
post-WWI restoration of gold standard, 42
WW II losses by, 76
Franco-Prussian War of 1871, 35
free trade. *see also* trade
defined, 3–4
during "first era of globalization," 21–22
free trade areas, 116
GATT and, 87
Free Trade Agreement, 121. *see also* North American Free Trade Agreement (NAFTA)
Friedman, Milton, 54, 55–56, 57, 61, 65

G
G20, 141
G5, 197
Galbraith, John Kenneth, 51–52, 63
Gandhi, Rajiv, 182
General Agreement on Tariffs and Trade (GATT)
Bretton Woods System and, 75, 80, 86–88, *87*
China in, 174
NAFTA and, 121
on regional trade agreements, 117

226 Index

General Arrangements to Borrow (GAB), 89
General Theory (Keynes), 73
Germany. *see also* East Germany; West Germany
    ECSC formation and, 127
    European financial crisis of 1931, 67
    European sovereign debt crisis, 145
    Exchange Control Area, 69
    financial crisis of 1992 and exchange rate
        mechanism (ERM), 133–134
    "first era of globalization" and, 17
    Great Depression and, 49–50, *50*
    Great Depression and clearing agreements, 69–70
    Great Depression and fiscal expansion, 71
    hyperinflation following WWI and effect on
        government, 39
    post-WW I boom and slump, 34
    post-WW I hyperinflation, *34*, 34–39, *36*
    post-WWI reparations, 38, 42–43
    subprime mortgage crisis of 2007 and Great
        Recession, 114
    WW II losses by, 76
Ghana, imports from China to, 216
glasnost, 158–159, 166–167
globalization
    defined, 98
    first era. *see* "first era of globalization"
    international financial crises, globalization, and
        capital mobility, *97*, 97–100
    non-oil-exporting Middle Eastern states and, 212
    "political elites" and European sovereign debt
        crisis, 146–147
Gold Bloc, 69
gold standard
    Bretton Woods System and, 82, 84–86
    Bretton Woods System and gold reserves of
        selected countries (1950-1971), *85*
    classical gold standard during "first era of
        globalization," *23*, 23–25
    as fixed exchange rate system, 12
    Great Depression and, 57–58, 66–68, 72–73
    Great Depression and recovery of 1933, 63–64
    restoration following WW I, *40*, 40–42
    suspension of, during WW I, 29
Gorbachev, Mikhail, 158, 162, 166–167
Gosplan, 156
government debt. *see also* government deficit
    China as funder of U.S. government debt, 180
    euro zone creation and government debt to GDP
        ratios, 135
    WW I and, *32*, 32–33

government deficit
    euro zone creation and government deficit to GDP
        ratios, 135
    monetary policy and, 14
government expenditure
    defined, 1, 2
    exchange rate and, 11
    fiscal policy, 12–13
government's role
    demand and Great Depression, 53
    Great Recession and, 114–115
    market failure and government failure, 202–203
    WW I and economic role of, 30–31
gradualism," 168–169, 180–181
Great Britain. *see also* United Kingdom
    Bretton Woods System and, 81, 89
    Brexit, *145*, *145–148*, *146*
    British Commonwealth Preferences (Imperial
        Preferences), 70–71
    colonialism by, 19
    Great Depression and, 49–50, *50*, 57, 58
    Great Depression and monetary expansion in,
        71–72
    Sterling Area, 67, 68
    WW II losses by, 76
Great Depression, 49–74
    aggregate demand-aggregate supply and wage and
        price rigidity, 59, *59*
    Bretton Woods System and, 80–81
    credit hypothesis, 61, *61*
    deflationary expectations, 62
    Great Recession (2008-2009) compared to, 72–73
    international aspects of, 64–68, *65*
    international economy (1933-1940), 68–72
    monetarism and money creation process, 54
    monetarism and wage rigidity, 54–58, *57*
    Open Economy Trilemma, 15–16
    overview, 49–50, *50*
    post-WW I boom and slump, *33*, 33–34
    recovery from and recession of 1937-1938, 63–64
    stock market crash, *62*, 62–63
    in U.S., *50*, 50–53, *53*
    wage rigidity, 60–61
Great Leap Forward, 172
Great Purge, 154
Great Recession
    BRICS emerging economies and, 170
    subprime mortgage crisis of 2007 and, 113–115,
        114
Greece
    European sovereign debt crisis, 139–145, *140*

hyperinflation after WW II, 76
Greenspan, Alan, 114, *114*
gross domestic product (GDP)
    aggregate demand - aggregate supply framework, 59, *59*
    defined, 1–2
    euro zone creation and government deficit/debt to GDP ratios, 135
    during "first era of globalization," 22
    index at constant prices, before and after WWII, *78*
    real GDP and nominal GDP, 1
    WW I and, 30
gross national product (GNP), defined, 2
Growth, Employment and Redistribution (GEAR) strategy (South Africa), 187
Gulf War, 182
gunboat diplomacy," 19

H

"haircut," European sovereign debt crisis and, 140–141
Hansen, Alvin, 53
hard budget constraints," 157
"hard peg," 101–102
Hayek, Friedrich, 51
"high yen" recession, 197
Hong Kong, as East Asian "development state," 190
Hoover, Herbert, 51
housing
    Asian Crisis of 1997, 111
    Great Depression and, 53
    Nikkei (1980s-1990s) and, 198
    subprime mortgage crisis of 2007 and Great Recession, 113–115, *114*
    WW II losses, 76
Hume, David, 24
Hungary
    Great Depression and clearing agreements, 69–70
    hyperinflation after WW II, 76
    socialist economies of Central and Eastern Europe, 160
Hussein, Saddam, 211
hyperinflation
    beneficiaries and losers from, 39
    cause of, 36–37
    end of, 37–38
    German wholesale price index (1914-1923), *36*
    overview, *34*, 34–36, *36*
    as WW II legacy, 76

I

Immigration
    Brexit and, 146
    "first era of globalization," 22, *22*
imperialism
    globalization through, 18–21
    Tsarist Russia, 151–152
imports. *see* regional trade agreements (RTAs); trade
import substitution industrialization (ISI)
    Africa, 216
    BRICS countries, 184–185
    Middle East, 212
    regional trade agreements, 122–123
Impossible Trinity, 15–16
"improvement engineering," 195
income
    dependency theory, 218
    Great Depression and distribution of, 51–52
    inequality of, in South Africa, 188
    Japanese "bubble economy," 197
    modernization theory, 218–219
    North American countries, compared, 120
India, as BRICS country, 181–184, *183*
Indonesia. *see also* Asia
    Asian Crisis of 1997, 110–113
    as East Asian "development state," 190
industrialization
    in China, 173–174, 175–177
    by East Asian "development state," 190–192
    in India (1980s), 181–182
    Japan (late twentieth century), 195–196
    manufacturing, post-WWI production, 43–44
    (*see also* production)
    second industrial revolution, *17*, 17–18
inflation
    BRICS emerging economies and, 169
    euro zone creation, 135
    exchange rates and, 10
    hyperinflation following WW I, *34*, 34–39, *36*
    "lost decade" (Brazil), 185
    following WW I, 33–34
Institutional Revolutionary Party (PRI), 124
interest
    euro zone creation, 135
    interest rates and exchange rate, 11
internal capital markets, 205
International Bank for Economic Cooperation (IBEC), 161
International Bank for Reconstruction and Development (IBRD), 84

228   Index

international financial crises and international institu-
    tions. *see also* General Agreement on Tariffs and
    Trade (GATT); International Monetary Fund (IMF);
    World Bank; World Trade Organization (WTO)
    Asian Crisis of 1997, 110–113, *111*, *112*
    contagion and, *96*, 96–97
    Debt Crisis of 1980s, 106–109, *110*
    exchange rate policy, 101–102
    globalization and capital mobility, *97*, 97–100
    inception of international institutions (*see*
        Bretton Woods System)
    macroeconomic imbalances and, *95*, 95–96
    moral hazard and Basel Accords, 100–101, *101*
    overview, 95, 105
    role of IMF and World Bank, 102–105
    subprime mortgage crisis of 2007 and Great
        Recession, 113–115, *114*
international institutions. *see* Bretton Woods System;
    General Agreement on Tariffs and Trade (GATT);
    international financial crises and international insti-
    tutions; International Monetary Fund (IMF); World
    Bank; World Trade Organization (WTO)
International Labour Organization (ILO), 92
International Monetary Fund (IMF)
    Asian Crisis of 1997, 112–113
    on balance of payments, 6
    Bretton Woods System and, 75, 80, 81–84, *82*,
        88–89, 91, 94
    BRICS economies and, 168, 178, 185–187
    European sovereign debt crisis, 139, 140, 141
    international financial crises and role of, 102–105
    loan categories of, 103
    NAFTA and, 123, 125
    regulatory framework and East Asia, 205
    "Washington Consensus," 104–105, 109
international trade. *see* trade
International Trade Organization (ITO), 87–88
intraregional trade, in Asia, 192
investment
    defined, 1–2
    investment income, 5
    investment-led growth model of China, 178
    by Japan, 195
Iraq, Persian Gulf War in, 182
Ireland, European sovereign debt crisis and, 139, 140
Islamic banking practices, 214
Israel, Yom Kippur War and, 211
Italy
    ESCS formation and, 127
    European sovereign debt crisis, 143
    Great Depression and, 49–50, *50*

J
Jamaica Agreement of 1976, 91
Japan. *see also* Asia
    Asian Crisis of 1997, 111, *112*
    as East Asian "development state," 190, 193, 194
    economic "miracle" of, 193–197, *194*, 195, 197,
        200
    economic setbacks following Plaza Accord (1985),
        197–199, *198*
    during "first era of globalization," 20
    "Flying Geese" model, 193, 199, *199*
    post-WW I boom and slump, 33
    WW II losses by, 76
    Yen Area, 69
Johnson, Lyndon, 210

K
Keiretsu, 193
Kennedy Round, 87
Kerensky, Alexander, 152
Keynes effect, 62
Keynes, John Maynard, 72, 73, 81, 82, 86
KGB, 158
Khrushchev, Nikita, 155–156
Kindleberger, Charles P., 65–66
Kochin, I. A., 60
Kornai, Janos, 157
Krueger, Anne, 105, 118
Krugman, Paul, 201
kulaks, *152*, *154*, *155*
Kuwait, Persian Gulf War in, 182

L
labor force. *see also* regional trade agreements
    (RTAs); wages/wage earners
    Bretton Woods System and, *3*, 91–94, *92*
    in China, 175–176
    collectivization of agriculture, in Soviet Union,
        154–156, *156*
    in East Asia, 192
    in India (1990s), 183
    Japanese dualism and, 194–195
    NAFTA and, 125–126
    in South Africa, 188
    unemployment of Great Depression, *50*, 50–51
    wage rigidity and Great Depression, 54–58, *57*,
        60–61 (*see also* Great Depression)
Latin America. *see also individual names of countries*
    Debt Crisis of 1980s and, 106, 108, 109, *110*
    Mexican Peso Crisis of 1994-1995, 95–96, 100
League of Nations, 66

"leave campaign". *see* Brexit
legal systems, in Middle East, 214
Lenin, Vladimir, *20, 152*, 152–153, 161
Leopold (king of Belgium), 19
less-developed countries (LDCs), 106
"License Raj," 182
liquidity
  Bretton Woods System and, 89–90
  Liquidationists school of thought about Great
    Depression, 51
  monetary policy and, 13
Lisbon Treaty, 147
London. *see also* Great Britain; United Kingdom
  Brexit and financial center of, 148
  Marshall Plan and financial center of, 79
  post-WWI restoration of gold standard, 41
"lost decade" (Brazil), 184–185
Lula da Silva, Luiz Inácio, 186, *186*

M

M (quantity of money), 25
Maastricht Treaty, 134–136, 142–143
Macmillan Committee, 67
macroeconomics and global economy, 1–16
  balance of payments, *5*, 5–7, *7*
  economic orthodoxy and Great Depression, 52
  exchange rates, 7–12, *8, 9, 10*
  fiscal and monetary policy, 12–16, *13, 16*
  international financial crises and macroeconomic
    imbalances, *95*, 95–96, *109*
  macroeconomics, defined, 1n1
  national accounting definitions, 1–2
  overview, 1–2, *2*
  trade and protectionism, 2–5, *3*
Malaysia. *see also* Asia
  Asian Crisis of 1997, 110–113
  as East Asian "development state," 190
managed exchange rates, 12
Mandela, Nelson, 187
Mao Zedong, 172–173, 176
maquiladora, 124–125, 126
Marshall, George, 78, 159n3
Marshall Plan, 77–80, *78, 84*, 159
Marxism, in "first era of globalization," 20, 21
Marx, Karl, 152–153
material balance method," 156–157
May Committee, 67
Mbeki, Thabo, 187
Medieval cloth hall (Ypres, Belgium), *32*
Meiji Restoration, 193
Mellon, Andrew, 51

Mercosur, 116, *149*, 149–150
  NAFTA compared to, 119
Mexican Peso Crisis of 1994-1995, 95–96, 100
Mexico. *see also* Latin America; North American Free
    Trade Agreement (NAFTA)
  Chinese competition with, 180
  Debt Crisis of 1980s and, 108
  Mexican Peso Crisis of 1994-1995, 125
Middle East
  Arab Spring in, 212, 215, *215*
  defined, 209
  non-oil-exporting states, 212–214
  OPEC and oil-exporting states, 209–212, *210*
    (*see also* oil industry)
  Ottoman Turkish Empire and, 19
minimum wage, 92
mint parity, 24
mobility, "first era of globalization" and, *22*, 22–23, *23*
modernization theory, 218–219
Monetary History of the United States (Friedman,
    Schwartz), 54
monetary policy
  defined, 13
  in era of gold standard, 25–27
  EU and, 132–136
  exchange rates and, 15–16
  fiscal policy compared to, 12–15
  Great Depression and monetarist explanation,
    54–58, *57*
  Great Depression and monetary expansion
    (Great Britain), 71–72
  international monetary system as Great Depression
    cause, 80
  money creation process, 54
  overview, 12
  twin deficit hypothesis, 15
money. *see* monetary policy
money supply, 54
Mongolia, Comecon and, 161
moral hazard, 100–101, *101*, 203
"Most Favoured Nation Clause" (GATT), 87
Mundell effect, 62
Mundell, Robert, 16, 132

N

National accounting definitions, 1–2
national control, Brexit and, 146
National Health Service (NHS) (United Kingdom),
    146
nationalism, protectionism and, 46
net exports, defined, 1, 2

230 Index

Netherlands, ESCS formation and, 127
net international capital flows, "first era of globalization" and, 22–23, *23*
New Deal, 63–64
New Economic Policy (NEP), 153, 155, 161, 166
newly industrialized countries (NICs), 190, 200–204.
see also East Asia
New York City. *see also* United States
Great Depression and New York banking industry,
55
post-WWI restoration of gold standard, 41
Nikkei stock market, 198
"Nixon Shock," 91
nominal GDP, 1
nongovernmental organizations (NGOs), 93–94
nontariff barriers," 5
North American Development Bank (NADB), 126
North American Free Trade Agreement (NAFTA),
118–127
Canada and U.S. trade, 121–122
environmental issues, 126, *126*
EU compared to, 127
impact of, 126–127
labor issues, 125–126
maquiladora, 124–125, 126
Mercosur compared to, 149
Mexico and U.S. trade, 122–124, *123*
overview, 116, 118–119
Peso Crisis, 125
population and GDP for countries of, *119*
U.S. dominance of, 119–120, *120*
"Norway option," 147, 148

O

October Revolution, 152
oil industry
Comecon and socialist economies, 162
crisis of 1973-1974, 98, 184
crisis of 1973 and 1979, 210–212
crisis of 1978, 107
Debt Crisis of 1980s, 95–96, 106–109, *110*
dominance of oil-rich states in Middle East, 212
NAFTA and, 123
OPEC and oil-exporting states, 209–212, *210*
(*see also* Middle East)
Open Economy Trilemma, 15–16
Organization for Economic Cooperation and Develop-
ment (OECD), 79
Organization of Petroleum Exporting Countries
(OPEC), 106–109, 209–212, *210*

Ostry, Sylvia, 93–94
Ottawa Agreement of 1932, 71

P

P (price level), 25
Partido Revolucionario Institucional (PRI), 124
pauper labour argument," 125–126
payments agreements, 70
peasants *(kulaks)*, 152, 154, 155
People's Bank of China, 86
perestroika, 158–159, 166
Perry, Commodore, 193
Persian Gulf War, 182
Peru, Mercosur and, 149–150
Philippines. *see also* Asia
Asian Crisis of 1997, 110–113
as East Asian "development state," 190
Plano Real (Brazil), 185
Plaza Accord (1985), 197–199
"political elites," European sovereign debt crisis and,
146–147
politics, market/government failure and, 203
population change
demographic changes, China, 177
demographic changes, Japan, 200
demographic changes, Middle East, 212, 213–214
European Union (EU) population and GDP,
136–137
population control by China, 174
WWI and demographic changes, 29, 31, 45–46
WWI losses, 29, 31, 45–46
portfolio investment, 6
Portugal, European sovereign debt crisis and, 139, 140
pound/pound sterling
Bretton Woods System and, 84–86, 89–91
Brexit's effect on, 147
Sterling Area, 89
Poverty Reduction and Growth Facility (IMF), 103
predatory behavior, by state officials, 203
price elasticity, 210
price-specie flow mechanism, 24
privatization, BRICS emerging economies and, 169
production
Great Depression and, 49–50, *50*, 52–53
Marshall Plan and, 78–79
post-WWI manufacturing, 43–44
WWI and patterns in, 29
WW I and patterns in, 43–44
proletariot, defined, 153
protectionism
defined, 2–5

Great Depression and, 64–65
following WW I, 30, 46
"public financing identity," 13
purchasing power parity, 10
Putin, Vladimir, 170–171

Q

Quotas
Bretton Woods System and, 83
defined, 4–5
free trade areas, 116
Great Depression and international monetary
arrangements, 70

R

Reagan, Ronald, 163
real GDP, 1
real income
defined, 25
WWI and, 47
recession
Great Depression and recession of 1937-1938,
63–64 (*see also* Great Depression)
Great Recession (2008-2009), 72–73, 113–115, *114*
"high yen" recession, 197
"stagflation" era, 106
Red Guards, 172
regional disparities, in China, 179
regional trade agreements (RTAs), 116–150
Brexit, *145*, 145–148
Canada-U.S. Free Trade Agreement (CUSTA),
118, 121, 122, 126
European sovereign debt crisis, 139–145
European Union (EU), 127–138, *134, 136–137*
Mercosur, *149*, 149–150
North American Free Trade Agreement (NAFTA),
118, 118–127, *119, 120, 123, 126*
overview, 116–117
trade creation and diversion by, 117–118
regulatory framework, financial sector and, 205–206
Reichsmark (Germany), 37
religion, as economic factor in Middle East, 214
renminbi (RMB), 180n4
Rentenbank, 37–38
rent-seeking activities, 202
Reparations Commission (Allied Powers), 38
reserves, exchange rate and, 11
reserve tranche, 83
restrictions, of trade. *see* protectionism
Rhodes, Cecil, 19
Rhodesia, 19

riba, 214
Ricardo, David, 2, 4
Robertson, Dennis, 47
Rogoff, Kenneth, 105
Romania, as socialist economy, 160
Romer, Christina, 58, 60, 63
Roosevelt, Franklin D., 63–64
ruble, collapse of, 170
Russia. *see also* Soviet Union and socialist economies
of Europe
Bolshevik power in, 151–154 (*see also* Soviet
Union and socialist economies of Europe)
as BRICS country, 165–171, *167*, 168, *170*, 171,
180–181
"first era of globalization," 24
physical destruction from WW I, 32
population loss from WW I, 31

S

Salinas, Carlos, 123–124
Sarkozy, Nicholas, 143
savings, by Japan, 195
Say, Jean-Baptiste, 51
Say's law, 51
Scarce Currency Clause, 81–82, 90, 104
Schuman, Robert, 127
Schwartz, Anna J., 54, 55–56, 57, 61, 65
second generation transmission, 97
second industrial revolution, *17*, 17–18
securitization, 113–114
semiconductor industry (Japan), 196
"sexenio crisis," 124
shallow integration regulations, 91
sharia, 214
"shock therapy," 168–169, 180–181
short-term capital, mobility of, 99–100
Siemans-Martin steel process, 17
silver standard (China), 23
Singapore. *see also* Asia
Asian Crisis of 1997, 110–113
as East Asian "development state," 190
Singh, Manmohan, 182
Single European Act (1987), 130–132
Smiley, Gene, 60n6, 61
Smithsonian Agreement, 90–91
Smoot-Hawley tariff, 52, 60, 64–65
Smoot, Reed, 65
social capital, BRICS emerging economies and, 169
"social dumping," 93
socialist economies. *see* Soviet Union and socialist
economies of Europe

232 Index

Social Security, inception of, 64
soft budget constraints," 157
South Africa
    as BRICS country, *187*, 187–188, *188*
    colonialism in, 19
    imports from China to, 216
South Korea. *see also* Asia
    Asian Crisis of 1997, 110–113
    as "development state," 201
    as East Asian "development state," 190
Soviet Union and socialist economies of Europe,
    151–164
    collectivization of agriculture in Soviet Union,
        154–156, *156*
    communism and "first era of globalization," 20–21
    Council for Mutual Economic Assistance (CMEA)
        ("Comecon"), *161*, 161–162, *162*
    economic planning in, 156–158
    failure of, 163–164
    historical development of Soviet economic system,
        151–154, *152*, *154*
    overview, 151
    reform attempts, 158–159
    socialist economies of Central and Eastern Europe,
        159–160
    Soviet Union and WW II losses, 76
Spain, European sovereign debt crisis and, 143
Special Drawing Rights (SDRs), 83*n*3, 86, *86*, 90–91
special economic zones (SEZs) (China), 174, 179
Stability and Growth Pact (1997), 72, 135, 142
stagflation" era, 106
Staiger, R. W., 93
stalinism, 166
Stalin, Joseph, 78, 153–154, *154*, 155, 157, 160, 166
Standard and Poor, 139
stand-by arrangements (SBAs), 103
State Enterprise law (Soviet Union), 157
state-owned enterprises. *see also* Soviet Union and
    socialist economies of Europe
    in China, 179, 180–181
    in India, 182–183
    in Japan, 193
State Planning Commission, 172
static effect, 62
steel industry, 17, 174
Sterling Area, 89
Stiglitz, Joseph, 104–105, 141, 168
Stinnes, Hugo, 39
stock market
    Nikkei (1980s-1990s), 198

stock market crash (1929) and Great Depression,
    60, *62*, 62–63
Stolypin reforms, 151–152
Strong, Benjamin, 57
Structural Adjustment Facility (SAF), 91
structural adjustment loans (SALs), 102–103
structural deficit, defined, 142*n*7
subprime mortgage crisis, effect on East Asian "devel-
    opment state," 204
subprime mortgage crisis of 2007, Great Recession
    and, 113–115, *114*
"subsidiarity" principle, of EEC/EU, 129
Suez Canal, 21, *21*
Supplemental Reserve Facility (SRF) (IMF), 103
Supplemental Reserve Facility (SRF), 91
Sweden
    Great Depression and fiscal expansion, 71
    post-WW I boom and slump, 33

T

Taiping Rebellion, 19
Taiwan. *see also* Asia
    Asian Crisis of 1997, 110–113, *111*
    as "development state," 201
    as East Asian "development state," 190
tariffs
    defined, 4–5
    free trade areas, 116
    Great Depression and international monetary
        arrangements, 70
    Smoot-Hawley tariff, 52, 60, 64–65
taxes
    exchange rate and, 11
    fiscal policy, 12–13
    Tobin tax, 99–100
    WW I financing with, 30–31
technology. *see also* industrialization
    international financial instruments and, 99
    WWI and, 47
Temin, Peter, 51–52, 67, 72
Thailand. *see also* Asia
    Asian Crisis of 1997, 110–113, 111
    baht collapse (1997), 110
    as East Asian "development state," 190
Tobin, James, 99–100
Tobin tax, 99–100
Tokyo Round, 87
Torrens, Robert, 47
total factor productivity (TFP), 185, 201, 213
trade. *see also* currency; regional trade agreements
    (RTAs); World Trade Organization (WTO)

balance of trade surplus and Great Depression, 52

bilateral trading agreements, 69–70

Bretton Woods System and, 80, 91–94, *92*, *93*

by China, 174

comparative advantage, 2–3, *3*

creation and diversion of, 117–118

by East Asian "development state," 190–192

"first era of globalization" and, *21*, 21–22

free trade, 3–4, 21–22, 87, 116

in goods and services, 5

international trade during "first era of globalization," *21*, 21–22

by Japan (mid-late twentieth century), 196–197, *197*

post-WWI, 29–30, 44–45, *45*, 47–48

protectionism and, 2–5

socialist economies of Central and Eastern Europe, 160

tariffs and quotas, defined, 4–5

"trade rounds," 87

WW I and, 44–45, *45*

WWI and diminishing trade hypothesis, 47–48

transboundary effects, environmental standards and, 93

transfers

current transfers, 6

defined, 2

transfer unions, 145

Transparency International, 214

transportation

during "first era of globalization," 18

Great Depression and fiscal expansion (German autobahns), 71

Marshall Plan and, 79

Treaty of Asunción of 1991, 149

Treaty of Rome of 1957, 127–128

Treaty of Versailles, 35

Triffin dilemma, 84–86, *85*, *86*, 89

"Trilemma," 15–16

Tripartite Monetary Agreement, 70

Trotsky, Leon, 153

Truman, Harry, 77–78

twin deficit hypothesis, 15

U

United Kingdom. *see also* Great Britain

Brexit, 145–148, *146*

"first era of globalization," 17, 22–23, 24–25

Great Depression and, 56

post-WW I boom and slump, 33

post-WWI restoration of gold standard, 41

subprime mortgage crisis of 2007 and Great Recession, 114

WWI and decline in trade, 29–30

WW I and decline in trade, 47–48

United Kingdom Independence Party (UKIP), 145

United Nations

International Labour Organization (ILO), 92

International Trade Organization (ITO), 87–88

Monetary and Financial Conference (Bretton Woods Conference), 80–84 (*see also* Bretton Woods System)

Relief and Rehabilitation Administration (UNRRA), 77

United States. *see also* government debt; North American Free Trade Agreement (NAFTA); *individual names of agencies*

Bretton Woods System and, 81–82, 89

Canada-U.S. Free Trade Agreement (CUSTA), 118, 121, 122, 126

China as funder of U.S. government debt, 180

Dollar Area, 68

"first era of globalization" and, 17, 25–27

Great Depression and, 49–50, *50*

Great Depression and recession of 1937-1938, 63–64

Great Depression in, *50*, 50–53, *53* (*see also* Great Depression)

international institutions and international financial crises of, 95–96, 98, 106–109, *110*, 113–115, *114* (*see also* international financial crises and international institutions)

post-WW I boom and slump, 33

post-WWI chain of debt, *42*, 42–43

post-WWI restoration of gold standard, 41–42

post-WWI trade, *45*, 44–45

WW II legacy of, 77

Uruguay, Mercosur and, 116, *149*, 149–150

Uruguay Round, 87

U.S. Federal Reserve

building of, *57*

creation of, 26–27

Great Depression and, 49, 54–58, 64, 66, 68

monetary policy and, 13

NAFTA and, 123

subprime mortgage crisis of 2007 and Great Recession, 113–115, *114*

USSR. *see* Soviet Union and socialist economies of Europe

U.S. Treasury

Debt Crisis of 1980s, 108–109

Great Depression and, 64

"Washington Consensus," 104–105, 109

234 Index

V

V (velocity of circulation), 25
value added tax (VAT), 131–132
Venezuela, Mercosur and, 116, *149*, 149–150
Vietnam
    Comecon and, 161
    Vietnam War, 20, 89, 210
Viner, Jacob, 117
virgin lands" campaign, 155–156
von Mises, Ludwig, 51
vote-seeking politicians, 203

W

wages/wage earners. *see also* labor force; regional
    trade agreements (RTAs)
    hyperinflation following WWI, 39
    income in North American countries, compared,
        120
    "pauper labour argument," 125–126
    wage rigidity and Great Depression, 54–58, *57*,
        60–61
"war communism" era, 152–153
"war on poverty," 210
"Washington Consensus," 104–105, 109
wealth effect, 59
Weimar Republic, 34. *see also* Germany
West Germany
    ESCS formation and, 127
    financial crisis of 1992 and exchange rate
        mechanism (ERM), 133–134
White, Harry Dexter, 81
World Bank
    Bretton Woods System and, 75, 84, 94
    international financial crises and role of, 102–105
    regulatory framework and East Asia, 205
    "Washington Consensus," 104–105, 109
World Trade Organization (WTO)
    Bretton Woods System and, 75, 88, *88*, 93
    Brexit and "WTO option," 148
    China in, 174, 179
    on regional trade agreements, 117
World War I, 29–48
    chain of debt, 42–43

decline in trade and, 47–48
demographic changes, 45–46
economic role of government, 30–31
"first era of globalization" and, 17, 21, 22, 23
gold standard restoration, *40*, 40–42
hyperinflation, *34*, 34–39, *36*
immediate costs of, 31–33, *32*
international trade and, 44–45, *45*
period between WWI and WWII, overview, *29*,
    29–30, 65–66, 75 (*see also* World War II)
postwar boom and slump, *33*, 33–34
production and demand, 43–44
protectionism following, 46
World War II
    Bretton Woods System following, 75, *76*, 76–77
    Comecon formation after, 161
    ECSC formation and, 127 (*see also* European
        Union (EU))
    "first era of globalization" and, 23
    international financial crises and, 98
    international trade growth following, 47
    period between WWI and WWII, overview, *29*,
        29–30, 65–66, 75 (*see also* World War I)
    Russia and, 151–152 (*see also* Soviet Union and
        socialist economies of Europe)
    Soviet Union postwar reform attempts, 158–159

Y

Y (real income), 25
Yeats, A. J., 150
Yeltsin, Boris, *167*, 167–170
yen (Japan), 197
Yen Area, 69
Yom Kippur War, 211
Young, Alwyn, 201
yuan, 180*n*4

Z

Zaibatsu, 193
Zhou Xiaochuan, 86

$16^{1/8}$

$16^{1/8}$

$\log_2 1/8 = x$

$2^x = 1/8$

$2^3 = 8$

$2^{-3} = 1/8$